Testing Industrial Skills

Testing Industrial Skills

**Alan Jones
Peter Whittaker**

A HALSTED PRESS BOOK

JOHN WILEY & SONS
New York – Toronto

First published in Great Britain by
Gower Press Limited, Epping, Essex, 1975

© Alan Jones and Peter Whittaker, 1975

*Published in the U.S.A.
by Halsted Press, a Division
of John Wiley & Sons, Inc.
New York*

Library of Congress Cataloging in Publication Data

Jones, Alan.
   Testing industrial skills.
   "A Halsted Press book."
   Bibliography: p.
   1. Employment tests. I. Whittaker, Peter,
joint author. II. Title.
HF5549.5.E5J65 1975   658.31'12   75-255
ISBN 0-470-44871-7

Printed and bound in Great Britain

Contents

Acknowledgements		*xii*
Preface		*xiii*
1	**Introduction**	1
	Discussion	1
	The purposes of testing	4
	References	7
	Suggested further reading	7
2	**Skill**	8
	The concept of skilled performance	8
	Categories of skill	10
	Summary	11
	Suggested further reading	12
3	**Analytical Techniques for Test Development**	13
	Analysis of a task	13
	How to collect the information	18
	The behavioural specification	26
	Summary	33
	Suggested further reading	34

4	**Testing Techniques**	**35**
	Introduction	35
	Hands-on testing techniques	36
	Hands-off tests	41
	References	70
	Suggested further reading	70
5	**Choosing between Testing Techniques**	**71**
	Skill and knowledge to be tested	72
	Purpose of testing	72
	Attitudes towards testing	74
	Type and level of personnel	74
	Administrative situation	75
6	**Assessing the Test Performance**	**79**
	Marking schemes	79
	Use of on the job measures	83
	The assessment of quality	84
	Measuring quantity	93
	The assessment of speed of work	93
	The assessment of process	97
	Scoring fault-finding and situation diagnostic tests	100
	Scoring tests for planning and similar skills	106
	Summary	109
	References	113
	Suggested further reading	114
7	**Implementing and Administering the Test**	**115**
	Task specification	115
	Candidate instructions	116
	Instructions for examiners	119
	Marking schemes	119
	Mark sheets	122
	Pilot testing	123
	Timetabling and layout of tests	125
	Security	130
	The test manual	130
	References	131
8	**Interpreting and Utilizing Test Results**	**132**
	Determination of results in a pass/fail type situation	132
	Trouble-shooting with results determination methods	139
	Utilizing tests and test results	140
	Suggested further reading	151
9	**The Process of Validation**	**152**
	The validity of performance tests	153
	Reliability	157

Reliability of criterion – referenced tests	163
A validation checklist	165
Process of evaluation	167
Examples of assessing the validity of tests	168
Summary	179
References	179
Suggested further reading	180

Glossary 181

Index 189

Illustrations

Figure
2.1	A categorization of skills	10
3.1	A test in adjusting tractor wheel tracks	19
3.2	Questionnaire used to assess the importance of various bricklaying tasks	25
3.3	Basic hydraulic course content	28
3.4	Interim statement of skills	29
3.5	Hydraulics course — behavioural specification	30
3.6	Extract from behavioural specification for tractor driver	31
3.7	Extract from behavioural specification for a short hydraulics course	32
4.1	Testing the reading of a micrometer scale	35
4.2	Relation between speed and accuracy for three groups in operating a small punch press	37
4.3	A pipeworker carrying out a work sample test in a ship under construction	37
4.4	A work sample test designed by the Road Transport Industry Training Board requiring removal and replacement of a clutch plate	39
4.5	SITB planned experience checklist	40
4.6	Taper plug test piece	42
4.7	Engineering test (CGLI)	42
4.8	SITB phased test in joinery	43
4.9	Hems in a short answer test for motor mechanics	46

Figure

4.10	A multiple-choice item for a hydraulic test	49
4.11	A high fidelity multiple choice item testing recognition of a hydraulic valve	50
4.12	A matching item using hydraulic circuit symbols	54
4.13	A complex objective item	55
4.14	A complex item assessing ability to read engineering drawings	58
4.15a	A complex high-fidelity matching item	59
4.15b	Current to pulse converter circuit diagram	60
4.15c	Current to pulse converter circuit board	60
4,15d	Current to pulse converter printed circuit	60
4.16	Method of assessing operation sheets	61
4.17	A comparison of essay, short answer and multiple choice items on a number of factors	62
4.18	Basic hydraulics test	67
4.19	The Wilkes and Son simulator	69
5.1	Areas of consideration in choosing a testing technique	71
5.2	Types of skill and associated testing techniques	73
5.3	Relation between administrative considerations and testing techniques	77
5.4	A summary of testing techniques – their content, use and method of assessment	78
6.1	Different levels of discrimination which may be required in assessment	80
6.2	A marking scheme for the taper plug test piece	84
6.3	A more objective marking scheme for the taper plug test piece	85
6.4	Taper plug test piece and specially constructed go/no go gauge for measuring the taper	86
6.5	The go/no go gauge in use	86
6.6	Another go/no go gauge – this time for the 10 DIM – note the minimum and maximum dimensions	87
6.7	Using the dial test indicator (DTI) for measuring the taper plug test piece	87
6.8	A test in assembling jacks for a harpsichord	89
6.9	Assessment of performance of a number of candidates on a five point rating scale by a harsh and a lenient rate	90
6.10	Three rating scales	91
6.11	A scheme for the assessment of speed of work	94
6.12	A skill sample test in basic bricklaying	95
6.13	Matrix illustrating a combined speed and quality assessment	96
6.14	A work sample test in plastic injection moulding	96
6.15, 6.16	Two views of a candidate tuning a fuel injector pump	97-8
6.17	A work sample test in plastic injection moulding	99
6.18	A rating scale for use of tools	100
6.19	A marking scheme for a fault diagnosis test in injection moulding	103

Figure

6.20	Examiner's notes for marking a test in fault-finding	104-5
6.21	A comparison of two methods of testing faults diagnosis	105
6.22	A hands-off test for planning skills	106-7
6.23	Another hands-off test for planning skills	108
6.24a	Cards used in the test of planning skills	110
6.24b	Answer sheet for planning test	111
6.24c	Candidates instructions for planning test	112
6.24d	Specimen conection list for test planning test	112
7.1	Marksheet for joiners and woodcutting machinist phased test	117
7.2	Candidate instructions for an electrical test	118
7.3	Instructions for a test in faults diagnosis	120
7.4	Examiners instructions for a hands-on test battery	121
7.5	A marksheet for a test battery on motor mechanics	124
7.6	A work sample test used in the agricultural industry	126
7.7	Timetable for a battery of tests	127
7.8	Possible layout for the tests in stripping down hydraulic valves	128
7.9	Computer used in the feedback classroom to record trainees' responses	129
	(a) General view of the feedback classroom	
	(b) Response unit used in the feedback classroom	
	(c) Digital response	
8.1	Norm-referenced and criterior-referenced standards	134
8.2	A check list for a test in stripping a harpsichord	136
8.3	A minimum acceptable performance profile	136
8.4	A work-sample test illustrating parallel marking systems	137
8.5	A specimen weighting system	138
8.6	Trouble-shooting with results determination methods	140
8.7	Performance of trainees who received less than 60% marks on a fitting test	142
8.8	Some trainees' reactions to a phased test	142
8.9	Results on a self-testing in recognition of road signs	143
8.10	Instructions for giving fork truck trainability assessment test	145
8.11	Trainability assessment sheet	146
8.12	Table of reference norms for trainability rating	147
8.13	Proportion of candidates achieving criterier on various operations	147
8.14a	Centre statistics for an End Test Centre	149
8.14b	Centre statistics for a Phased Test Centre	149
8.15	Table showing relative performance of two groups of trainees	150
9.1	Stages in the development of a performance test	153
9.2	Types of performance test validity	155
9.3	Shipboard performance test blueprint	158

Figure

9.4	Methods of determining test reliability	160
9.5	Division of scores into halves for reliability estimate of valve stem and hex fitting test	162
9.6	Statistical techniques for reliability control	166
9.7	Ratings of five performance tests for machine trades on a variety of factors	169
9.8	Ratings on 12 written tests for machine trades on a variety of factors	170
9.9	Disparity in number of test items in major areas covered in all tests	170
9.10	Results of past experience group/post training group on four test batteries	174
9.11	Questionnaire used to assess phased testing schemes	177
9.12	Frequency distribution of general tolerance worked to on machining test pieces for firms and colleges	178
9.13	Frequency distrubition of general tolerances worked to on fabrication testpieces for firms and colleges	178

Acknowledgements

The authors would like to acknowledge and thank the following organizations, publishers and authors for their permission to reproduce figures and photographs:

City and Guilds of London Institute
City and Guilds of London in conjunction with the British Steel Corporation
City and Guilds of London Institute in conjunction with the Shipbuilding Industry Training Board
British Steel Corporation
Shipbuilding Industry Training Board and Appledore Shipbuilders Ltd
Road Transport Industry Training Board
Road Transport Industry Training Board in conjunction with the Industrial Training Research Unit
Princeton University Press
Dr E. Belbin and John Wellens Ltd
National Occupational Competency Testing Project
Human Factors Research Inc
Central Electricity Generating Board
J. Tiffin and E.J. McCormick and Prentice-Hall Ltd
P.H. Sharpe and the Institution of Training Officers

The authors would also like to thank Garrett Green Technical College for allowing them to take photographs.

Preface

The aim of this book is to present a comprehensive and realistic guide to the development of tests to measure the acquisition of industrial skills. Since it refers to past and present practices in this field it can also be looked upon as a review of the 'state of the art' of testing performance and related job knowledge although this is not the authors' chief concern. We attempt to describe the process of test development through its various stages, from job analysis to methods of assessment and the interpretation of tests results. We should also like to warn any reader and prospective test developer that for the purposes of exposition we have split up the process of test development itself into some half dozen chapters; in reality the various aspects are not so conveniently compartmentalized and they interact at all stages.

The authors would like to acknowledge a debt of gratitude to City and Guilds of London Institute where they developed many of their ideas and gained much experience whilst on the staff of its Skills Testing Service. Since no test developer would have much of interest to say without his clients and contacts in industry, we should also like to thank all the members of firms, colleges, and industrial training boards who provided the opportunities and facilities for test development. Special personal acknowledgement is due to Colin Clegg who offered useful advice and criticism on our efforts.

1

Introduction

DISCUSSION

Tests and examinations have become something of an industry over the last few years. Besides examinations in traditional academic areas, the increasing emphasis on qualifications has caused a boom in assessment. In the selection of industrial personnel and students there has been an increasing use of psychological tests of intelligence, aptitude, interest, or whatever. All these developments are linked ultimately to the efficiency of performance in an industrial, commercial, or educational context. One important area that has been relatively ignored is the field of testing the individual's acquisition of industrial or commercial skills and the knowledge needed to support these skills. To this area the authors have given the title 'performance testing', emphasizing that it is the successful performance of a job in which one is interested. A performance test attempts to establish what a person can do as distinct from what he knows or what he claims to be able to do; where related or supporting job knowledge is dealt with the authors do not feel that a measure of knowledge alone is adequate but rather that tests of knowledge or similar 'hands-off' procedures can help to round off the picture of an individual's level of attainment.

It is surprising that such an obviously useful method as performance tests has for so long remained a rather neglected member of the testing family whereas paper and pencil tests of aptitude and achievement have been in widespread use. It is not necessary to look very far to see why paper and pencil tests have enjoyed such popularity since in many cases they can be an efficient and economical method of testing. The economic aspect is a particularly important one since

Introduction

written tests can be given to large groups at a single sitting and marked quickly. Performance tests on the other hand are usually longer and require a higher ratio of examiners to candidates.

Until recently, however, there was another reason for the lack of interest in performance tests, that is a widely held belief that a high relationship existed between knowledge about a job (sometimes thought of in 'educational' terms) and actual performance. It was therefore believed that a measure of knowledge (which was easier and cheaper to obtain anyway) would serve as an indirect measure of actual proficiency. A brief visit to any firm would, no doubt, yield contrary instances to this belief. There is the trainee who is very poor at written tests or examinations, but when it comes to doing the job is first class. On the other side of the coin, one has a trainee who receives top marks in a written examination but who is regarded as 'hopeless' by his supervisor.

Many studies have shown that there may be little relationship between written tests and tests of actual performance (eg Stuit[1]) while others have shown that knowing about a job is not the same as being able to do it. Arny[2] for example found little relationship between knowledge of the principles underlying cooking and the actual quality of cooking. One may therefore conclude that a direct measure of how well a person can perform a task is essential in assessing his proficiency. Even if knowledge were highly correlated with performance in general terms it would still be necessary to ascertain whether any one individual would perform the task satisfactorily.

Today it is probably generally accepted that written tests of trade knowledge alone are not a valid way of measuring proficiency and that without some type of direct or indirect measure of actual performance it is unlikely that one can make an accurate assessment of an individual's competence on a job. While knowledge about a job may be a necessary condition for competence, it is rarely a sufficient one.

It may often be the case that written tests are too theoretical and therefore unrelated to any given practical situation. They may also put emphasis on how articulate the candidate is, which in many job situations will not be of great consequence. We shall, however, deal with paper and pencil and similar testing techniques under the broad heading of performance testing, because these technique can be made relevant to the job or skill in question and therefore give a measure of job proficiency. Often these techniques can be used to fill out, in an economical manner, our picture of the candidate's ability.

Of course the view that observation of actual performance is the best way of measuring competence is not a new one and in fact it has been implicitly accepted for centuries by those responsible for passing on skills from one generation to the next. Informal assessment of performance has always been made by instructors, supervisors, craftsmen looking after apprentices, and so on. Where performance testing differs is that in place of informal observation one has a candidate doing a set task under specified and controlled conditions, and his performance is assessed in as standard and as objective a way as possible. Information about the test is also built up so that one has more idea of what a particular score of assessment means and how efficient the test is.

Performance testing is often thought of as being restricted to engineering-type skills. This is not the case; the method of development is applicable to any industrial task and often to commercial ones also. Such diverse areas as agriculture, piano-tuning, bacon-cutting, and typing, have all been subject to test development. Readers will probably be familiar with the testing of industrial skill and knowledge from three areas: Practical examinations for technical subjects, such as those offered by national examining bodies, further education written papers, and trade testing.

The latter has the oldest history, since in medieval times the guilds of craftsmen demanded that at the end of an apprenticeship, the apprentice should display his skill by making a 'masterpiece' to be submitted to the Masters of the Guild for their inspection and assessment. For example, a silversmith would make an intricate piece of silverware, a clockmaker a complete clock, and so on. Obviously, such a test would be very lengthy, and the apprentice might work at it over a number of months or even years.

Unfortunately, this concept of the masterpiece has held such sway that many people in industry feel that only a lengthy task involving the actual performance of all the skills of the trade is a valid way of 'passing out' a trainee. The marking, etc, may have been tightened up but the philosophy is the same. For example, a colleague visiting a large training establishment was invited to watch a test in progress. The test was a lengthy one involving stripping down and repairing a large unit from a motor vehicle on site. The greater part of the test consisted of relatively unskilled work such as unscrewing nuts in order to get at the interior of the unit. When asked what he thought of their testing system, the authors' colleague inquired how often mechanics had to do this task in the field. The answer was very rarely, if at all; the unit would be replaced in the field and any repair done in the workshop. The staff of this centre nevertheless considered that this was a 'good test' although they were not quite so sure what it was a test of!

The practical examination although logically separate has itself been affected by the above philosophy. In essence, the true practical examination complements a further education course and is intended to determine whether a student has absorbed the theoretical elements of the course. This is done by making him demonstrate his grasp of these principles in a practical task. For historical reasons, such as the fact that much industrial training has been done in technical colleges, practical examinations often became a mixture of the practical examination and trade test. However, it should be admitted that since educational courses as such are not related to specific jobs or indeed necessarily to industrial practice, success or failure in a practical examination need bear no relation to success or failure at doing a job itself. Indeed, such examinations may lead to the adoption of inappropriate training objectives. An examination for fitters in one of the power supply industries for example restricted itself to installation skills, although fault-finding and diagnostic skills had become increasingly important. Because training centres tended to be examination-orientated, trainees were taught installation skills to get them through the examination rather than diagnostic skills to help them in doing their job.

Written educational examinations in technical subjects, since they are educational and test knowledge and not actual performance, do not measure proficiency on-the-job. A student may learn up facts about a given occupation such as the different types of welding, the gases used, the merits of different types of equipment, etc, and pass the examination. Yet he could not bluff his way

Introduction

through a performance test actually involving welding. As we said previously, knowledge or the appreciation of principles may help one do a job but it does not mean that one will be able to do it. Performance tests are needed to see if an individual can actually do a job, and as such must be related to specific industrial situations and skills.

A further important point is the distinction between norm-referenced and criterion-referenced measures of performance. A norm-referenced measure is intended to place candidates in relation to one another or to other candidates; for example, to decide who are the top five pupils in a class. Most educational examinations are norm-referenced, although this is often not made clear. Pass/fail decisions in such cases are often made on the basis of allowing a certain fixed proportion of candidates to pass. Such a system is unavoidable if the exact level of attainment required is difficult to specify. A criterion-referenced measure on the other hand is intended to place candidates in relation to a criterion or standard of performance; for example, typing x words in an hour with only y errors. From the above description it can be seen that criterion-referenced tests are usually more applicable to the testing of industrial skills.

Norm-referenced and criterion-referenced tests can be differentiated on the following bases:

1. The purpose of testing; whether a candidate's performance is described in terms of that of other candidates or in terms of a standard of performance.
2. The method of construction of the tests; criterion-referenced measures are based on an extensive analysis and definition of the required behaviour.
3. Criterion-referenced tests given highly specific information, such as that a candidate can or cannot weld to a given standard. Norm-referenced tests tend to be general rather than specific.
4. How far one can generalize from the test to the area for which the test is devised; with a criterion-referenced test, since it is based on analysis and is specific, it is known to what extent it can say 'Because he can do the test, he can do x'. With a norm-referenced test, since it is not too difficult to devise a test which differentiates between candidates on some basis or another, it is not immediately clear to what degree one can generalize to non-test behaviour. Often an extensive study is required to determine the relationship between norm-referenced test performance and performance in an allegedly related area.
5. Norm-referenced measures are intended to place candidates in some order of merit and test results are used chiefly for that purpose. Criterion-referenced test results, since they have a fixed reference point, can be used for a variety of purposes, some of which are given below. Other uses will emerge throughout the course of the book.

THE PURPOSE OF TESTING

To measure a trainees readiness for another stage in his career

This is the traditional passing-out function of tests and is probably the one that springs first to mind. The test establishes that the individual has achieved a

Introduction

given level of performance during a course of training. Care must be taken, however, to ensure that no greater value is placed on the test result (often formalized in terms of a certificate) than it deserves. For example, if the trainees have only been tested on part of the course or assessed at a lower standard than on-the-job work, the certificate should not be taken to mean that he can do the job immediately. Hence one trend in certification is to state in exactly what areas the candidate was tested and the standard achieved rather than having broad global descriptions such as 'engineering craft practice'.

Providing information on performance to trainees and trainers

Although the passing-out function is an important one, it has been pointed out that testing somebody only at the end of a course loses a lot of information. For example, if a trainee's performance is unsatisfactory, there may be little that can be done about it. A phased testing system, on the other hand, involves trainees being tested at discrete stages of training so that both trainer and trainee can be made aware of any areas of strength of weakness. The phased test can provide the type of feedback which is essential in the development of any skill.

Determining training needs

Chaney and Teel[3] report that in one factory it was decided that the quality control inspectors of machined parts were not performing well enough. An experimental study established that an efficient way to improve performance on this task was to give the inspectors a test. This consisted of four parts fabricated to contain a representative sample of known defects. Deficiencies in the ability to identify faults were discovered in this way and an appropriate training programme developed.

Setting training objectives

Teachers are often accused of teaching only 'towards the examination', an apprehension of the fact that a set system of assessment serves as an objective towards which teachers aim. This is a bad practice where the objectives as specified by the test or examination are inappropriate or when teachers should be teaching something which is, for whatever reason, not included in the examination. Performance tests because they specify the task to be performed and have a standard way of assessing performance on the task can present a good set of behavioural objectives. Just how a rather vague set of objectives can be transformed in this way is shown in Chapter 3. This function is particularly important where those involved in training may otherwise be unaware of the exact nature of their objectives.

To assess the effectiveness of training methods and suitability of training content

In 1954 a US Army survey showed there was a widespread opinion that the training of tank crewmen left a lot to be desired. A research project described by Crawford[4] was initiated which looked first of all at current training and the tasks

Introduction

themselves. As a result of this various training packages were developed involving different amounts of instruction and practice time. Trainees from each package were then tested and the results showed little increase in proficiency even with large increases in instruction time. A new course was then developed on the basis of this study and the 'Armor Mastery Performance Test' was constructed consisting of 21 subtests; six on driving, nine on gunnery, four on loading, and two on special weapons.

In order to validate the new training programme, two groups of trainees were used, one undergoing the conventional eight-week training and one the new six-week programme. The trainees on the new course were superior on 11 subtests, were equal on seven tests, and were inferior only on three. These results showed that the 25% reduction in training time involved in the new programme improved overall proficiency of trainees and so the new programme was instituted for all tank crewmen.

The above is a very interesting example of how the intelligent use of tests can give information of how good various training methods are. The test acts as a yardstick against which the effectiveness of training can be measured.

To assess the suitability of an individual for employment or for a particular salary grade

So far tests within the training situation have been discussed but there is no reason why a test embodying relevant tasks and standards cannot be used for other purposes. Since most, if not all, companies must at one time or another recruit personnel trained in other organisations, it is often useful to apply a performance test as a selection device. The test need not be used only to pass or fail the prospective employee, but also to provide a profile of his strengths and weaknesses. The organization may then feel it worth its while to redress the latter. Similarly if there are grade differentiations within the organization, both employers and employees may consider a suitable performance test the fairest means of deciding into which grade a man should be placed. Short tests could also be used by employment agencies to screen personnel before sending them onto prospective employers.

To validate selection procedures

Many selection procedures, notably psychological tests, are validated by comparing test performance with some measure of job performance. All too often such measures may be unreliable or invalid (eg supervisor's ratings). A suitable performance test can provide a valid and reliable measure against which selection techniques can be validated. For example, Stuit[1] reports that when scores on an aptitude test used for classifying US Navy recruits were compared with grades at training school, little relationship was found when the grades were based only on instructors' ratings. However, when grades were alloted on the basis of performance tests, the classification test was seen to be a much better predictor of training performance. One reason for this difference was that the instructors' ratings were considerably influenced by academic and intellectual abilities.

REFERENCES

1. Stuit D.B., *Personnel Research and Test Development in the Bureau of Naval Personnel*, Princeton University Press, Princeton, 1947.
2. Arny C.B., *Evaluation and Investigation in Home Economics*, Appleton-Century-Crofts, New York, 1953.
3. Chaney F.B. and Teel K.S., *Improving Inspector Performance through Training and Visual Aids* in Experimental Psychology in Industry, Holding D.H., Ed., Penguin Books, London, 1969.
4. Crawford M.P., *Concepts of Training* in Psychological Principles in Systems Development, Gagne R.M. Ed., Holt Rinehart and Winston, New York, 1962.

SUGGESTED FURTHER READING

Boyd J.L. and Shimberg B., *Handbook of Performance Testing*, Educational Testing Service, Princeton, USA, 1970, Chap.1 'Introduction to Performance Testing', Chap.2 'Why Measure Performance?'

Clegg C.R. and Jones A., *Skills Testing Service*, Industrial and Commercial Training, Volume 2, Number 6, 1970.

Glaser R. and Klaus D.J., *'Proficiency Measurement: Assessing Human Performance'* in Psychological Principles in Systems Development, Gagne R.M., Ed., Holt, Rinehart and Winston, New York, 1962.

Jessup G. et al, *Manual of Trade Proficiency Testing,* Ministry of Defence, 1968, Chap.3 'The Functions of Tests'.

2

Skill

THE CONCEPT OF SKILLED PERFORMANCE

The aim of a performance test is to assess the proficiency or level of performance of an individual by setting him a standard task (or number of tasks) which embodies the important or critical elements of the relevant skills.

Taking this as a very broad objective for performance testing, it is worth noting that the term skill sets a limit to the concept of performance testing. This means that human skills of various types will be looked at throughout the subsequent pages so it will be valuable to examine the term skill to see exactly what limits it imposes.

Here are some typical definitions of skill provided by people involved in industrial training:

> 'The ability to perform a task as opposed to the knowledge required.'
>
> 'The observable actions that a person performs when performing his job. The skill of calculation for example is being able to do the calculations including obtaining the necessary information to perform the calculations.'
>
> 'A practised ability or change in behaviour which results from training or experience.'
>
> 'The practical ability to perform a defined range of mechanical tasks requiring the intelligent application of related technical knowledge.'
>
> 'Practical ability coming from knowledge in combination with expertness and discrimination.'
>
> 'Skill is the ability to perform a task to a satisfactory standard.'

Skill

It can be seen then that most people tend to see skill as a *complex, practical* activity that requires the support of theoretical and factual knowledge. Also the idea that this activity is learned and purposive is fairly common.

But these definitions tend to restrict the concept to the area of mechanical skills like turning, fitting, etc, while skill may cover a wider area than this, and if some well known skills are now examined it is possible to see which aspects of skill these definitions ignore.

Take two dissimilar activities like driving a car and playing chess; most people would accept these as representatives of skilled performance. But they differ in one fundamental way in that the outstanding facet of driving skill is manual dexterity and perceptual skills such as discrimination of speeds etc, while with chess this facet takes on a lesser role compared with the ability to manipulate ideas. Clearly both types of manipulation are present in both activities but their relative importance is reversed. Thus the concept of skill can be seen to include both a predominantly physical type of skill and a predominantly 'mental' type of skill.

Now, although these two activities are dissimilar in some ways, they must have similarities or one would not be prepared to call them both skill. One similarity of course is manipulation. Another is that these activities are organized into complex sequences. There are different levels of organization in that muscle movements must be organized to say change gear and memory traces must be organized to remember the valid moves in chess but the concept of skill usually refers to the total activities so one has a higher level or organization in that all the simple sequences are recombined to produce a complex sequence of activities.

Another characteristic common to both chess and driving is that they are goal directed in a rather human way in that it can be seen why people drive cars and play chess, but they are also human in that one is not obliged to do them in the same way that one is obliged to eat and breath. So far, then, skill is a goal directed sequence of activities with a high level of organization but a comprehensive description of skill has not yet been given here.

It was noted earlier that skill involves the manipulation of ideas and symbols or simply information. This may form the major part of the skill as in chess or a relatively minor part in driving, but it is always present. Information is essential before the organized sequence can start and continue. 'Would you like a game of chess?' might be an appropriate input of information to start one sequence and one important point here is that the input of information tells one that perception is involved; information is taken in via the senses, it is processed and an appropriate response made. Furthermore, it is often the response that is made or the outcome of that response which provides the necessary stimulus for the next response. Here one has feedback of information; the result of one action initiates another.

Skill, then, is a complex goal directed sequence of activities with a high level of organization and making extensive use of feedback.

This definition of skill is less restrictive than that which was put forward initially. It should be noted that the term skilled as used in industry has applied traditionally to those who have served an apprenticeship and does not necessarily

Skill

entail any particular level of competence. In the field of performance testing one is concerned with establishing whether or not a person can actually do something.

CATEGORIES OF SKILL

By now one should have a fair idea of what skill is but it has also been seen that different types of skill can be identified. For example, the reverse importance of the mental and physical aspects of skill in driving and chess has been named. As test development is described it will be found useful to be able to categorize these different types of skill since this will help one to see exactly for what one is testing.

There are several different approaches to the categorization of skill but the authors have found that for the purpose of test development the scheme shown in Figure 2.1 has provided a useful framework.

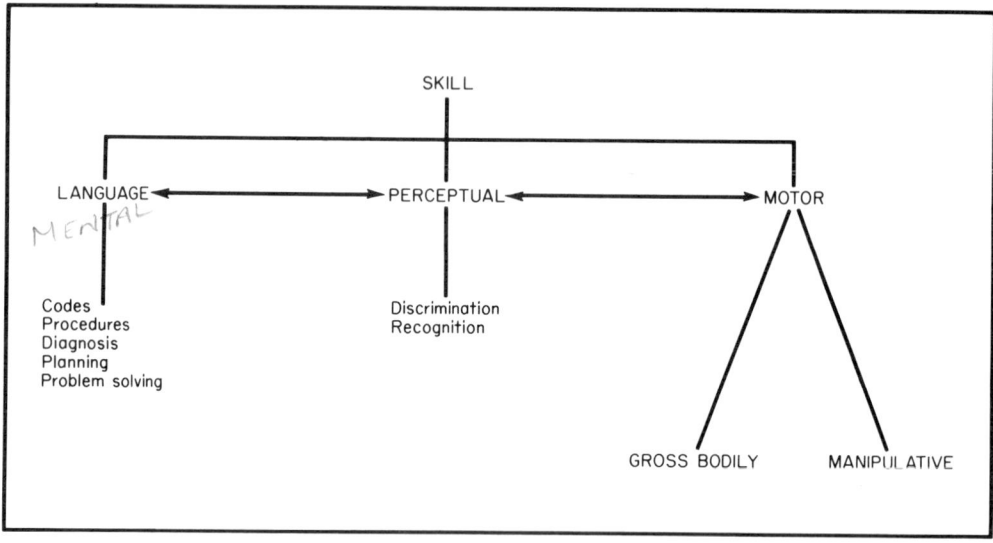

Figure 2.1 A categorization of skills

Reference to the figure shows three broad categories of skills; motor, perceptual, and language. It should be appreciated that in any particular skilled performance, skills from all three categories are likely to be present, but there is variation in their contribution to the overall performance. So, any reference to a particular type of skill is one of emphasis, and this is brought out in the figure by the interconnecting double-headed arrows.

Looking first at motor skills, these are skills which involve extensive use of the motor systems which produce movement. Motor skills are therefore always visible or overt; one can see them taking place. It is possible to identify two types of motor skills. Firstly, there are those like dancing, swimming, and running that involve the movement of the whole body; these can be called gross bodily skills. Secondly, there are those that involve relatively smaller, but finer, movements of few muscles; these are the manipulative skills like sewing, typing, and milling.

Perceptual skills involve the sensory systems, notably the eyes, ears, nose, and touch. Highly developed perceptual skills are needed in motor activities and language processes. These skills include discrimination between various types of perceptual input (for example, a piano tuner must be able to discriminate fine differences in pitch), estimation of speed and distance (as in driving), recognition of patterns (for example, recognizing correct and incorrect functioning of an engine), and so on.

Language skills are those referred to earlier as mental skills; since the word mental tends to indicate the opposite of physical and little else, the more descriptive term language skills will be used.

Language skills involve the manipulation of symbols and since language is a symbolic method of communication it may be used to describe this type of skill. The term language may at first sight appear to restrict this type of skill to the varied use of words, but since language has been described as a symbolic method of communication it is clear that language covers a much wider concept and as such will embrace such things as words, numbers, diagrams, codes, etc, in fact anything that is used to communicate. It is the perception and manipulation of this information that constitutes a language skill.

Thus reading and writing are basic language skills for most jobs in an industrialized society, while reading colour codes and technical drawings are examples of work-specialized but still relatively basic language skills. At a higher level, there are skills involving decision making and planning which are also language skills. For example, a TV service engineer must be able to diagnose faults on a subscriber's receiver and decide what remedial action to take, while a skilled bench fitter has to organize the operations required to produce a working part from the information contained in the production drawing.

Unlike motor skills, language skills need not necessarily be overt; in fact the major part of the skill, the manipulation of symbols, may only be detected indirectly in that the person will have to concentrate on the manipulation at the expense of other tasks. For example, one would not expect to be able to learn a poem or do mental arithmetic while concentrating on a game of chess.

It is worth noting that the type of skill classified here as motor is often referred to as psycho-motor, perceptual-motor, etc, since these terms stress the presence of perceptual and language skill in all motor skill. These terms may seem more descriptive but when one considers that it is impossible for a person to move without perceiving that movement and that perception is an equally important aspect of language skills it is obvious that the prefixes psycho and perceptual are rather redundant.

This point raises again the original statement about the three broad classes of skills. Remember that all classes will always be present: it is their relative importance or predominance that varies.

SUMMARY

The commonly held concept of skill as a sort of physical wizardry has been expanded to include wizardry with ideas and symbols or simply language. It has also been noted that skill relies on perception, the stimulus often arising as the result of a previous action (feedback). It was possible to identify language skill, motor skill and perceptual skill and to see that their emphasis varies with the skill under analysis.

Now that the authors' area of interest has been defined it is possible to go on to look at the initial stages of test development.

SUGGESTED FURTHER READING

Fitts P.M. and Posner M.I., *Human Performance,* Brooks/Cole, California, 1967, Chap. 1 'Skills of Civilized Man'.
Seymour W.C., *Industrial Skills,* Pitman, London, 1969, Chap. 1.
Wellens J., *Training in Physical Skills,* Business Books, London, 1974.

3

Analytical Techniques for Test Development

ANALYSIS OF A TASK

It was seen in Chapter 1 that there are many reasons for using performance tests, but the common factor in all situations where tests are required is the necessity to establish the level of competence held by some person in a particular skill or group of skills. Within this frame of reference it will always be necessary to establish what the person should be able to do.
 One may be required, for example, to find out whether or not trainees have benefited from a particular training programme. Or one may wish to select personnel for a particular job. Thus the performance expectancies will be contained to some extent in training programmes and job descriptions. In order to establish a specification of essential skills it will be necessary to analyse the situation and draw up a behavioural specification. The first step in this analysis is to decide what to analyse. It has already been stated that training programmes and job specifications will usually be examined but often this is not sufficient. If the case where tests are needed to establish the performance level of trainees is taken, it may be that one will wish to know whether or not these trainees are ready to enter the normal work environment. In this case it would be a mistake to work entirely from the training programme since this would assume a perfectly relevant and up-to-date programme. It would be necessary to confirm the contents of the training programmes by analysing the requirements of the actual job. If, on the other hand, one were concerned only with the acquisition of the training programme content it would then be unnecessary to study the job; it would,

however, be a mistake to work purely from the training programmes since these often seem to overstate what is being taught.

Whatever the situation the first step is to decide the exact purpose of the test in terms of the type of person that would be successful with the tests. In most cases this will lead to an analysis of a job or of a training programme.

As a result of various restricting conditions that may be present it will probably be necessary to select the skills or tasks to be tested. This means that one needs some criteria on which to base the selection. Occasionally it may be possible to test all the elements contained in a job. In this case, the problem of deciding what to test may not arise but the problem of defining a minimum acceptable level of performance is still present.

In very general terms only the essential skills and knowledge required for successful job performance need to be tested. The problem is how to identify these and distinguish them from the 'nice to know' components. One trap to avoid is the selection of those aspects of the job which are easy to measure, because tests are easy to prepare, administer, or score. A common example of this is the testing of job knowledge or theory by means of paper and pencil tests instead of a more expensive test involving the practical elements of the job.

Unfortunately, there is no simple formula that can be applied to a job to help one select the correct skills and knowledge to be tested. What can be done, though, is to identify the essential characteristics of a task and apply these as a set of criteria. To this end the analysis should bring out the following information:

1 Tasks performed   —   skills involved.
2 The frequency of occurrence of tasks.
3 The criticality of the tasks   —   the cost of performing the task inadequately.
4 The difficulty of the tasks.
5 The standard to which tasks should be performed.
6 The relative importance of the way a job is carried out (process) and the quality of the end result (product).
7 The conditions   —   amount of responsibility, physical and psychological conditions in which duties will be carried out.
8 Any supporting knowledge that is required.
9 Safety regulations   —   both company and statutory.

These points now require some more detailed explanation.

Frequency

If the test is to be a true reflection of the job it must reflect the frequency with which tasks occur. It is worth pointing out at this stage that the data collected need not be particularly detailed as long as it is reasonably accurate. Thus with frequency one could study the job situation at close quarters for several months and keep a record of the actual frequency with which tasks were carried out during that period. This level of analysis is not necessary for test development; it would often be sufficient to consult available records or ask people how often they have to perform a particular task.

Frequency is a useful measure of the importance of a task in that one would expect a man to be especially competent at the tasks he performs most regularly. But this is really only half the story for there may well be several tasks that only occur, say, once a month and yet it is essential that they be carried out well. These tasks could be described as critical and it is essential to consider frequency and criticality as interacting characteristics.

Criticality

If incorrect performances can lead to loss in production, damage to equipment or injury to personnel (ie failure leads to high costs) then that item must be included and be satisfactorily performed. Safety precautions are an obvious example.

High-cost tasks are critical tasks and frequency and cost should be considered together; a low-frequency but high-cost task is as important as a high-frequency low-cost task. For example, the use of thermionic valves in electronic equipment is becoming increasingly rare and so one might not expect an electronic service hand to know much about valves. At the same time it could be the case that valves are still used in some of the major control equipment that tends to be very reliable and so only break down on rare occasions. When that equipment does fail the hand will be expected to repair the fault quickly and it is therefore essential for him to have some knowledge of valve equipment.

Difficulty

The tests should measure a man's ability to carry out difficult parts of the job. There are several indications of this as noted below.

Time

If a task has a long average time factor and wide variations in the individual times and some can perform it more efficiently than others then it is apparently a difficult task. The test developer should try to identify the cause of difficulty and look for different methods of approach, use of special tools, job aids, jigs, etc.

Errors (Number and Type)

A large percentage of errors can point to difficult tasks and/or inadequate training.

Requests for Assistance

How often men seek the assistance of more qualified men can provide a useful index of difficulty.

Analytical Techniques for Test Development

Standard of Performance

If the tests are to have any meaning to production departments it is essential that a comparable standard of performance is used so one must be in a position to say that the candidate, having passed the test, can perform a job to a given standard.

The standard must be defined as rigorously as possible, and usually in terms of the following.

Output

For most manual and clerical jobs, it is fairly easy to establish objective output standards. The expression of these will vary with the kind of work involved for production work, units produced per unit of time is a good measure; in clerical work there are obvious measures like words per minute (shorthand and typing) and the number of forms processed. In service industries it may be necessary to establish a set time for performance of the task.

Quality

Where quality standards already exist these should be used. In production quality can often be defined in terms of finish while in service industries the quality is often expressed in the process or procedural aspects of the job. In other fields it may be necessary to resort to less objective measures such as ratings of pleasantness and politeness when answering telephone calls.

Product or Process

Different types of industry and different departments within an industry place varying emphasis on the product and process aspects of a job. With some tasks the quality of the finished product is the main consideration whereas with others it may be the process which is utilized that is the most important. In the case of motor vehicle overhaul, for example, one is not only concerned that the engine is running but also with the way in which the unit was reconstructed; if the mechanic has not payed sufficient attention to the significant points of reconstructional methods (such as lubricating parts, torque ratings etc) the engine may run for a short period only.

Thus with many jobs it would be short sighted to look at the end-product only, while in pure production work one is interested only in the fact that the components are produced to the desired standard. The way in which they are produced may be of less interest as long as safety precautions are not violated and equipment is not ill-treated. When it comes to assembling components, however, one will become more interested in process aspects.

In some cases the end-product may be an inevitable outcome if all significant procedural points are carried out, but care must be taken not to ignore the product too hastily since it may be possible to leave out a critical significant point but still pass the tests in terms of an acceptable end-product. So, to avoid excessive detail in process both product and process could be defined as necessary conditions for success.

For example, in a test for tractor drivers which involves an alteration of the wheel distances (see Figure 3.1) one can list the significant aspects of the procedure but it would be quite possible for the testee to omit say the thirteenth point. This omission would leave the task unfinished but may not show up in the definition of the final result.

What is being pointed out is that product and process are always present and it is their relative importance that should be established.

Working Conditions

There are two basic types of condition to be considered, these being the psychological and physical or environmental conditions.

Psychological conditions can often be examined in terms of the amount of personal responsibility; whether the man is able to call assistance when faced with difficult or new problems or must solve them himself.

Environmental conditions such as temperature, noise level, confined spaces, level of illumination, etc, may affect the difficulty of performing the task; for example, driving a car at night can be an exacting experience for a new driver.

The tempo of required performance can change a job; fault diagnosis in commercial aircraft must be fast since turn-round time must be kept to a minimum and it is important that the maintenance team is able to trace and correct faults in the minimum time.

Fitters in the quarry industry are required to work in difficult situations because of the location of plant and the possibility of adverse weather conditions. It would be unwise to assume that a man who can do the job in a warm well lit workshop can also do it on a cold windy cliff top.

Clearly it is important that the testing environment should as far as possible reflect any relevant adverse conditions that will exist in the actual job if the test is designed to measure on-the-job performance.

Supporting Knowledge

This refers to any knowledge that it is essential for the man to know before he can successfully perform the task. This source of information will vary so one must establish whether he will be expected to learn the necessary facts so that he carries them in his head or whether he will be able to refer to algorithms, flow diagrams, decision trees, tables, service manuals, etc.

A good example of the use of both these sources of information can be found in the agricultural industry. If one goes back to the test for adjusting tractor wheel track (Figure 3.1), it will be seen that the distance between the wheels of a tractor can be varied. This adjustment is brought about by moving the wheels into various alternative mounting arrangements. The tractor driver is expected to know how far apart his wheels must be when working with a particular crop. But he is not expected to know the exact arrangement of wheel positions needed to give that particular wheel width; he will refer to the instruction manual for this information.

So the source of knowledge should always be established but the true practicality of the findings must also be noted. It may be the case that electricians are allowed to use algorithms to assist speedy fault finding but it must be

Analytical Techniques for Test Development

considered whether any algorithms are available. If they are available in the training school it must be taken into account whether they will also be available in the works.

Safety Regulations

It is very important that all candidates should adhere to the safety regulations as laid down both by the State and by the company. This is especially important where breach of the regulations could lead to death or injury. It is equally important that the tests should not lead to dangerous situations. In a test of pig castration it was laid down that the candidate should load the scalpel at the start of the test and disinfect the blade at the end. Since scalpel blades are sharp enough to castrate a whole litter before they are discarded the test administrators naturally removed the blade disinfected by one candidate and left the dismantled scalpel ready for the next. The next candidate therefore had to handle a wet blade which put him in considerable danger of cutting himself quite badly. The test specification was subsequently revised to indicate that each candidate was to be provided with a dry blade.

Other Information

The analysis situation provides an ideal opportunity for collecting other items of information.

There are some items which, although they may not be essential to the analysis itself, will be essential to the later stages of test development. These are mainly items of administrative interest and as such are very important.

1. The amount and type of equipment available.
2. The availability of candidates — in terms of time.
3. The availability of examiners to carry out testing (and mark tests) in terms of time and numbers.
4. The number of candidates that will need to be tested during any one session.
5. The frequency with which candidates will be ready for testing (once a year, one a month, etc).

The importance of these factors and the way in which information relating to them can be used will be discussed in Chapter 7.

HOW TO COLLECT THE INFORMATION

The type of information which is needed about a situation before adequate and relevant tests can be produced has already been discussed. Now it has to be decided how to collect that information. There are several techniques available and each situation may call for a different combination of these and one must decide which methods are applicable for the problem at hand. In order to give some guidance, however, the advantages and pitfalls of each technique can be considered.

Analytical Techniques for Test Development

C/E/III
Test No. T101
Time: 1 hour

Adjusting wheel track — front and rear

The tractor, which must not have rear wheel weights fitted or rear tyres ballasted, should be standing on ground that is unsuitable for jacking.

The adjustment to be made must require a change in the position of rims relative to centres and an interchange of wheels (rear wheels).

It should be established before the test begins that all appropriate nuts and bolts are easily freed with suitable spanners, ie the nuts should not be seized or badly rusted. The candidate must be told which crop the tractors is to be used for.

Procedure

Adjust the front and rear wheel tracks to the correct width to *suit the given row crop*

Significant points

Front wheels
1. Tractor moved to firm level ground (concrete if possible)
2. Rear wheels blocked and parking brake applied
3. Nuts on axle bolts released before jacking
4. Sensible placement of jack
5. Axle stands (or blocks) placed in position as safety measure
6. Axle bolts refitted in correct holes after changing wheel setting
7. Toe-in checked and adjusted as necessary
8. Axle bolts finally tightened after lowering to ground

Rear wheels
9. Front wheels securely blocked
10. Stud nuts (or outer rim nuts) released before jacking
11. Sensible placement of jack
12. Axle stands (or blocks) placed in position
13. Wheel refitted in correct position without damage to threads on studs or bolts
14. Tyre tread checked — facing correct way
15. Wheel correctly located on spigot or lugs
16. All nuts finally tightened after lowering to ground

Result

Wheels adjusted to correct width and toe-in correct. All safety precautions adhered to.

Score: A, B, C

Score [15 or 16]

© Copyright Skills Testing Service

Figure 3.1 A test in adjusting tractor wheel tracks

Personal Experience

This can be a useful approach since it sometimes provides information which would otherwise be difficult or impossible to obtain, but it suffers from several obvious flaws.

Firstly, it is only useful when one is dealing with one's own areas of skill and even then it may be limited to a narrow selection of the full activities of the trade.

Secondly, procedures may well vary with different parts of the country, plant, or company. Also the information which can be supplied may not be up-to-date and may be at the wrong level.

So personal experience will have only limited use and should never be relied upon as the main source of information.

Consulting Colleagues

This can help to some extent in counteracting the drawbacks of using personal experience but the above points should still be kept very much in mind.

Written Information

In the preliminary stages of analysis it will be useful to consult written information such as training programmes, existing job descriptions, manufacturers' handbooks, British Standards, etc. Some care must be exercised here since the information may be incomplete, out-of-date, incorrect or inappropriate for some conditions in which the job is performed.

These first three stages are most useful as a preliminary analysis which will help guide the more detailed techniques that follow.

Survey

A systematic enquiry directed at various levels of personnel can provide information for both training and test construction. Questions can be directed at:

1 *Supervisors*   What do you expect your men to be able to do?
2 *Tradesmen*   What does your job involve?
3 *Training*   What do you expect your trainees to be able to do at the end
  Instructors   of the course.

The survey can be carried out by either interview or questionnaire or both.

Interview

The interview is usually the simplest method to arrange in that relatively little preparation is required. This does not mean that one can saunter into an interview and take it all off-the-cuff. The earlier stages of analysis should involve a fairly detailed study of the training programme or job specification and from them one may find areas that leave one suspicious or in doubt. Thus it may be found hard

Analytical Techniques for Test Development

to believe that trainees do so much in so little time. These are the sort of questions that should be answered during the interview.

Before starting interviews, then, one should prepare a list of questions that are to be answered. This list will then be used as a skeleton structure around which the interview should be constructed. But one must be prepared to let the interview branch out where appropriate so that one allows oneself the opportunity to collect unexpected information. Indeed the skeleton itself will probably evolve as more people are interviewed.

It is of course of the utmost importance to record the results of the interview as accurately as possible. Although it may be necessary to *summarize* what the interviewee has said, interpretation of the data should wait until all relevant personnel have been interviewed. Tape recorders, if acceptable to the interviewee, are useful to record what takes place and to avoid the distractions of writing notes.

Who to interview

It is important to interview personnel from different levels of the working heirarchy. Thus when developing tests for a training course the following persons should be interviewed:

1   Training officers
2   Training instructors
3   Trainees

To check how training relates to the actual job:

1   Managers
2   Foremen
3   Supervisors

Where a training programme is not involved the interview should be directed at:

1   Plant engineers
2   Works managers
3   Foremen
4   Supervisors
5   Tradesmen and operators

It is essential to motivate interviewees to give truthful and accurate information. In order to do this, the interviewee should be informed of the purpose of the project and how he can contribute towards it. Every effort should be made to put him at ease and to create a situation where he feels free to express his opinions.

For the majority of the situations the interview will probably be the most useful technique at one's disposal but there are situations where the interview becomes very time-consuming and expensive. For example, if one is dealing with a situation where personnel are dispersed between several establishments over a wide geographic area, then it is quite possible that local practices have caused a divergent trend. This means that staff would have to be interviewed at all

21

these establishments to ensure that any divergent practices are taken into account. Clearly the interview becomes very costly in these circumstances and a questionnaire may well be more useful. Another type of interview is the group interview where a number of people can be interviewed simultaneously; they provide the necessary information under the direction of the interviewer, often in an atmosphere of free discussion. Such a technique can be useful in tidying up the behavioural specification (see below) or other details. Care must be taken, however, to avoid any individual or group of individuals dominating the interview. Groups of three to five are a practical size.

Questionnaire

Questionnaires can be used to save the day in the type of situation described above. They will gather vast amounts of information from a wide range of people for relatively little cost. But a questionnaire must be well designed if it is to be of any use. This means that all the questions must be unambiguously stated, easily understood and relevant to the situation. In order to be certain of this it may be necessary to carry out other stages of development, including interviews, before the questionnaire can be written.

Decisions to be made prior to construction

The main and auxiliary methods of data collection. The final form of the questionnaire cannot be decided until some pilot work has been carried out. Early work will probably be in the form of a structured interview with open questions. This approach should give some ideas about alternatives to use in multiple-choice questions.

It cannot be assumed that the respondent holds any opinion at all towards the content of the questionnaire let alone that he will be able to choose a suitable answer (to one of the questions) from a set of say four answers that have been invented. Therefore, it may be necessary to include some fairly open questions to ascertain whether or not the respondent has any opinion at all before going on to more specific questions.

Method of approach to respondents. Anonimity seems to be valuable. Stated aim is important since the respondent tries to answer in a way that he feels is appropriate to the problem at hand. Small details such as reply-paid envelopes can considerably increase the response rate.

Question sequences. The order in which questions are asked can play a large part in the 'rapport' set up between the questionnaire and the respondent. Thus, as in an interview one should start by asking the respondent questions about himself. If one is comparing training departments with production departments two questionnaires are needed, one starting with questions about training, the other in the reverse order.

Order of questions within each sequence. There are two useful approaches to question sequencing. The *funnel approach* starts by asking very broad questions to find out whether or not the respondent has relevant knowledge or opinions on that subject and then gradually the field is narrowed down to specific questions. This method gives the respondent every opportunity to give the required response spontaneously and as such it may be useful in pilot work. Also responses to earlier questions will show whether answers were spontaneous or steered. The *Quintamensional Plan* differs slightly in that it starts by asking open questions to find out if the subject is aware of the relevant issues. Then asks questions of his general opinions. It finally presents multiple-choice questions dealing with the specific issues. One may also ask some questions to find the reasons for the given responses.

Use of precoded or free responses   —   Open and closed questions

Open questions give the subject a great deal of freedom and thus provide a lot of illuminating material. But analysis is difficult and requires some kind of coding technique to convert answers to numerical values, so the waffle is reduced to a rating anyway. This type of question is possibly most useful in pilot work where one is not quite sure of the type of responses to be expected. Its use in the final study would seem to be limited, however, since one must do twice as much work for equally valuable information.

With the closed question, on the other hand, the answers provided play an essential part since they steer responses in the required direction. This is reasonable if good pilot work has pointed one in that direction.

It is possible to ask some questions in open and closed form, this tends to lower the respondent's resentment since he is allowed some freedom to give his own ideas.

Question wording

A few hints on question wording are given below:

1 Define precisely what it is you want to know; meanings must be unambiguous.
2 Do not assume that the respondent has any opinion or knowledge about the subject.
3 Avoid leading questions   —   much leading comes from a failure to state suitable alternatives, thus a positive question tends to rule out negative answers. The use of multiple-choice questions with positive and negative alternatives avoids this problem to a large extent.
4 Avoid prestige bias   —   a question must not be worded in such a way that any particular answer may be more derogatory to the respondent than any other, eg 'Can any of your trainees read a micrometer?' should read: 'How well do your trainees get on with reading a micrometer?' The second version does not put the respondent on the defensive regarding his trainees' abilities.
5 Questionnaire rapport can be maintained in several ways:
   (*a*)   Explain aim of study (or stated aim).
   (*b*)   Tell the respondent why he was selected.
   (*c*)   Stress confidentiality and anonymity.
   (*d*)   Avoid putting respondent on the defensive.
   (*e*)   Be polite.
   (*f*)   Avoid abbreviations and terms which are too technical.

Analytical Techniques for Test Development

6   The type of item used will depend on the type of information required. This can range from a simple factual question such as 'Have you ever used a transistor analyser? Yes ( ) No ( )' to a tabular format that asks several questions about each point. Examples of tabular questions are shown in Figure 3.2. In most circumstances the tabular item will be the most useful since it easily provides much of the information required.

This type of question can easily be elaborated to cover say, the purpose of using the equipment, any difficulties experienced, etc.

7   *Pilot-Tests* With questionnaires, it is necessary to check their content before actually administering to large numbers of people. One should ensure that the questions are clear, and do not tend to lead the subject, etc.

There are two main drawbacks to questionnaires; the first is fairly obvious from what has been said so far; that there is a great deal of work and skill involved in the preparation of an effective questionnaire. It is usually necessary to carry out earlier stages of analysis or interview etc, before the questionnaire can be produced.

Another difficulty with questionnaires is that they present a rigid framework in which to collect information. This makes them more reliable but may lead to loss of information. Unlike the interview situation you cannot gain unexpected information. But a questionnaire should be used when the interview is not feasible due to dispersed personnel.

Direct Observation

This may appear to be the ideal method but in fact it has many drawbacks. The classical method of task analysis involves the construction of a detailed description of the procedures and action required to accomplish each task and the times taken to carry them out.

This sort of detail may be useful for the production of a training programme but it is too detailed to be used for test development.

Data collection by itself is not analysis: both interpretation and selection of data are required.

For the purposes of test development a detailed task analysis written up on the basis of extensive observation contains too much information but this does not mean that observation has no place in test development.

It can be useful to verify the data collected by other methods and can often show up the type of short cuts and incorrect procedures that are used.

Problems with direct observation

The chief difficulties are given below:

1   It is difficult to weed out the relevant information unless one has considerable knowledge of the job.
2   Direct observation can be very time-consuming especially with lengthy and/or infrequent jobs.
3   The performance one observes may not be ideal or even optimum, eg in fault finding experienced men often do not use the optimum strategy, so a marking

Analytical Techniques for Test Development

BRICKWORK QUESTIONNAIRE

Listed below is a series of tasks that might be expected of a bricklayer. For each task decide whether or not it is essential, useful, or irrelevant to you as an employer of bricklayers and enter a tick in the appropriate box.

Definitions:

Essential means that you would not employ a man who could not perform that task.

Useful means that you would employ the man even if he could not perform that task but you would be *more likely* to employ him if he could perform that task

Irrelevant means that you are not interested whether or not a man can perform this task.

Tick one box for each task listed.

	Essential	Useful	Irrelevant
Build cavity brickwork			
Build solid brickwork			
Build walls up to damp course including sleeper walls			
Build manholes			
Build solid or cavity work in blocks			
Build boundary walls			
Pointing and jointing			
Build partitions in bricks and blocks to receive surface finish			
Lay or fix cills and copings			
Build in brackets, pipe supports etc			

Figure 3.2 Part of a questionnaire used to assess the importance of various bricklaying tasks

scheme based on observation might be quite inappropriate. But direct observation can be useful for simple repetitive tasks where detailed analysis may be necessary. The test developer is often unfamiliar with the job in question and observation can provide an overall impression of the job, and also help him to check other data.

The appearance of the test developer on-site 'getting his hands dirty' may help in the ultimate acceptance of the tests. Therefore the test developer should carry out some observation to help him appreciate the difficulties of the job and the way in which environmental conditions affect it.

THE BEHAVIOURAL SPECIFICATION

The analysis will have provided a list of skills and supporting knowledge that are necessary for effective performance. The list will also contain information about these skills such as their frequency and criticality.

In most cases the list will be somewhat different to the original training programme or job specification in that some areas will have been rejected and others added on. This usually occurs if the original specification is out-of-date but sometimes they are just badly written in the first place. The extent to which one's list varies from the original will also depend on the frame of reference; it was noted earlier that tests may be produced to assess a person's readiness to enter the plant as say an electrician or they may be required to assess the extent to which a trainee has benefited from a period of training. In either case a training programme could have been the basis of the test development. The main difference is that the former will entail an analysis of the actual job to confirm the contents of the training programme, while with the latter one would concentrate on the training only. It is clear that the final list of skills and knowledge is more likely to differ from the original documents when a job as well as a training programme has been analysed. But changes will still occur when the training programme only has been studied.

The most common failing in existing documents like job descriptions and training programmes is that they tend to be vague since they are usually written in non-behavioural terms with frequent use of all embracing words such as 'understanding' and 'appreciation'. Thus the most important step at this stage is to write the specification in behavioural or doing terms so that the behavioural components of the skills and knowledge to be tested are clearly stated.

Another important procedure at this stage is to reject obvious overstatements, aspects of the course or job that were in the original documents and have proved to be either irrelevant or just overstated. An example of a more extreme case was an in-company electronics course where tests had to be developed to ensure that trainees had acquired the relevant skills. Analysis of the job showed that thermionic valves were virtually non-existent in the plant while almost half the training course was devoted to the understanding of valve characteristics; in this case then, although the training emphasized valves, the plant foreman was more concerned that electricians be familiar with transistors. Although the specification ignored valves and concentrated on transistor circuits, this should

Analytical Techniques for Test Development

not imply that analysis led simply to the dropping of any references to valves; it was also necessary to restate the description of tasks in behavioural terms. For example, 'an appreciation of simple transistor circuits' became:

Given circuit diagrams and photographs of the following circuits:

1 Simple amplifier
2 Differential amplifier
3 Current to pulse converter

the candidate must:

1 Name the circuit.
2 State where to test the overall performance of that circuit.
3 Select (from a choice of four) the correct output from that circuit.

If the tests are aimed only at the effectiveness of a training scheme it is unlikely that large chunks of that scheme will be rejected but it is often the case that some aspects of the course are overstated. The course manual for a short (five days) hydraulic course (Figure 3.3) for example contained the statement, 'Understanding of graphical symbols for components'. This may seem clear at first, but rather vague terms like understanding are still being used. A more surprising point, however, is that the manual contained several hundred symbols and it seemed unlikely that trainees could learn all of these in five days. Subsequent interviews revealed that symbols were made up from combinations of basic symbols and it was the latter that the candidate was expected to be familiar with.

To illustrate the gradual progress from course objectives to behavioural specification three steps have been reproduced that were taken during test development for the hydraulics course mentioned above.

The three stages shown are:

1 The original course content, Figure 3.3.
2 The authors' first specification of skills, Figure 3.4.
3 The final behavioural specification, Figure 3.5.

Examination of a single item will make its evolution clearer. Take 'the ability to maintain the following equipment and rectify faults. Valves . . . etc'.

At stage 2 the maintenance and fault rectifying function has been redefined in clearer terms:

Check and repair components (pumps, valves, motors):
(a) Strip down components.
(b) Checks to be done on components.
(c) Recognize faults in components.
(d) Reassemble components.

At the behavioural specification stage, (Figure 3.5) the whole selection has been expanded in terms of what the trainee is actually expected to do:

Analytical Techniques for Test Development

1 Training Objective
To provide trainees with a basic understanding of hydraulic components and circuitry applied to the control of plant and equipment.

2 Duration   One week (40 hours)

3 Training Analysis
 (a) Skill requirement
    The ability to maintain the following equipment and rectify faults.
    Pumps: Constant and variable volume
                   Single vane
                   Double vane
                   Two stage
                   Combination
                   Radial piston
                   In line piston
                   Angle piston
    Reservoirs, strainers, filters
    Valves: Pressure relief
                   Pressure reducing
                   Sequence
                   Pressure switches
                   Directional control
                   Check
                   Flow control
                   Deceleration
    Motors: Variable and fixed displacement
                   Piston and vane types

 (b) Knowledge requirement
    The understanding of basic principles of hydraulics
    Method of pump operation   Constant and variable volume
                                    Single vane
                         Types {   Double vane
                                    Two-stage
                                    Combination
                                    Radial piston
                                    In line piston
                                    Angle piston
    Typical pump faults and trouble shooting procedures.

    The method of operation of the following types of valves.
    Their interaction in a circuit with relevant limitations of use:
        Pressure relief   — Simple and compound types
        Pressure reducing sequence
        Pressure switches   — Two and four way
        Directional control check   — Simple, restricted, and pilot operated
        Flow control   Pressure and temperature compensated
        Deceleration   and overload relief

    The method of operation of hydraulic motors with relevant faults and trouble shooting procedures of:
                   Piston and vane types
    An appreciation of reservoir design
    The importance of filters and strainers
    The interaction of component parts in a hydraulic system
    An appreciation of hydraulic fluids
    The understanding of graphical symbols for components
    An understanding of hydraulic circuit drawing with particular reference to sequence of operations.

Figure 3.3 Basic hydraulics course content

Analytical Techniques for Test Development

Trainee should be able to strip down, service, and reassemble each of the following:
(a) Single vane pump.
(b) In-line axial piston pump.

Trainee should be able to recognize wear in parts of the following:
(a) Single vane pump.
(b) Double vane pump.
(c) Two-stage vane pump.
(d) In-line axial piston pump.

Trainee should be able to strip down report on condition and reassemble as appropriate valves of the following type:
(a) Pressure relief valve.
(b) Pressure reducing valve, etc.

Apart from the fact that the tasks are now stated in behavioural terms there have been other changes taking place during the two steps from the original. In general, these have classified and restricted the tasks. Thus, for example, it is now stated that the candidate must strip down service and reassemble only one example of two major types of pumps. This means that a basic similarity has been established between all vane pumps and all axial piston pumps. Another interesting point is that the recognition of wear in pumps has been isolated and a separate test would now be produced for that function. This allows one to test the candidate's knowledge of a wider variety of pumps in a quick way, but this will be enlarged upon when the variety of testing techniques that are available are discussed (Chapter 4).

1   Identify components
    Function of components in circuits
    JIC symbols of components

2   How to check and repair components (pumps, valves, motors)
    (a) Strip down components
    (b) Checks to be done on components (such as pumps)
    (c) Recognize faults in components
    (d) Reassembly

3   Function of given circuit, ie given function you want performed, what kind of circuit would you use?

4   Fault finding in simple circuits.
    What to check and in what order.
    How to check (any measuring or other instruments) and any criteria.
    Use of algorithms?

Note: This is an unadorned version of the short notes used by the authors in this analysis.

Figure 3.4 Interim statement of skills

Analytical Techniques for Test Development

1. Trainee should be able to name from their appearance the following types of Vickers valves:
   (a) Pressure relief valve
   (b) Pressure reducing valve
   (c) Sequence valve
   (d) Simple directional valve
   (e) Standard check valve
   (f) Restriction check valve

2. For each of the above types of valve trainee should be able to identify the correct version from a selection of functional diagrams only one of which is functionally correct.

3. Trainee should be able to recognize the following JIC symbols (pp.154–155)
   (a) Pumps
   (b) Lines and functions
   (c) Miscellaneous units

4. Trainee should be able to indicate inlet and outlet ports on a variety of symbols.

5. Trainee should be able to strip down, service, and reassemble each of the following:
   (a) Single vane pump
   (b) In-line axial piston pump (with compensator control)
   NB This would require say six pumps, preferably cast-offs. Trainee would strip down, indicate which parts need to be replaced (but does not replace) and reassemble.

6. Trainee should be able to recognize wear in parts of the following:
   (a) Single vane pump
   (b) Double vane pump
   (c) Two-stage vane pump
   (d) In-line axial piston pump (with compensator control)

7. Trainee should be able to strip down, report on condition, and reassemble as appropriate valves of the following type:
   (a) Pressure relief valve
   (b) Pressure reducing valve
   (c) Sequence valve
   (d) Simple directional valve
   (e) Standard check valve
   (f) Restriction check valve

8. Trainee should be able to determine (from its number) whether a valve is two or four way and how many positions are possible (two or three), and from its symbol the type of spool centre condition where appropriate for Vickers simple directional valves.

9. Trainee should be able to indicate what component would be needed to complete a given circuit with a given purpose.

10. In simple circuits (circuits with no more than two interrelated actuators) the trainee, given a set of symptoms, a circuit diagram and information regarding the circuit's purpose, should be able to trace a fault in the circuit using a logical approach.

Figure 3.5 Hydraulics course – behavioural specification

Analytical Techniques for Test Development

Having drawn up the list of behavioural specifications, one has a clear picture of the activities required of a competent person. However, this list is incomplete since the behavioural specification will be used as a reference document for actual test production and each item should be accompanied by other details collected during analysis. The following is a list of the information which needs to be collected and some suggestions as to how it may be qualified.

1. *The Task* — in behavioural terms.
2. *Frequency of Occurrence* — simple rating on three or five point scale, eg infrequent, regularly, very frequent.
3. *Criticality* — simple rating again such as high/medium/low.
4. *Difficulty* — rating.
5. *Major Skill Component* — language, manipulative, gross-bodily, etc.
6. *Any supporting knowledge.*
7. *Conditions* — well lit workshop, all weather conditions, low level lighting, etc.
8. *Acceptable Standard of Performance* — time to complete, whether job should be acceptable to production departmental inspection department; important procedural points etc.

Example lists are shown in Figures 3.6 and 3.7

Once all this information has been collated a much clearer picture of the tasks required can be built up and so how they might best be tested. It will also become easier to select areas to test where necessary and to draw up a suitable marking scheme.

Task: Given tractor, type of crop, appropriate tools and tractor instruction manual the candidate will be able to set front and rear track at correct spacing.

Frequency: High and throughout the year.

Criticality: High — wrong setting could damage crops.

Difficulty: Low.

Major Skill Component: Manipulative.

Knowledge: Candidate must know the required spacing for given crop but may refer to manual for actual setting.

Conditions: Usually outdoor and could be poor weather.

Acceptable Standard of Performance: One hour for both front and rear with change of rims and wheels — Process important.

Figure 3.6 Extract from behavioural specification for tractor driver

Analytical Techniques for Test Development

Task: Trainee should be able to strip down, report on condition and reassemble as appropriate Vickers valves of the following types:

(a) Pressure relief valve

(b) Pressure reducing valve

(c) Sequence valve

(d) Simple directional valve

(e) Standard check valve

(f) Restriction check valve

Frequency:

Criticality: } Expected behaviour for trainees leaving course.

Difficulty:

Major skill component: Recognition, manipulative, decision making.

Knowledge: Type and location of wear that occurs in all valves, degree of wear that is acceptable, any significant points to be attended to during reassembly.

Conditions: Normal work-shop.

Acceptable Standard of Performance: Acceptable times for servicing of each type of valve to manufacturers specification:

(a) 20 mins

(b) 20 mins

(c) 15 mins

(d) 15 mins

(e) 10 mins

(f) 15 mins

Process important.

Figure 3.7 Extract from behavioural specification for a short hydraulics course

So far the actual selection of skills to be tested has not been discussed except to say that in many cases it is possible to include them all. This does not mean that the man will simply be put onto the job and his output assessed, because there are several different ways of testing performance as will be seen in the next chapter. There will, however, be occasions when one either cannot or does not wish to test every aspect of the job. The main reasons for not being able to test everything will be economic; there may be too little time for testing or too little money for materials. When restrictions like this are present, the most important aspects of the job will have to be selected and this means weighing up all the information on the behavioural specification relating to frequency, criticality, etc. Another thing that one should look for is repetition of skills; if one has concentrated on making your behavioural specification realistic in terms of the job one may have several tasks that are basically the same except for, say, some additional knowledge. In bricklaying, for example, the main difference between normal brickwork and reinforced brickwork is the introduction of metal reinforcing wire between certain courses of bricks.

One could argue in this case that to test a man's ability to build plain brickwork and reinforced brickwork is rather a waste of time when he could be tested on plain brickwork and then his knowledge of reinforced brickwork assessed by means of paper and pencil tests.

Depending on the situation then one will end up with a list of the skills and knowledge that one intends to test. This may be identical to the behavioural specification or it may be a shortened version of it, but either way it will differ radically from the original documents.

SUMMARY

Job descriptions and training objectives are often not detailed enough or in the necessary form for immediate use in test development. The areas of skills and knowledge to be tested must be expressed in behavioural terms, so that the task, the conditions under which it is to be performed and the acceptable standards of performance are explicitly defined. In order to do this an analysis must be carried out.

One should remember to ask questions about administrative restrictions and working conditions as well as about the tasks.

In most cases the best way to collect information is by the use of structured interviews, having previously carried out a preliminary analysis of written information. However, when large numbers of personnel are spread over several establishments and divergent practices are expected, a questionnaire should be administered.

Direct observation should always be included but this should not be used as a major source of data unless one is dealing with short repetitive tasks.

The information needed for this specification indicates the level to which the analysis needs to be taken except that marking schemes may require more detail, particularly with regard to any procedural points.

The analysis should be stopped when one can produce a list of skills to be tested and specific details about test conditions, levels of performance, etc.

SUGGESTED FURTHER READING

Annett J., Duncan K.D., Stammers R.M., and Gray M.J., *Task Analysis*, HMSO TIP 6, 1971

Boyd J.L. and Shimberg B., *Handbook of Performance Testing*, Educational Testing Service, Princeton, USA, 1970, Chap.3 'Planning the Performance Test'.

Oppenheim A.M., *Questionnaire Design and Attitude Measurement*, HEB Paperback, 1966.

Kahn R.L. and Cannell C.F., *The Dynamics of Interviewing*, John Wiley and Sons, New York, 1957.

4

Testing Techniques

INTRODUCTION

There are two main methods of testing performance, that is by means of either a hands-on test or a hands-off test. A hands-on test is one which involves the use of the tools or other hardware of the actual job. A hands-off test does not do this. Thus for a bench fitter a hands-on test may require him to produce two mating parts while a hands-off test might require him to state the reading given on a diagram of a micrometer like that shown in Figure 4.1.

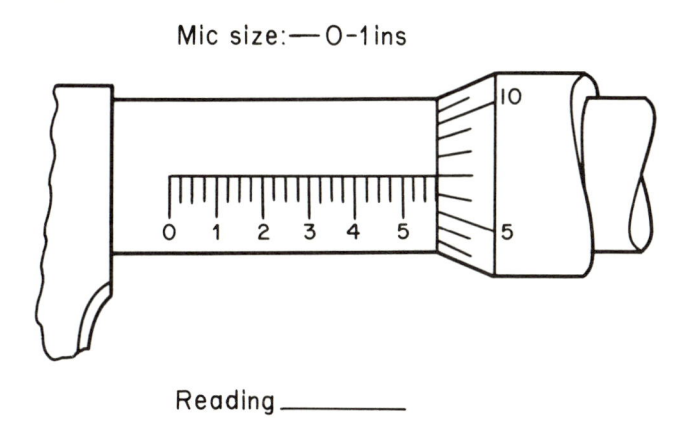

Figure 4.1 Testing the reading of a micrometer scale

Testing Techniques

A point worth noting here is that hands-off tests are not necessarily 'paper and pencil' tests since one might, for example, use a series of oral questions and a hands-on test might involve the use of paper and pencil; a hands-on test for storekeepers, for example, involves the monitored handling of various types of stores requests (eg verbal, telephone, written). Needless to say the candidate must make considerable use of paper and pencil because he must complete the associated paper work, but within the context of the normal working situation. A hands-off test, on the other hand, may require him to complete the paper work for a fictitious stores request without actually seeking the part required.

HANDS-ON TESTING TECHNIQUES

There are two approaches to hands-on testing, each being appropriate to different situations. These two techniques are perhaps characterized by the question of whether or not one should 'sample' the required behaviour contained in the behavioural specification. The question is, in other words, whether one should test the entire specification or just some of it.

The non-sampling technique is conveniently called a 'total job' test in which the candidate is required to carry out the job under reasonably controlled conditions. One might be inclined to say that this is not really a test but simply doing the job, the difference being in the conditions under which the job is carried out. Whether the test is carried out in an on- or off-the-job situation, it will be under controlled conditions in that there will be a set time during which the candidate's behaviour will be observed and this possibly by a trained examiner. Furthermore the candidate will not be able to rely upon help from his fellow workers or superiors and there will be a well-defined expected outcome that will be assessed with the aid of an objective marking scheme or automatic recording devices.

An example of a total job test is the miniature punch press which is a replica in all essential features of a small industrial punch press. It differs from a real punch press in that it is fitted with a device to count mispunches. Assessment involves the 'punching' of two items while a record is made of the time taken and number of mispunches.

The performance of three different groups of candidates is described in the graph of Figure 4.2. It can be seen that experienced press operators have a lower rate of mispunches than students and operators of other types of machinery. This indicates that the test is probably a valid and relevant measure of punching ability.

There are many similar tasks which one might assess in the actual job situation with the aid of some marking system, possibly employing automatic recording devices. Clearly, short circle repetitive tasks are most appropriate for total job testing since it would be difficult and probably meaningless to test anything less than the total job, and the time involved in each cycle is short enough to make total job testing feasible from an administrative point of view. Siegel, Richlin, and Federman[1], for example, assessed the performance of parachute riggers after training by selecting a number of critical tasks such as 'inspecting and checking continuity of lines', 'cutting material', and 'sewing pieces together'. Riggers were assessed on-the-job.

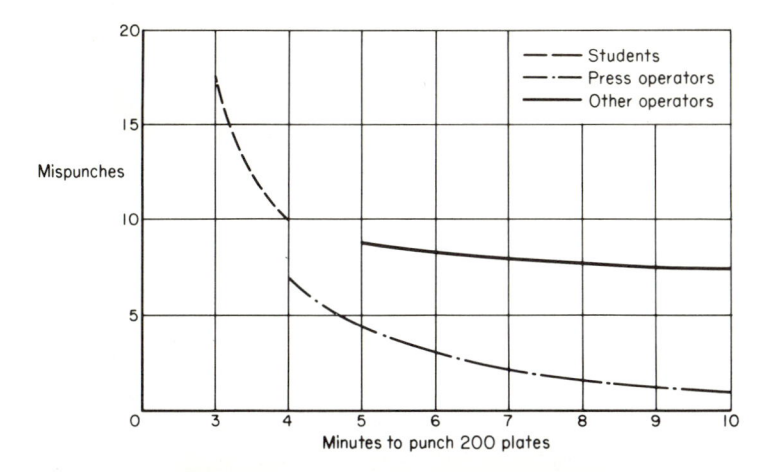

Figure 4.2

Relation between speed and accuracy for three groups in operating a small punch press

Figure 4.3

A pipeworker carrying out a work sample test in a ship under construction

(Joseph Tiffin and Ernest J. McCormick, Industrial Psychology, *Fifth Edition (c) 1965. Reprinted by permission of Prentice-Hall, Inc., Englewood Cliffs, New Jersey.)*

The punch press test involves the use of a simulator but is still hands-on because it represents an exact replica of a real punch press and so the candidate is effectively using the same tools as he would on the job. One could equally well ask the man to operate the actual press in the plant and this sort of situation has the advantage of undeniable validity (see Chapter 9) providing that the standards of performance are relevant, but there are many administrative drawbacks that reduce the attraction of this one advantage (see Chapters 6 and 7). Perhaps the most obvious disadvantage is the possible danger of allowing non-tested people to use an expensive machine. Other problems such as wasted material, wasted machine time, and difficulty of controlling conditions do need to be considered. Perhaps the most suitable application for on-the-job total testing is when one is concerned with the grading of personnel rather than allocation. Where short cycle repetitive tasks are involved and people must be graded in terms of their performance it is relatively easy to produce an assessment procedure for timed output.

Clearly the total job tests have limited use, especially in an on-the-job setting, since they must really be restricted to fairly simple repetitive tasks. It would be difficult to produce a total job test for an airline pilot or a motor mechanic even though very sophisticated assessment devices are available in the form of simulators.

Hands-on Sampling Techniques

There are two sampling techniques available to the performance test developer: the work sample and the skill sample. Work sample tests involve the performance of sections of a job that can usually be identified as a part of that job; weighing pigs might be a work sample test for pig handlers. The skill sample on the other hand measures the important skills and does not necessarily take the job situation into account; skills are often combined for convenience of testing rather than job relevance. The skills tested will be relevant but the particular combination may not; the classical 'engineering test piece' is an example.

One can also discern a difference of emphasis between the two types of sample: the skill sample approach says that the composite skills are all important provided the man has acquired these skills he will be able to apply them to any situation. The work sample on the other hand says that sections of the job that may well contain several different skills can be looked at and as long as these sections are performed adequately all will be well.

Clearly, neither of these two viewpoints is wholly correct and one must decide which is most appropriate to ones own situation, but in general the work sample seems to be more relevant where the job involves a larger number of fairly simple skills represented in discrete tasks that are combined together often with the aid of considerable job knowledge. An example of this type of job is the motor mechanic whose skill lies in the ability to manipulate hand tools and diagnose faults but this does not mean that anyone who can handle a spanner is a motor mechanic because the mechanic must have the associated job knowledge.

The performance of certain aspects of a motor mechanics duties, then, could be adequately assessed with a work sample test. An example of this type of test is shown in Figure 4.4. This test is part of a battery produced by the Road Transport Industry Training Board. Note that a discrete task is defined; 'Remove and replace clutch plate' and a marking scheme is provided. Another example of a work sample test was referred to earlier, involving the adjustment of a tractor wheel track (Figure 3.1).

Another work sample test developed as part of a battery of tests for shipyard apprentices, is reproduced in Figure 4.5. This example shows the variety of administrative arrangements that are possible with work sample tests. These planned experience tests, as they are called, can be taken as part of the normal working day rather than in the 'formal' testing situation that would be used for the agricultural tests. The photograph Figure 4.3 shows one of these tests being carried out in a shipyard.

Work sample tests should be designed to allow standardization of the content and objectivity of the assessment. As far as possible, the cost and number of materials, tools and equipment should be kept as low as possible so long as the skills are still adequately tested. With this in mind, the test should not be of undue length and involve as little repetition of identical procedures as possible. Little is gained, for example, by having a candidate remove and replace a series of nuts and bolts if competence in this area can be adequately assessed by carrying out the operations once or twice and then ascertaining that the candidate knows the correct procedure for the whole series.

Testing Techniques

PRACTICAL TEST

No. P11a05

Assembly	Clutch
Task	Remove and replace clutch plate
Time allotted	(According to task difficulty)
Marks	(Maximum) 100
General	Set apprentice at ease; explain task; explain marking schedule

Testers Notes

This task commences after the clutch housing has been removed, it does not include adjustments.

Marks are deducted as shown on the marking schedule.

In order to arrive at the marks awarded the penalty marks should be entered on the marking schedule. The marks are then deducted from the maximum marks in order to find marks awarded.

Explain marking schedule eg

You will be marked on:
- (a) Condition and use of tools.
- (b) Workmanship in tackling the job.
- (c) Cleanliness of work.
- (d) Answering of questions.
- (e) Time taken for the completion of task (extra time taken carries a low penalty).

If you are delayed by anything outside your control the time lost will not be counted against you.

MARKING SCHEDULE

No. P11a05

	Penalty	Marks
Use of tools		
Selects wrong tools (each time)	5	
Uses worn or damaged tools	10	
Uses tools incorrectly (each time)	5	
Workmanship		
Does not work systematically	10	
Damages any part	20	
Strip		
Does not release clutch assembly bolts evenly	10	
Does not mark clutch assembly before removal (for balance)	20	
Does not mark intermediate plate before removal	10	
Assemble		
Does not fit clutch driven plate correctly	20	
Does not use aligning tool	20	
Does not tighten clutch assembly bolts evenly	20	
Does not align clutch assembly to balance marks	10	
Does not remove or fit any additional part correctly (each time)	5	
Obtains incorrect part	20	
Does not lubricate correctly where necessary	10	
Does not tighten bolts to the correct torque	10	
Cleanliness		
Does not work in a tidy manner	10	
Does not check that flywheel face is clean	20	
Time		
For every minute over time allowed deduct one mark		

Name .... Date .... Total ....

Name .... Date .... Total ....

COURTESY: RTITB

Figure 4.4 A work sample test designed by the Road Transport Industry Training Board requiring removal and replacement of a clutch plate

39

Testing Techniques

JOB No. 22

Take Deflections and Bearing Wear-down
Bridge or Poker Gauge Reading

Specification

Main or auxiliary engine requiring readings during alignment.

Brief Details of Actual Job ....

....

Assessment Points

Correct use of measuring instruments   ...   .   ☐

Correct procedure for taking deflections   ...   .   ☐

Deflections correctly recorded   ...   .   ☐

Understands purpose   ...   .   ☐

Safety   ...   .   ☐

Correct procedure for measuring wear-down   ...   .   ☐

Wear-down correctly recorded to within limits of accuracy of measuring instruments   ☐

Proposed time   ...   ☐

Time taken   ...

Overall Assessment   General Comments
                           (If job unsatisfactory overall, briefly state why)
Satisfactory   ☐

Unsatisfactory ☐

Assessor's Signature ....   Date ....

Trainee's Signature ....
COURTESY: SITB

Figure 4.5 SITB Planned Experience Checklist

Work sample tests are usually relatively brief (up to say 30 minutes) and formed into a test battery. The candidates usually take a number of work sample tests whereas with skill sample techniques the various skills are combined into one test. There are several common factors to these tests that should be noted. The most important one at this stage is the way the tests attempt to either use or recreate the actual job situation. Since they do this, they are testing a real part of the job but are not attempting to test everything at once.

The skill sample test is similar to the work sample in that a sample of the relevant skills is tested. The difference lies in the fact that the main interest is the skills tested rather than the situational aspects of the job being tested. To this extent the skill sample test may require the production of a somewhat bizarre item which the candidate may never encounter again but which does necessitate the candidate displaying the relevant skills.

An example of the skill sample, which is probably the commonest performance test used, is the classical test piece for craftsmen in the engineering industry. This type of test will contain all or most of the relevant skills. Thus, for a turner it would include various aspects of turning such as producing external diameters, screw cutting, undercutting, taper turning, etc. Since the purpose of this type of test is to demand the use of as many relevant skills as possible, one often ends up with a test piece that is rather unrealistic in terms of an everyday industrial task. However, one could argue that the skills would apply equally well to various situations and it is therefore more useful to test aspects of the skill abstracted from the job situation. A common factor with these tests, then, is that they are less specific than the work sample and total job tests, and tend to be used for production rather than maintenance and service jobs.

For the benefit of readers who are not familiar with this type of test examples are included from both the engineering (Figure 4.7) and the shipbuilding industry (Figure 4.8). As it happens, both examples are useful objects which might be produced by the craftsman in the work situation. Note that the same engineering test piece (the taper plug) has been used as an example throughout the book. Figure 4.6 shows a completed taper plug.

Skill sample tests should be designed whenever possible for ease of measurement, as well as with a view to testing the relevant skills and operations. This is an important consideration both from the point of view of speeding up marking and making it as objective as possible.

HANDS-OFF TESTS

Hands-off tests do not normally utilize the actual tools (or other hardware) of the job, but may attempt to recreate the same perceptual cues that occur in the job situation. There are various ways in which this can be done the most obvious being the use of photographs or film to reproduce visual cues and tape recordings to reproduce auditory cues. Reproduction of cues to other sensory systems is rather restricted; it would be difficult to reproduce an odour accurately even though odour may play a crucial part in the normal job procedure. Similarly, touch is difficult to reproduce in a well-controlled situation, but the use of special blocks may go someway towards this. The main point to remember here is that although hands-off tests are being used realism need not be sacrificed.

Testing Techniques

Figure 4.6 Taper plug test piece

THIRD ANGLE PROJECTION

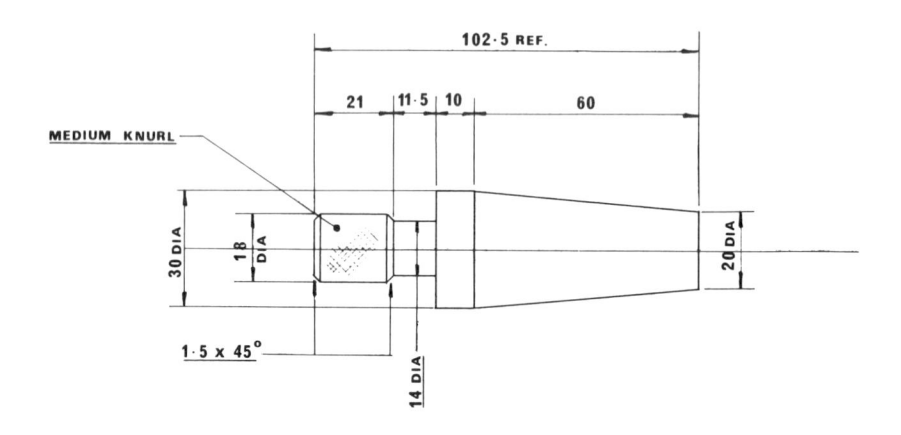

Figure 4.7 Engineering test (CGLI)

Testing Techniques

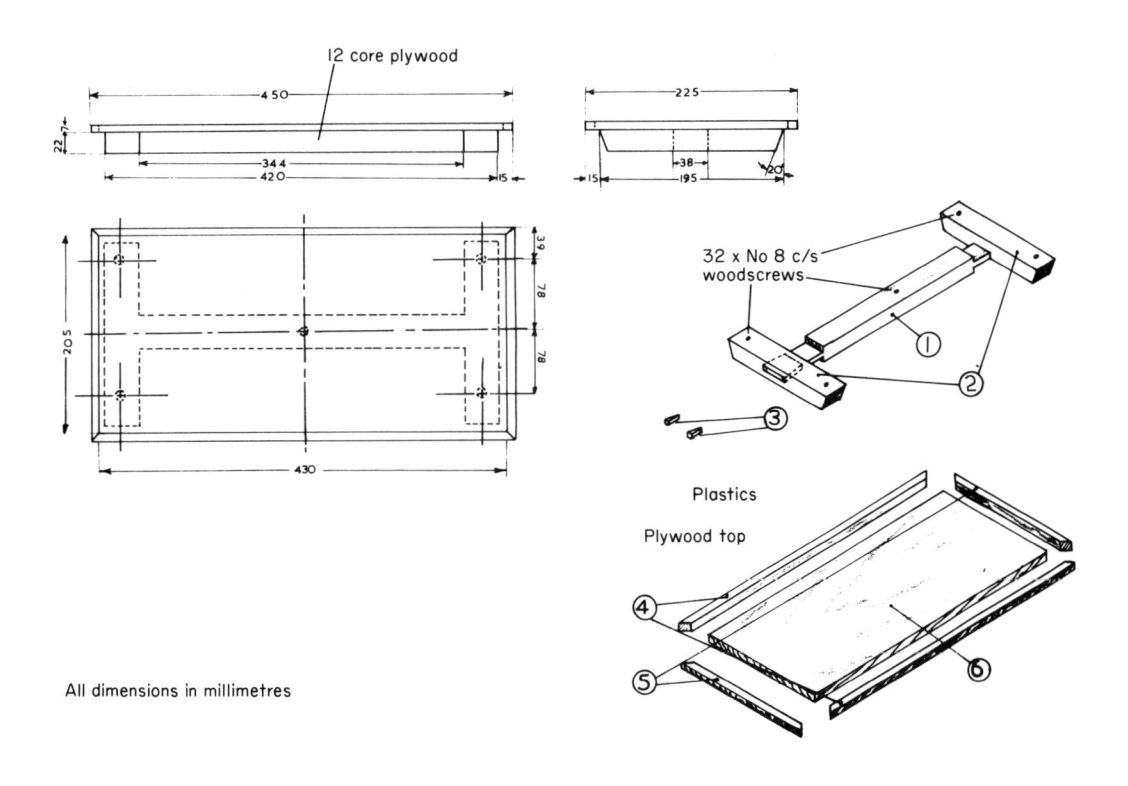

All dimensions in millimetres

Item number	Number off	Material	Description
1	1	AGBA	38 x 22 x 420 long
2	2	AGBA	38 x 22 x 195 long
3	4	AGBA	12 x 9 x 33 long
4	2	AGBA	10 x 15 x 455 long
5	2	AGBA	10 x 15 x 230 long
6	1	Plastics	1.6 x 210 x 435

Figure 4.8   SITB phased test in joinery

43

The extent to which a test recreates the actual job can be called the fidelity of the test. Fidelity has been described[2] as a complex multidimensional phenomenon but for the present purposes it is adequate to treat it as a dichotomy where a high-fidelity test attempts to reproduce the perceptual aspects of the job and a low-fidelity test does not. Low-fidelity tests usually involve the presentation in verbal terms of information which the candidate would have to hear, see, or feel in the actual job situation. In addition to fidelity, there is a further characteristic of hands-off tests that needs to be considered. Most readers will be familiar with straightforward question and answer tests of one sort or another, but when testing more complex skills such as decision-making and fault-finding, it becomes necessary to utilize a variable sequence test. In such a test the candidate is presented with a small portion of information and the receipt of subsequent information is contingent upon the candidate's response to previous information. This type of testing is analogous to a treasure hunt where the solution of one clue leads to the presentation of the next clue and so on until the final clue is solved and the prize won. Fixed sequence tests, on the other hand, present all their information at the start of the test. Obvious examples of this are the various types of objective test items.

There are, then, two characteristics of hands-off tests that combine to give four broad classes of testing techniques. It is worth noting at this stage that one may decide on the degree of fidelity or variability to use on the basis of different criteria. Thus variable sequence and fixed sequence tests will only be relevant to testing particular skills and knowledge. Fidelity may be desirable in terms of the degree of face validity required or whether important perceptual skills are being tested. More will be said about this later but to make the point clearer at this stage, one should imagine a fault-finding test which would need to be of the variable sequence type by virtue of the type of skill involved whereas the ability to diagnose a particular fault in a component could be tested with a fixed sequence test. Either type of test might be either high or low fidelity depending on whether one is interested in assessing the decision-making process in isolation or whether there is also interest in the candidate's ability to recognize the actual job components or in his level of perceptual skill.

Having discussed the two characteristics of hands-off tests one can now go on to look at specific examples of these tests.

Fixed sequence testing techniques

In this area test items can be divided into two types; those where the candidate has to supply an answer and those where he has to select the correct answer from a number of items.

Items requiring the candidate to supply an answer

Examples of this type of item are essay questions and short-answer questions. Questions involving calculations may be treated as short-answer questions if one is only concerned that the candidate gets the right answer. If the interest is in how he arrives at the answer, then either an essay or a series of short answers may be used.

Essay-type questions. This type of question will be familiar to readers as the standard method of assessment in many educational systems. The chief characteristic of essay questions is the latitude given to the way in which a candidate can respond and the subjectivity involved in marking. When testing knowledge related to industrial skills essay questions should be avoided because:

1. The quality of the candidates response will depend a great deal on how articulate he is. This is a very different thing from how well he knows the area in question.
2. The marking of essay questions is not objective and often examiners differ greatly in the marks awarded for the same answer. Downie[3], for example, found that teachers gave grades ranging from 'A' to 'F' (failure) when grading the same paper independently. Even the same teacher regrading the same paper after a few months gave a similar variation in grades.
3. The area covered by an essay-type test is usually small since only a few questions can be asked. The test is therefore unrepresentative of the total subject and so high or low scores may indicate strengths or weaknesses in the small area tested rather than overall. There is more 'luck of the draw' in essay-type tests.
4. Marking of essays always involves expert knowledge on the part of the markers, whereas objective-type items can be marked on a clerical basis.

If for some reason, essays are chosen as a testing technique, one should bear in mind the following:

1. Since there is usually no interest in the candidates ability to write prose, the candidate could be asked to list points or answer in other 'rough' ways.
2. It is preferable to use several short essay items rather than a few long ones, since this can provide a better coverage of the topic.
3. It is often helpful to indicate the approximate length of the answer required.
4. Do not allow any choice in questions; all candidates should attempt the complete test.
5. Prepare a marking key or schedule, showing specimen correct answers and how many marks an item or an element of an item should receive.
6. It is better for examiners to mark the first question for all candidates, then the second question and so on. This avoids the possibility of the halo effect which will be discussed in Chapter 6.
7. Check that the same standard is being used throughout the papers, and if possible have more than one examiner mark the test.

Short-answer items. Short-answer items, require the candidate to supply a word, phrase or number, or even a sentence in response to the question. For example a test on reading engineering drawings might include the items:

'What is the size of dimension A'.
'What instrument would you use to measure dimension A to within 0.01 mml'

Such items, particularly if only a one word or number answer is required can be marked with a high degree of objectivity and several can be included in a test.

Testing Techniques

They are particularly useful for testing the recall of factual information. The chief problem in constructing such items is in posing the questions in such a way that they will produce answers which can be clearly seen to be right or wrong, and unless great care is paid to this factor either ambiguous answers will be produced or trivial but easy-to-write items will be used.

Before using items it is important to inspect them (and have others inspect them) for any possible differences in interpretation. It may be helpful in this respect to consider the answer first and then build up the question from this. To illustrate this technique an example is given in Figure 4.9. This consists of four photographs of motor car components and the candidate is required to carry out four operations with regard to each component:

1. Identify the component.
2. Describe the defect.
3. Describe the probable cause.
4. Suggest remedial action.

This could be done either orally or by providing an answer layout that would give some indication of the length of answer required. A completed answer key is also shown. Clearly, there is some room for subjectivity of marking with this type of item where maximum use is made of the available material. It would be difficult to ask all four questions about each component using a multiple-choice item, because later questions might provide answers to earlier ones.

The use of photographs rather than the actual equipment has several advantages, the most important being that photographs provide a standard presentation of information for all candidates. Related to this is the actual cost of having equipment standing idle in the training department when photographs can provide a perfectly adequate stimulus (see Chapter 9).

No.	Component	Defect	Probable Cause	Action
1	Valves (exhaust)	Burnt seats	Over-heating due to wrong tappett clearance, valve not seating, or local build up of carbon	Replace, and check seats
2	Weight from advance mechanism of distributor	Edge of weight damaged and burred	Weak or broken advance springs	Renew weights and springs
3	Reverse gear idler	Worn teeth	Length of service and/or brutal engagement	Replace and inspect associated gears
4	Connecting-rod little end	Fractured	Metal fatigue or manufacturing fault	Replace, and check piston, bore, valves

Figure 4.9 Items in a short answer test for motor mechanics

Testing Techniques

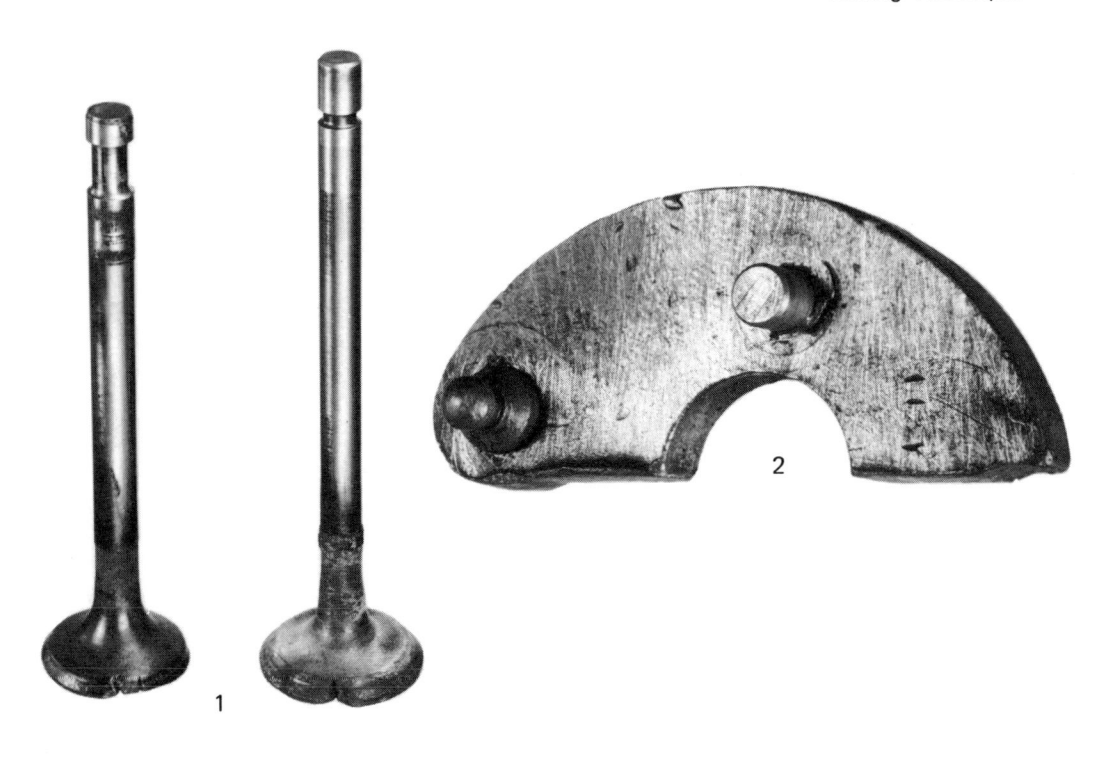

Figure 4.9 Items in a short answer test for motor mechanics

Items requiring the candidate to select the correct answer

These types of items are commonly referred to as objective test items since they can be marked with a high degree of objectivity. The literature on these items is quite voluminous and for more details the reader is referred to the books mentioned at the end of the chapter. The account will be relatively brief and confine itself to the main types of objective item, the chief problems are their construction and how they can be used to assess industrial skills and knowledge.

Multiple-choice items. The multiple-choice item is made up of a 'stem' which represents the question part of the item, and a selection of 'alternatives' which are the answer part. Within the alternatives will be found the correct answer (known as the key) and usually two, three, or four 'distractors'. An example of a multiple-choice item is given below:

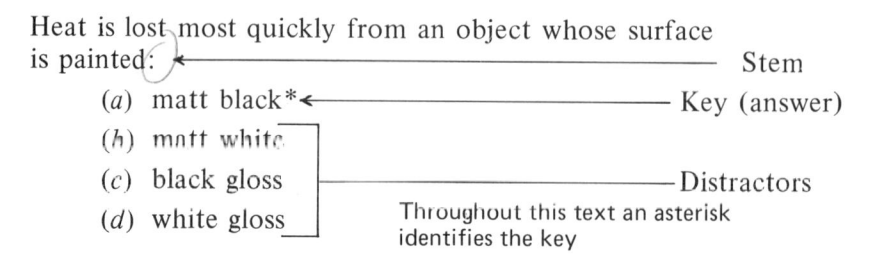

Heat is lost most quickly from an object whose surface is painted: ──────────────────────────── Stem
- (a) matt black* ──────────────────── Key (answer)
- (b) matt white
- (c) black gloss ──────────────────── Distractors
- (d) white gloss

Throughout this text an asterisk identifies the key

The example given is one that measures the candidate's knowledge of a particular aspect of the subject. The objectivity of such an item is apparent since there can be no dispute as to whether or not the correct answer has been chosen, assuming that the item was well written. There are other advantages in that these items take only a few seconds to answer and so one can subject candidates to large numbers of questions thereby covering a large part of the syllabus without producing an over-demanding marking task. The type of examination paper is now being used in a large number of educational examinations up to first degree level. In this context these items may be useful when we wish to assess supporting job knowledge. The item below is from a battery of bench fitting tests.

What would you use to check the diameters of a stepped shaft, with four diameters ranging from 1 inch to 7 inches to an accuracy of ± 0.005?

(a) A micrometer
(b) Outside callipers
(c) A steel rule
(d) Venier callipers*

Items of this type do measure knowledge but knowledge with a very practical slant.

The item in Figure 4.10 was part of a battery of tests designed to assess performance after the short course in hydraulics discussed in the previous chapter. To answer the question correctly the candidate must have a clear understanding of the method of operation of this type of valve.

Testing Techniques

Which of the cross-sectional diagrams shows the correct arrangement for a pressure relief valve?

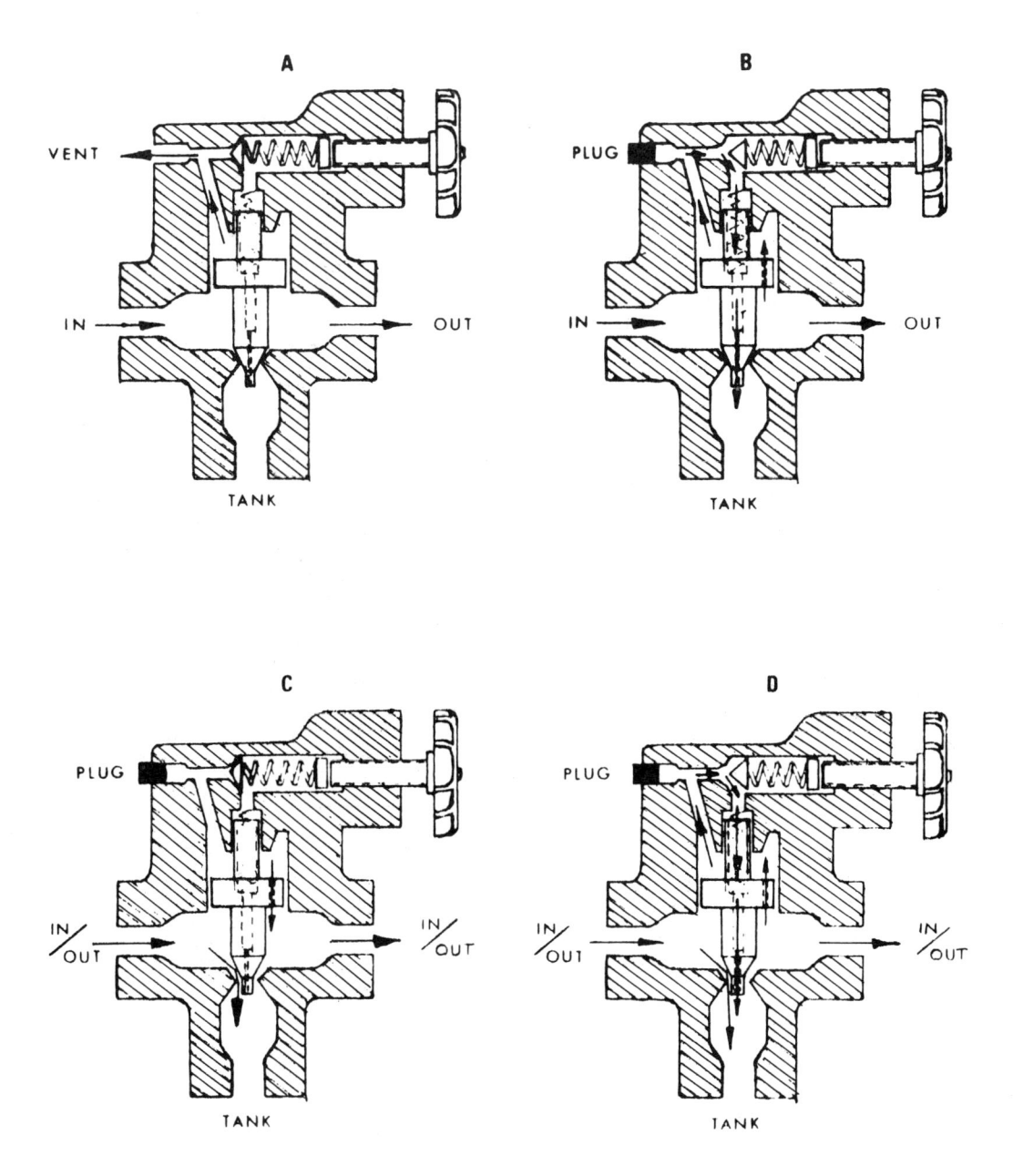

Figure 4.10 A multiple-choice item testing understanding of valve operation

Testing Techniques

One can begin to see then that the multiple-choice item can measure different types of knowledge and cognitive skills depending largely on the way in which information is presented. One can produce high-fidelity items simply by using photographs as in the stem of Figure 4.11 the candidate must identify the valve shown in the photograph by selecting the correct alternative. Clearly, this is a very practical type of test, since the man on the job must be able to recognize the different components of a system if he is to be able to maintain, trouble shoot, and repair it.

Multiple-choice items can have wide application provided some thought is put into the method of presentation and the rules that must be applied when writing them. Some of these rules are given below and more detailed accounts can be found in Gronlund[4] and Thorndike and Hagen[5].

Hints on producing multiple-choice and similar items. Although several books are available giving very detailed accounts of producing this type of item, below the authors give a list of some of the main points.

Photograph shows:

    (a)   Sequence valve
    (b)   Standard check valve
    (c)   Pressure reducing valve
    (d)   Pressure relief valve*

Figure 4.11 A high fidelity multiple choice item testing recognition of a hydraulic valve

1 Items should be worded as concisely as possible while at the same time including all relevant factors.
2 The statement of the problem should include as many as possible of the words common to the choices.

For example,

The law requires that lifting tackle should be inspected by a competent person
(*a*) At least every month
(*b*) At least every three months
(*c*) At least six months*
(*d*) At least every year

This question could be better phrased thus:

The law requires that lifting tackle should be inspected by a competent person at least every
(*a*) Month
(*b*) Three months
(*c*) Six months*
(*d*) Year

3 Stereotyped phrasing should be avoided, particularly phrasing found in textbooks, manuals, etc, since candidates may choose the correct alternative because it sounds familiar. Such terminology may however be used for the distractors.
4 The correct choices should usually be about the same length as the distractors, otherwise a pattern based on length may be discerned by the candidate.
5 The position of the correct answer should follow a random pattern. Thus, in the test overall these should be no more correct answers in position (*a*) than in position (*b*). Similarly a correct answer in (*c*) should not be followed by a correct answer in (*d*) and so on. However, if choices involve numbers or time, it is logical to present them in the usual order.

For example,

In general the mould temperature range for Nylon would be
(*a*) 45 – 60°C
(*b*) 65 – 80°C
(*c*) 85 – 100°C*
(*d*) 105 – 120°C

6 Irrelevant clues should be avoided in the wording of items, such as when a term used in the question (statement) is repeated in the correct answer only.
7 It should be ensured that all alternatives fit in grammatically with the stem.
8 Distractors, although obviously incorrect to those who know the subject adequately should be plausible to those who do not. Often previous short-answer items on the same area can provide good distractors when one examines the incorrect answers of candidates.

Testing Techniques

9 The use of the opposite to the correct answer should be avoided as a distractor, since the candidate may spot the pair of opposites and so guess that one of the two is the correct answer.

10 Overlapping choices should be avoided, such as:

In general the injection moulding temperature range for PVC would be
(a) 140 – 180°C
(b) 160 – 200°C
(c) 180 – 220°C
(d) 200 – 240°C

11 Present items in a positive form, since negative items are often unrealistic and do not get at what one wants to measure.

For example,

Which one of the following would cause flow-lines in the moulding?
(a) Dwell time too short
(b) Insufficient feed to cylinder
(c) Injection pressure too low*
(d) Injection pressure too high

Rather than:

Which of the following would not cause flow-lines in the moulding?
(a) Injection pressure too low
(b) Material too hot*
(c) Injection speed too fast
(d) Mould temperature too low

12 If a negative form is used, emphasize its negative aspect in order to ensure that candidates do not misread it as a negative item.

Which of the following is *not* self-extinguishing?
(a) Nylon
(b) Polystyrene*
(c) Unplastic PVC
(d) Polycarbonate

13 Do not use 'none of the above' as a distractor.
14 If one item depends upon a preceeding one, neither must reveal the correct answer to the other.
15 Sometimes the distractors can be derived from previous short-answer or essay questions covering the same area.

Analysing Objective-type test results. One of the advantages of using objective-items is that one can look at candidates' responses and obtain a large amount of information about them. Firstly one can obtain a difficulty value, ie the proportion of candidates responding incorrectly on that item (NB facility value is the opposite of the difficulty value, ie the proportion of candidates responding correctly). One can also obtain information of the popularity of distractors.

For example,

> The headlamp shown in the figure† will not work correctly because
> (a) The dip switch is incorrectly wired   19%
> (b) The earth connection is incorrect in both lamps   9%
> (c) The main drop connections are reversed in one lamp*   58%
> (d) The earth connections is not provided at the dip switch   12%
>   No answer   2%
>
> † not shown

Objective type items can also be analysed in terms of the correlation between the score on a particular item and total test score (known as r_{bis}). Thus a test made up of items with high item-total correlations is considered to be one measuring similar aspects of performance throughout the test. When reading literature from the further education world one is often advised to omit items of high- or low-difficulty value or with a low item-total correlation. However, in performance testing it may be necessary to determine whether or not a candidate knows a given fact, procedure, or whatever, irrespective of how difficult or easy the item is, or whether it has a lot in common with other items. Test developers should also remember an item may have a low facility value because of poor training and not because it is an intrinsically 'difficult' item.

True/false items. True/False items are in fact multiple-choice items with only two choices.

For example,

> The voltage used in domestic installations in this country is 250 volts AC
>   TRUE/FALSE

Their main disadvantage is that the candidate has a 50–50 chance of guessing correctly. Their use in testing for industrial skills is therefore not usually advisable.

Matching items. Again the matching item is a variation on the multiple-choice format. Figure 4.12 shows a matching item for recognition of hydraulic circuit symbols.

The same question could have been asked in the standard multiple-choice way, but five items would have been needed. It can be seen that the matching item can save a lot of time.

It is important that the number of alternative answers exceeds the number of keys; otherwise the candidate may work out the final answer by elimination.

Matching items can be very quick and efficient methods of testing, particularly for pictorial or diagramatic material. Such material may be used in one or more lists. A more complex matching item shown in Figure 4.13 requires the candidate

Testing Techniques

to complete a simple hydraulic circuit by selecting a symbol from a bank of symbols provided. This item requires not only knowledge of the symbols themselves but also an understanding of the function of components and the way they interact in a simple circuit.

Match the symbols in List 1 with the items in List 2 using the matching panel

List 1   List 2

A   ———⌵———   1   Rotating shaft

                                        2   Line to reservoir above fluid level

                                        3   Fixed restriction

B   ———▶———   4   Variable restriction

                                        5   Line to reservoir below fluid level

                                        6   Working line

C   ———⌒———   7   Flexible line

                                        8   Direction of flow

D   ⊔⊔

E   ⌣

Matching panel*				
A	B	C	D	E
4	8	3	5	7

*Correct answers: 1 mark for each correct answer

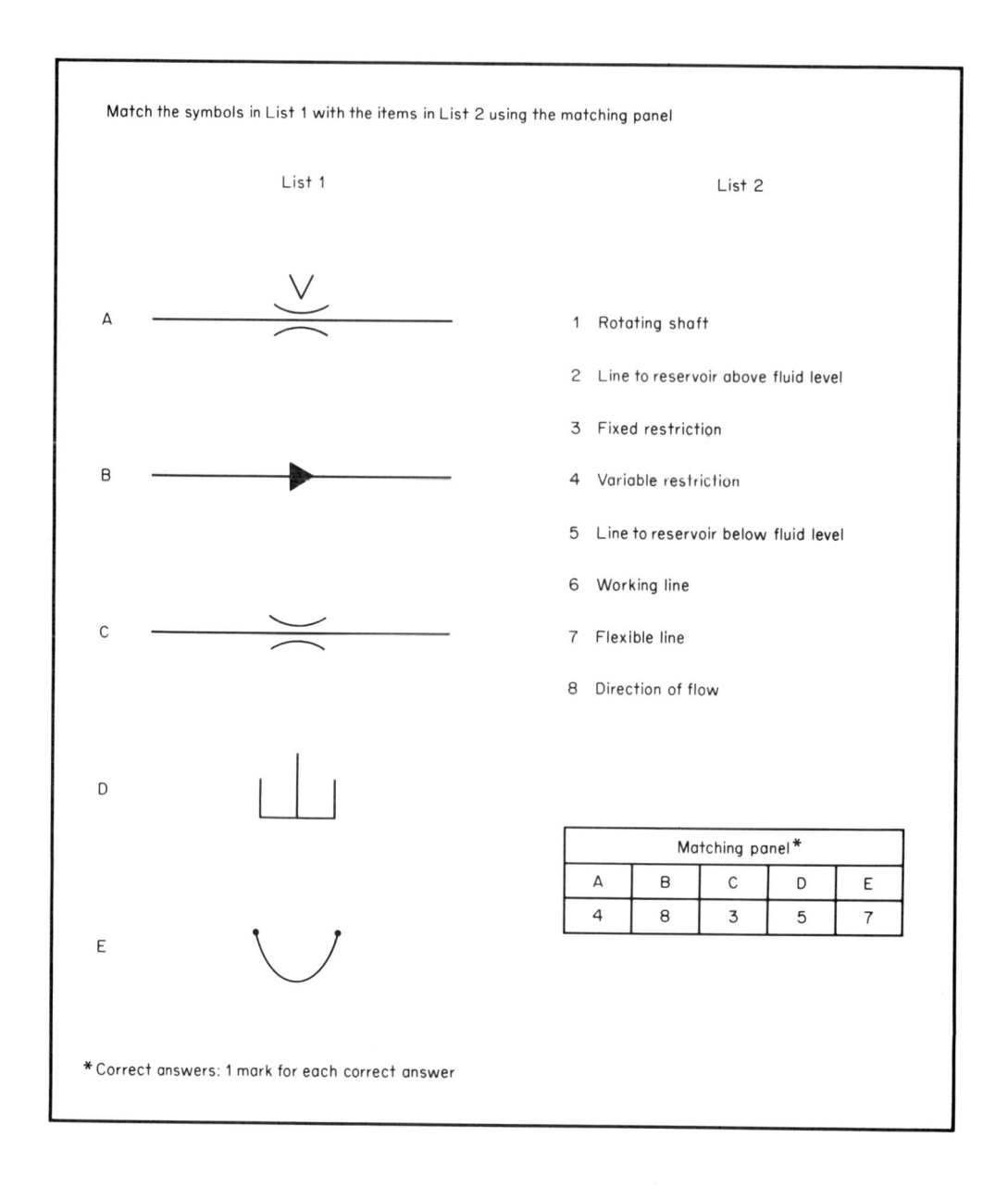

Figure 4.12 A matching item using hydraulic circuit symbols

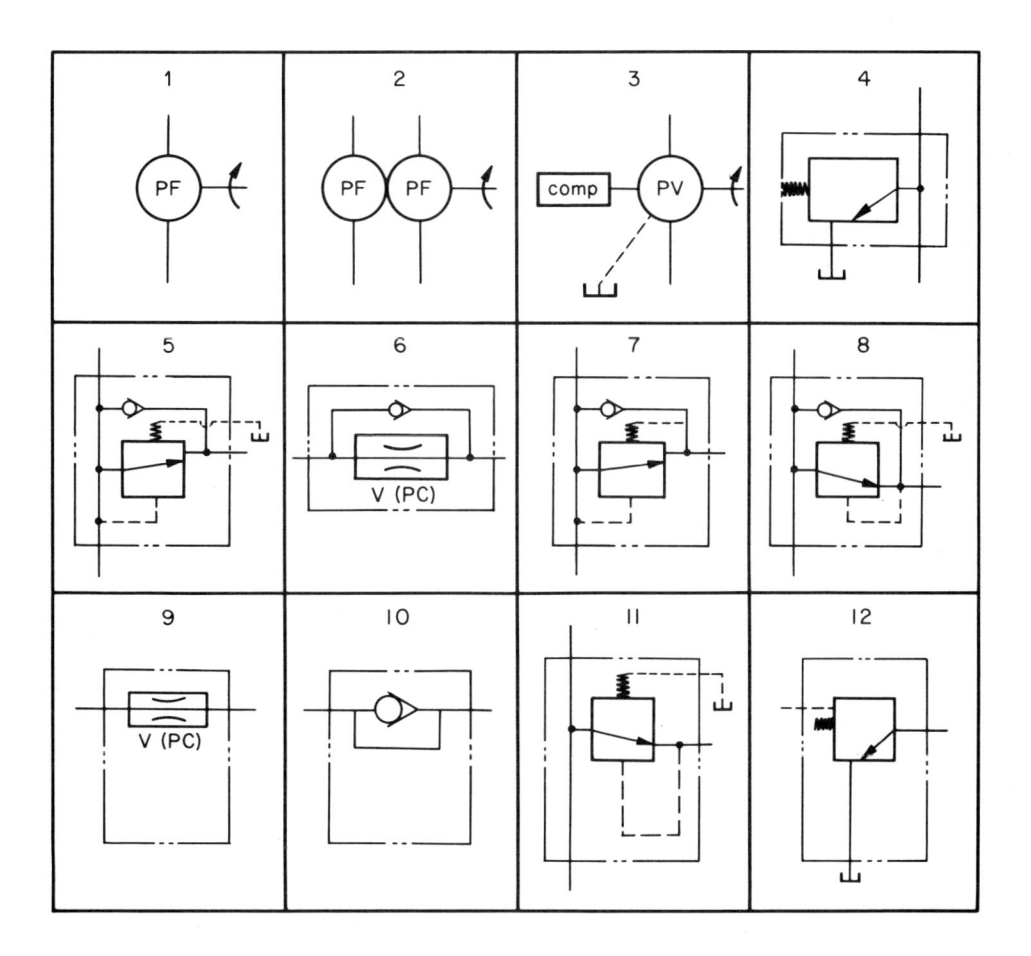

Figure 4.13 A complex objective item

Testing Techniques

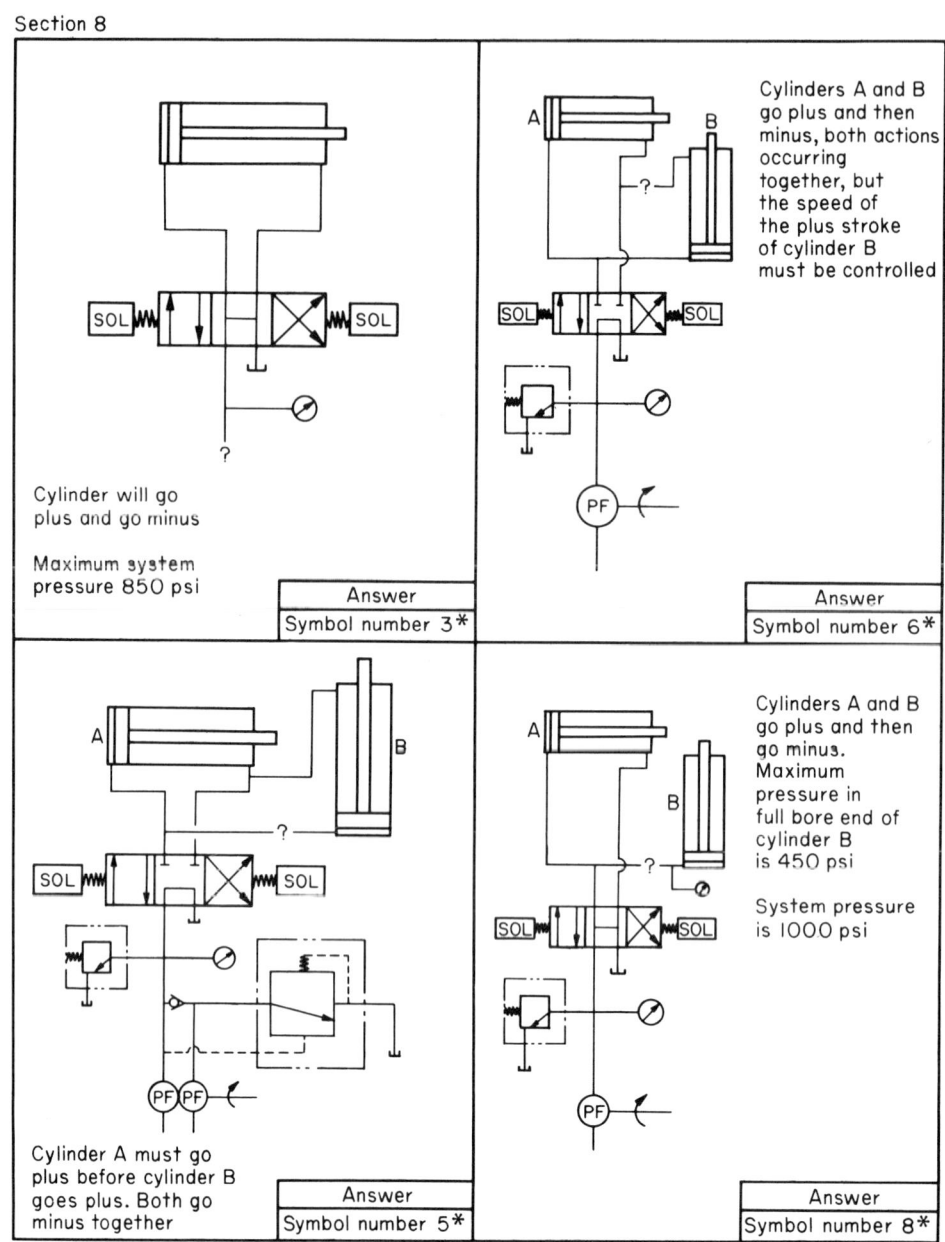

Section 8

Cylinder will go plus and go minus

Maximum system pressure 850 psi

Answer
Symbol number 3*

Cylinders A and B go plus and then minus, both actions occurring together, but the speed of the plus stroke of cylinder B must be controlled

Answer
Symbol number 6*

Cylinder A must go plus before cylinder B goes plus. Both go minus together

Answer
Symbol number 5*

Cylinders A and B go plus and then go minus. Maximum pressure in full bore end of cylinder B is 450 psi

System pressure is 1000 psi

Answer
Symbol number 8*

*Correct answer: 1 mark for each correct answer

Figure 4.13 concluded

Testing Techniques

The Central Electricity Generating Board[6] has developed a quite complex matching item to assess the candidate's ability to read engineering drawings in this test (shown in Figure 4.14) the various aspects of a production drawing are identified in different ways on different views. Thus a 'lug' numbered 1 on the plan view may be numbered D on the elevation. With this sort of detailed source of information one can either ask specific questions such as 'What is the corresponding label on the plan view for 7 on the elevation?' or one can draw up lists: 'List the numbers from the elevation corresponding to those on the plan'

A	
K	
F	
D	
M	

The fidelity of the matching item can be increased by the introduction of photographs or real objects. Figures 4.15 (a–b) shows the material for a fairly complex matching item designed to measure knowledge of electronic circuit diagrams, actual circuits, and the selection of appropriate measuring instruments.

The candidate is provided with a circuit diagram and photographs of a fairly complex circuit which in this case is a current to pulse converter. The circuit diagram is divided up into subcircuits which have been lettered A to G. Both the diagram and the photographs are either plastic covered or kept in clear plastic folders so that the candidate can indicate check points on them with a china pencil or crayon. It can be seen from the answer key that the candidate is required to indicate the points at which he would check the input and the output of each of the subcircuits (A–G) on both the circuit diagram and the associated circuit photographs.

It is clear that this test is measuring several different aspects of electronic skill but its main interest is whether or not the trainee can transfer his knowledge of the circuit on the circuit diagram to the actual circuit.

Tests for planning skills

There are occasions when one needs to assess the candidate's ability to organize or plan a particular job or operation. An example of this might be to plan the operations required to produce a particular production item. The traditional way to do this is to ask the candidate to complete an operations sheet where he lists in order the operations he would carry out and the tools and instruments he would use for each operation. This sort of test gives the candidate an opportunity to express himself freely but for this reason it requires him to be a reasonably descriptive writer and this may put a less articulate candidate at a disadvantage. Similar problems arise in the assessment of the completed sheet which is often left largely at the discretion of the examiner.

Testing Techniques

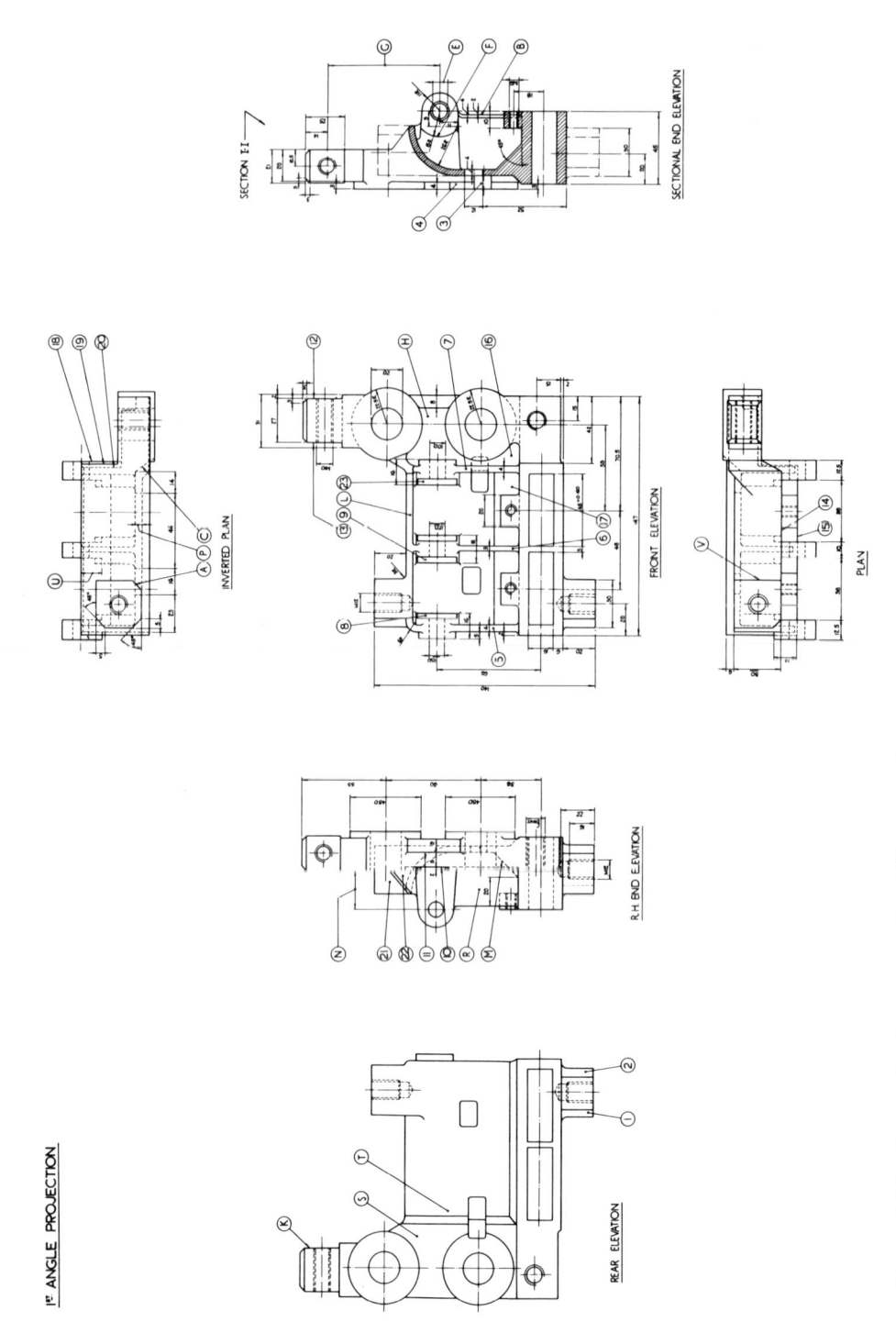

Figure 4.14 A complex items assessing ability to read engineering drawing

(a) **Instructions and answer key**

SECTION 5

This section tests if you know where and how to measure the input/output of subcircuits in a complex circuit.

You are provided with a complex circuit diagram (with certain subcircuits lettered) and a photograph of the same circuit. You have to indicate at what points you would test the input/output for these circuits on both the circuit diagram and the photograph by circling the points on the transparent sheet. Number these test points and record them together with the measuring instrument you would use in the answer box below

To help you the appropriate service sheet is available.

SECTION 5.1

Circuit being measured	Points tested (numbers)				Measuring instrument
	Circuit diagram		Photograph		
	Input	Output	Input	Output	
A Input Output					
B					
C					
D					
E					
F					
G					

Figure 4.15(a)   A complex high-fidelity matching item

Testing Techniques

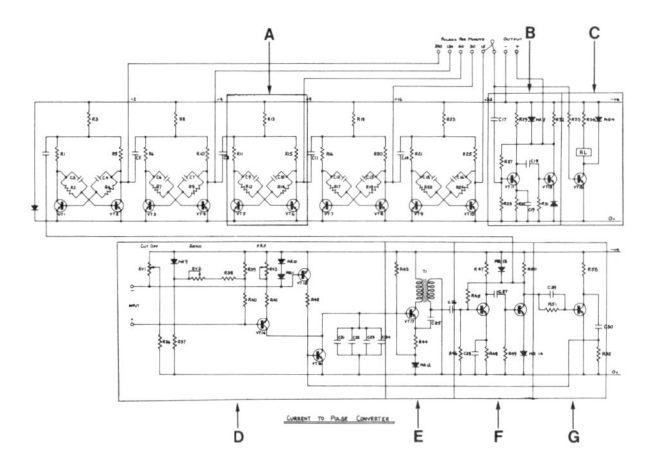

Figure 4.15(b)　Current to pulse converter circuit diagram

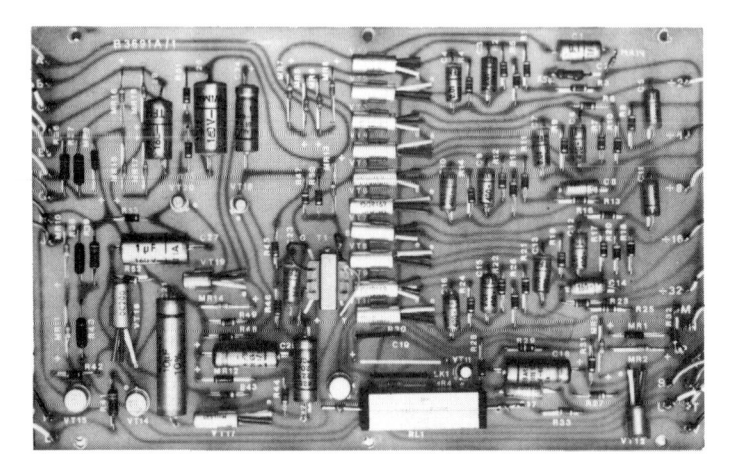

Figure 4.15(c)　Current to pulse converter circuit board

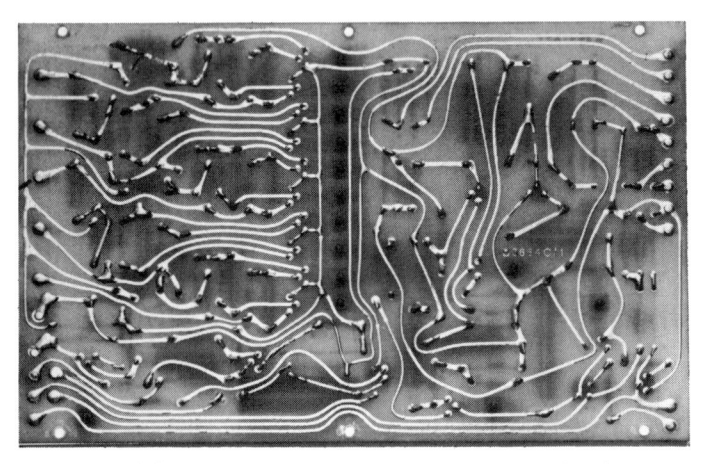

Figure 4.15(d)　Current to pulse converter printed circuit

Testing Techniques

Attempts have been made by the authors to make the marking of such operation sheets more objective. The first method employed required the examiner to ask various logical questions about each operation, in terms of the criterion of efficient production which can be defined as carrying out only relevant operations in the correct sequence with an appropriate method. It should be noted that the sequence of operations is fairly important for it will often be impossible to carry out some operations after others. An appropriate method would be one that achieved the desired effect in the shortest time. From this one can devise the necessary questions that must be applied to each operation. The question sequence is shown as a decision tree in Figure 4.16.

This appeared to be a reasonably objective system but it came up against severe operational problems. The main difficulty was the way in which candidates interpreted the term 'operation', some would break it down into quite small steps while others decided upon larger chunks of steps. It was necessary therefore to control the size of these steps. To do this it was argued that the important aspect of planning a job was not so much knowing what to do as knowing how to do it and the order in which the operations should be carried out. So the second method employed packs of cards on which the various necessary operations were described and the candidate was required to place these in the correct order and state which tools he would use. This overcame the problem of controlling the operation size while still testing the important planning aspect of the job.

The technique described was applied to a bench fitting job and both marking out and metal removal were assessed. It should be noted that this type of test assesses planning skills only.

Figure 4.17 compares the merits of short-answer essay and multiple-choice type questions as testing techniques. A glance at this table shows that essay questions are easy to prepare but difficult to mark, unreliable, and tend to be unrepresentative of the total subject area. Multiple-choice questions are difficult to construct but easy to mark, reliable, and give good subject coverage. Overall, short-answer questions fall between these two extremes.

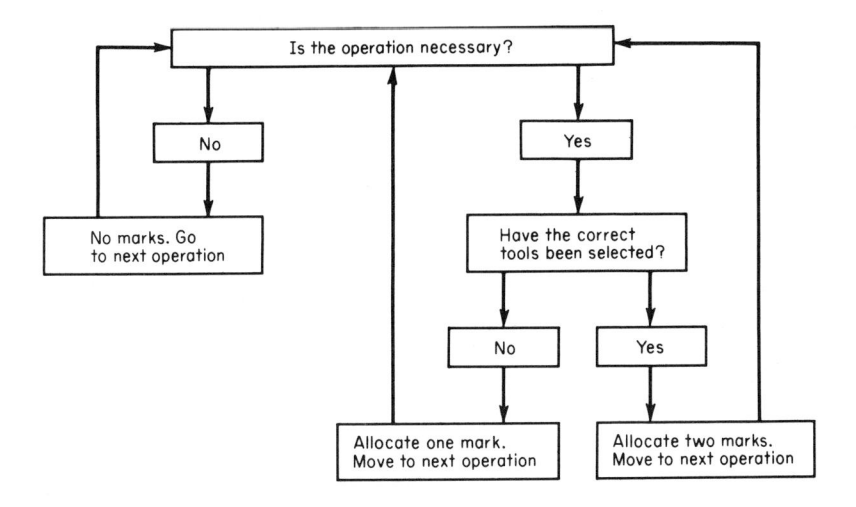

Figure 4.16 Method of assessing operation sheets

Testing Techniques

Most	E	M-C	M-C	E	M-C	M-C	SA	M-C	SA
Middle	SA	SA	SA	SA	SA	SA	M-C	SA	M-C
Least	M-C	E	E	M-C	E	E	E	E	E
	Ease of preparation	Level of skill required in preparation	Ease of marking	Skill required in marking	Coverage of subject	Susceptibility to guessing	Suitability for measuring factual knowledge	Reliability for long test	Reliability for short test

E = Essay   M-C = Multiple choice   SA = Short answer

Figure 4.17 A comparison of essay, short answer and multiple choice items on a number of factors

Relatively brief tests involving objective items can have quite high reliability (ie measure the area in question consistently). For example, the Short Occupational Knowledge Tests developed by Science Research Associates have alternate form reliabilities of 0.93 for motor mechanics (20 items) and 0.83 for electricians (20 items). Candidates are expected to complete the test in 10 to 15 minutes, and the test discriminates well between levels of achievement.

The application of fixed sequence tests

The fixed sequence test has its own particular place in testing and it is clear from the examples given that this lies mainly in the testing of perceptual skills and job knowledge. This is epitomized by the examples which combine the perceptual skills required for recognition with the job knowledge required to diagnose a fault and suggest a remedy. They have also been used to measure decision-making in terms of planning a job and this can be useful where one wishes to measure these skills in isolation. These tests will not tell us that a man can actually do the job but they allow us to assess some of the component skills and so help to identify the reasons why someone cannot do the job.

Job-knowledge tests aim to test the candidates retention and understanding of information that is necessary for the successful undertaking and completion of the job in-question. The types of information which commonly need to be tested are:

1 Names, sizes, and other identifying features of any tools, pieces of equipment, or parts of equipment necessary for the job.
2 Safety precautions or special procedures necessary in using tools, equipment, or materials.
3 Features and properties of materials which may affect their use or suitability.
4 Possible defects in materials and action to be taken.
5 Likely areas of difficulty and features of the job or work situation which may cause difficulties; ways of avoiding or overcoming such difficulties.
6 Features of work produced which should be checked and method of checking.
7 Care and maintenance of tools and equipment, both during and on completion of the job.

One question which springs to mind is 'To what extent do tests loose anything by being hands-off rather than hands-on?'

Baldwin[7] quotes two tests designed to measure a motor mechanic's ability to diagnose engine faults using an electronic engine analyser. In order to diagnose the fault the mechanic must interpret the visual pattern presented on an oscilloscope. The first test involved switching in a number of malfunctions into an ignition simulator and having the candidate interpret the analyser display. This test had moderately high reliability and appeared to be measuring predominantly perceptual skills. The second test used photographs of the scopes displaying the same patterns for the same malfunction. The test developers concluded that the static form using photographs could be substituted for the dynamic form so that candidates need not be tested on actual equipment.

On the other hand, if the fidelity of a test content is drastically reduced, the test may loose its validity. Cronbach[8] quotes a test system for naval gunners where originally gunners were assessed by actually operating the guns. In order to reduce cost, two new forms were developed, one involving pictures and one verbal. The areas tested were the same in each form, covering parts of the gun, duties of the crew and so on. The pictorial tests correlated highly with instructors' marks based on gun operation whereas the verbal test had a lower correlation and seemed to be influenced to a great extent by reading ability. Cronbach states that reading ability affects scores on almost all paper and pencil tests of achievement. Conrad[9] analysed the results of four sets of tests:

Mechanical knowledge tested pictorially
Mechanical knowledge tested verbally
Electrical knowledge tested pictorially
Electrical knowledge tested verbally

He found that the similarity of content produced lower correlations than similarity in form. In other words, the form of the test played a large part in the score the candidate obtained.

Oral tests

Traditionally many trade tests and assessments have involved the examiner asking the candidates questions about the job. It must be emphasized that such tests cannot measure manipulative skills and are usually aimed only at job knowledge. They are attractive to examiners as the latter like to 'pit their wits' against the candidate, the test situation sometimes taking on the aspect of a duel to the death. On the other hand, an examiner may be very sympathetic and attempt to 'draw out' the candidate's knowledge. Obviously if the examiner has choice in what areas he will cover and in the manner in which he poses the questions, different candidates will be facing very different testing situations. Since, if candidate performances are to be comparable, we must always aim for standardization of test situation and content, oral tests are often unsatisfactory. However, if the questions are specified and the examiner acts only as a medium of presentation then some of our objections are less relevant. Oral testing is useful if candidates are not particularly articulate in writing or may become anxious if anything like writing is involved. It will of course require a higher examiner/candidate ratio than corresponding paper and pencil tests.

The important thing with oral tests is to standardize the questions and, as far as possible, the conditions of administration. Tiffin and McCormick[10] describe a series of short tests (around 15 questions) developed by the US Employment Service, which were shown to be relatively efficient in discriminating between experienced workers, apprentices, and workers in other trades. For example, with the 15 question test for asbestos workers, experienced men scored between 7 and 15 with a median score of 14, apprentices and helpers between 0 and 12 with a median score of 6, other workers scored between 0 and 6 with a median score of 1. Thus anyone testing a candidate can be fairly confident that a person scoring six or below is unlikely to be an expert worker.

The tendency in oral and written tests of trade knowledge developed in the USA is for items to be selected on the basis of whether they discriminate between groups of known characteristics under test. Items which do not are discarded. While this may be valid in developing short tests to aid in selection, it can be argued that in certain circumstances items may have an intrinsic value irrespective of such factors as overall statistical discrimination. Suppose, for example, an item represents an essential area of knowledge as defined by a training programme or as required in new workers. It would then be of some importance whether a candidate passed the item, irrespective of how easy or difficult it was in general terms. Unsuccessful candidates could be given remedial training until this key area was mastered.

With oral tests, items requiring short, one or two word, answers are preferable, particularly if they require the answer to be in terms peculiar to the trade in question.

Variable Sequence Tests

The area of skill not yet discussed with regard to hands-off tests is fault finding and similar decision-making skills and it is this area that can be tested with variable sequence tests. It will be recalled that a variable sequence test does not present all information at the outset but makes presentation of information contingent upon earlier responses.

Dale[11] said of fault finding that the task encountered by the man will depend on the way he sets about doing the job rather than upon the job itself. He divides the process of fault finding into two major elements:

Testing Techniques

1 Recognition of symptoms of malfunction and use of these to determine course of action.
2 Location of test points and use of test gear to make physical checks.

From this it can be seen that the actual checking is a fairly minor part of the job while the major aspect is recognition and interpretation of symptoms and test data. All these can be tested with a variable sequence hands-off test.

As with the other hands-off tests described one can introduce fidelity in various ways.

Low fidelity variable sequence tests

The majority of low fidelity variable sequence tests are variations of the 'tab-test' first described by Glaser and coworkers[1,2]. The tab-test is comprised of a board or sheet bearing a series of flaps or tabs beneath which information relating to a particular check is contained. The candidate simply removes the tab to discover the result of the check that he would have carried out on the actual equipment. This technique has been modified by using sliding windows, rub-away masks, envelopes, and the like; but all are essentially the same.

An example using rub-away masks is shown in Figure 4.18. The test comprises a circuit diagram, symptom description, and test point data sheet. This latter is normally treated with a plastic coating so that some opaque substance such as black wax crayon may be placed over all the boxes that provide information, this being easily rubbed off by the candidate. Thus columns headed circuit reference contain the results and condition of physical checks carried out at the points indicated on the diagram. The remaining boxes indicate the test point or the component tested and the number of that step which is entered by the candidate as he proceeds through the test.

A candidate attempting the test would study the circuit diagram and the symptoms (eg slow feed) and then decide upon his first step which might be to check that the pump shaft is rotating. He then rubs away the covering from the appropriate box in the column headed 'condition'. The criterion of acceptable performance is that he uses a logical approach and sequence. Unfortunately, one cannot say that he should find the fault as quickly as possible because this would allow him to succeed by guessing and the main aim of this type of test is not to assess his ability to locate and remedy a fault but to isolate his decision-making and trouble-shooting skill as applied to a complex fault-finding task.

It will be noted that the test requires the candidate to record the order in which checks are carried out. This avoids the possibility of his rubbing out all the boxes to locate the fault. The 'Check No.' column is used in the marking of the test and is explained in Figure 6.20.

It is clear that the tab-test in this low-fidelity form requires the use of the decision-making aspect of fault finding rather than the perceptual recognition of symptoms although job knowledge is still necessary since the candidate must be able to interpret the symptoms that are described to him. One could decrease the amount of job knowledge and so isolate the decision-making completely by substituting a ready-made decision under the result of each check; thus rather than say 'clear and airtight', one would put 'result satisfactory'. On the other hand one could increase the amount of job knowledge required by making the check results more like the real thing by increasing the fidelity. Thus, rather than describe the outcome of a check as '950 psi' one might give a photograph of the appropriate test instrument showing the appropriate reading. By virtue of the contingent presentation of information which characterizes these tests, they will almost invariably be used to measure fault-finding ability or similar types of multiple decision-making skills. Clearly the important variation lies in the exact format of the test which can be varied in accordance with that aspect of fault finding that one wishes to measure.

It was seen earlier that the major aspect of fault finding is the ability to recognize and interpret the symptoms of malfunctions associated with the ability to locate test points, and use test gear to make physical checks. It has also been noted that the interpretation of symptoms can be tested in isolation with a low-fidelity test while recognition will require a high-fidelity test. The use of test gear can be measured separately by means of a skill or work sample test and the ability to isolate test points via a relatively high fidelity hands-off test like the one shown in Figure 4.15 or a similar hands-on test.

High-fidelity variable sequence tests – the simulator

It was seen in the previous section that the decision-making aspect of fault finding could be virtually isolated in the testing situation by reducing the fidelity of the information given to the candidate. Conversely the amount of job knowledge and perceptual skill required can be increased by raising the fidelity of the test in terms of the presentation of perceptual information. It is also possible to increase the realism of the test by introducing the actual test gear that is used on the job and it is here that the test begins to approach the hands-on type of test. When the actual job situation is approached in this way examples of high-fidelity simulators begin to be found.

The simulator was originally developed as a training aid since it allows trainees to gain experience of the use and rectification of equipment without the associated cost of using the equipment itself and despite the relative infrequency with which some faults occur. Probably the best known simulators are the full flight simulators for training pilots, which are often used before the plane itself is flight tested as was the case with the 747 Jumbo Jet. Similarly the American astronauts prepared for their moon shots in high-fidelity simulators. With all simulators of this kind there are facilities for switching-in faults so that the candidate's trouble-shooting ability can be measured in a realistic situation. There is probably little doubt in anyone's mind of the benefits offered by such advanced simulation, but there is also little doubt that the cost of this type of equipment is extremely high. It is probably not worth spending this much money unless the cost of damage to real equipment and associated personnel is even higher. Clearly the examples given so far do warrant such expenditure. It is worth noting that simulators used for testing may not be identical to those used for training. The former is designed to elicit certain behaviour under conditions where realistic assessment is possible, whereas the latter is designed primarily for modifying behaviour and therefore incorporates feedback and similar devices which are unnecessary if only testing is involved.

Testing Techniques

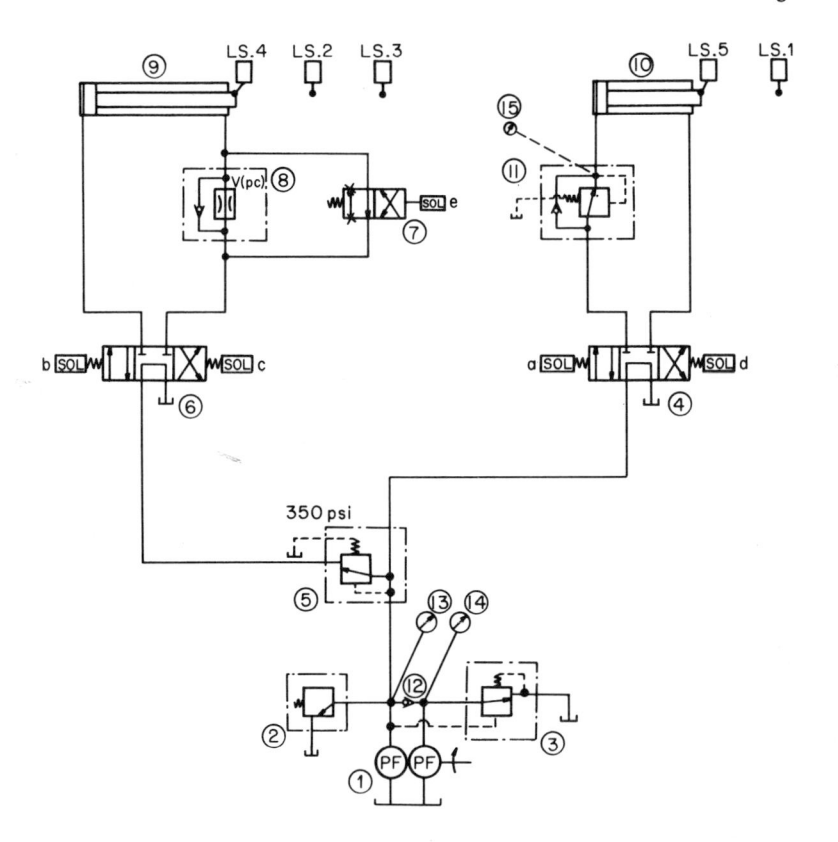

Item	Description
1	Pump-V-108-ED-10 — Vickers double vane type
2	Relief valve — CT-06-B-10 — Vickers balanced piston type
3	Unloading valve — RT-06-A-4-10 — Vickers 'R' series; Type 4 assembly externally operated; Internally drained
4	Directional valve — DG4S4-018C-41-ENU — Solenoid operated; 4 way spring centred, with 8 spool
5	Sequence valve — RT-06-D2-10 — Vickers 'R' series; Type 2 assembly internally operated; Externally drained
6	Directional valve — As item 4
7	Directional valve — DG4S4-012A-41-ENU — Solenoid operated; 4 way spring offset, with 2 spool
8	Flow control valve — FCG-02-1000-31-ENU — Vickers
9	Cylinder — 3" bore x 12" stroke
10	Cylinder — 3" bore x 4" stroke
11	Pressure reducing valve — XCG-03-B-10-ENT — Vickers
12	Check valve — C2-815-EN — Vickers
13	Pressure gauge — System 950 psi
14	Pressure gauge — Unloading 500 psi
15	Pressure gauge — Clamping 350 psi

Testing Techniques

Section 9   Circuit fault 1

Circuit symptoms: When start button is pressed, the sequence as described does take place but at a very reduced rate, ie the cylinders items (9) and (10) move very slow

Circuit reference	Condition	Check No.	Circuit reference	Condition	Check No.	Circuit reference	Condition	Check No.
Electric motor	Running	10	Gauge reading Item (13)	950 psi When system is in operation	P	Solenoid (E) of valve (Item – 7)	When energized gives flow P → B blocked A → T blocked	10
Motor speed	Correct	10	Gauge reading Item (14)	0 psi When system is in operation	P	Flow control valve (Item – 8)	Controlling the rate of flow as set	10
Pump shaft	Rotating	10	Relief valve Item (2)	Functioning correctly relieving at 950 psi	20	Pressure reducing valve (Item – 11)	Reduced pressure being delivered to cylinder 10	20
Pump assembly small volume	Correct	20	Unloading valve Item (3)	Passing oil valve is open	S	Pressure gauge reading (Item – 15)	350 psi when system is in operation	10
Pump assembly large volume	Correct	35	Sequence valve Item (5)	Functioning correctly opens at 350 psi	15	Cylinder Item (9)	Functioning correctly – No leaks	20
Wear on pump cartridge (small)	None	30	Directional control valve (Item – 4)	Functioning correctly	10	Cylinder Item (10)	Functioning correctly – No leaks	20
Wear on pump cartridge (large)	None	S	Solenoid (A) of valve (Item – 4)	When energized gives flow P → A and B → T	10	LS1	Functions correctly	10
Pump delivery	Full delivery	30	Solenoid (D) of valve (Item – 4)	When energized gives flow P → B and A → T	10	LS2	Functions correctly	10
Pump inlet line	Clear and airtight	15	Directional control valve (Item – 6)	Functioning correctly	10	LS3	Functions correctly	10
Strainer	Clean	10	Solenoid (C) of valve (Item – 6)	When energized gives flow P → B and A → T	10	LS4	Functions correctly	10
Pump leakages	None	10	Solenoid (B) of valve (Item – 6)	When energized gives flow P → A and B → T	10	LS5	Functions correctly	10
Check valve Item (12)	Functioning correctly	20	Directional control valve (Item – 7)	Functioning correctly	10			

Figure 4.18   Basic hydraulics test

Figure 4.19

The Wilkes and Son simulator

Fortunately, there are other types of simulators that, while not representing the whole job, do simulate various relevant aspects of it. One example of this is shown in Figure 4.19. This is the Wilkes and Son Simulator, which contains the entire electrical system of an average British saloon car in an easily accessible position, the moving parts being driven by a built in variable speed electric motor. Faults can be switched into or actually put into any part of the circuit. This type of simulator is useful not only for training but also for testing. Its convenience value is obvious since all parts are easily accessible and the problems of noise, fumes, and the cost associated with a real car are avoided. It is also possible with such simulators to build an automatic recording of responses to increase the objectivity of marking and avoid a high examiner to candidate ratio. Other simulators that can be used for performance testing are the Radar Maintenance Trainer, which is composed of units contained in typical radar sets, and the RCA training panels which incorporate either solid-state or vacuum tube subchassis in configurations simulating circuits used in a variety of electronic equipment. Components are plugged into the back of the subchassis and can be reached easily for trouble-shooting purposes. Both of these simulators have been used for training and testing at the US Army Signal Centre and School[13].

It is obvious that simulators of the sort just described have both advantages and disadvantages. They are quick and easy to use; they do represent important elements of the trouble-shooting task and they can be used in locations where real equipment cannot. They suffer from their representing only a part of the real environment. For example, the competent car mechanic listens to the way an engine runs or fails to run; he feels and sees differences in the vibrations of the engine under varying operating conditions. As was stated earlier it is feasible to represent the auditory input quite accurately by recordings. Indeed, tests of auditory diagnosis have been developed in the USA (see Chapter 9) but a greater problem is posed by the vibrations as perceived by the mechanic and other types of input such as the smell of petrol at various places.

It can be seen then that once again the rule holds that realistic hands-on testing is always important but where more detailed information regarding a performance is required or when some other restrictions limit the use of actual equipment, then hands-off tests will be extremely useful.

REFERENCES

1. Siegel A.I., Richlin M. and Federman P., *Post-training Performance Criterion development and application*, Wayne Pa. Applied Psychological Services, 1958.
2. Fitzpatrick R. and Morrison E.J., 'Performance and Product Evaluation' in Educational Measurement, Thorndike R.L., Ed., American Council on Education, 1971
3. Downie N.M., *Fundamentals of Measurement*, Oxford University Press, New York, 1966, Chap.9 'The Essay Test'.
4. Gronlun N.E., *Constructing Achievement Tests*, Prentice Hall, New York, 1968, Chap.3 'Constructing Objective Tests of Knowledge'.
5. Thorndike R.L. and Hagan P., *Measurement and Evaluation in Psychology and Education*, John Wiley and Sons, New York, 1955, Chap.3 'Planning a Test' and Chap.4 'Preparing Test Exercises'.
6. Slade R.E., *Report on Mechanical and Electrical Craft Apprentice Assessment — Post First Year*, Central Electricity Generating Board, Personnel Dept, Education and Training Branch, 1972.
7. Baldwin T.S., 'Evaluation of Learning in Industrial Education' in Handbook on Formative and Summative Evaluation of Student Learning, Bloom B.S., Hastings J.T. and Madaus G.F., Eds., McGraw Hill Book Co., New York, 1971.
8. Cronbach L.J., *Essentials of Psychological Testing*, Harper and Row Ltd, 1961, Chap.13, 'Proficiency Tests'.
9. Conrad H.S., *Statistical Analysis of the Mechanical Knowledge Test*, Princeton College Entrance Exam. Bd., 1944.
10. Tiffin J. and McCormick E.J., *Industrial Psychology*, Prentice-Hall, Englewood Cliffs, New Jersey, 1965, Chap.8 'Achievement Tests'.
11. Dale H.C.A., 'Fault Finding in Electronics Equipment', *Ergonomics*, Volume 1, pp.356-85, 1958.
12. Glaser R., Damrin D.E., and Gardner F.M., *The Tab Item: a technique for the measurement of proficiency in diagnostic problem solving tasks*, Bureau of Research and Service, College of Education, University of Illinois, Preliminary Report, 1952.
13. US Army Signal Centre and School, *Performance Testing for Systems Engineered Courses*, Ft. Monmouth, New Jersey.

SUGGESTED FURTHER READING

Boyd J.L. and Shimberg B., *Handbook of Performance Testing*, Educational Testing Service, Princeton New Jersey, 1970, Chap.6 'Variations on a Theme'.

Developing a Programme of Testing for Trainee Craftsmen in the Shipbuilding Industry, Industrial and Commercial Training, Volume 5, Number 1, 1973.

Ryans D.G. and Frederiksen N., 'Performance Tests of Educational Achievement' in Educational Measurement, Lindquist E.F., Ed., American Council on Education, Washington D.C., 1951.

5

Choosing Between Testing Techniques

The choice of testing techniques is a complex one that must take into account a great deal of the information collected during our original analysis. It should be clear at this stage that one of the most important factors to consider is the type of skill being tested. It was seen, for example, that fixed sequence tests are most appropriate for measuring perceptual skills, job knowledge, and planning, but there are other factors such as cost, availability of materials, and standardization of presentation that must also influence the choice.

The factors to be considered can be conveniently grouped into general areas and the whole task of choosing a testing technique in terms of these aspects is summarized in Figure 5.1. The factors within each area will be examined and it will be considered how they relate to the different techniques of testing.

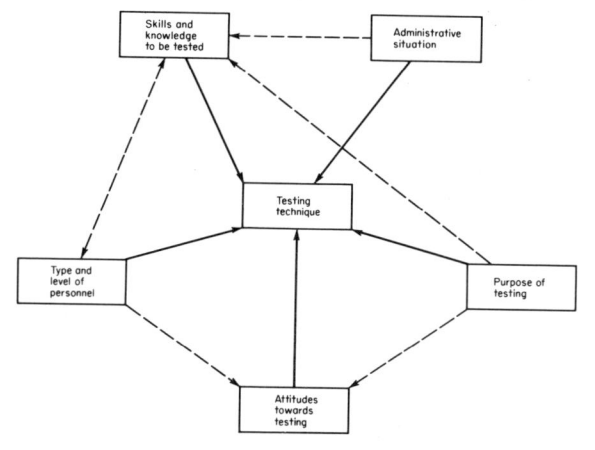

Figure 5.1   Areas of consideration in choosing a testing technique

SKILL AND KNOWLEDGE TO BE TESTED

The application of testing techniques to the various classes of skill is shown in Figure 5.2. This diagram requires some explanation for it shows the hands-on test as embracing all types of skill, which for some jobs it will do, although this depends on the type of job and whether or not the job requires all the types of skill shown. What this amounts to is that hands-on tests will cover most or all of the skills contained in any particular job, so if one's sole concern is to measure all the skills then hands-on tests will be the answer, but if one wants to assess the component skills individually then one will have to consider alternative techniques. Also a hands-on test may often measure only a sample of the knowledge component. For example, finding a fault in an electronic circuit may require a knowledge of only a small sample of electronic circuit symbols involved in that particular test.

One can see that all the factors relating to choice of testing technique are interactive for the discussion now is about the purpose of the test or test battery. The question is whether the concern is with purely effective performance or knowledge of the reasons for failures when they occur.

PURPOSE OF TESTING

As hinted in the previous section the test may be required to do more than just discriminate between satisfactory and unsatisfactory performance; it may also be desirable to know why a particular performance was not up to standard. This will be particularly so if one is concerned also with training since it will then be necessary to know what is required to bring an unsatisfactory performance up to par. In order to do this, the total job must be broken down into its various component skills and these tested individually so that performance can be assessed on each of these skills.

This does not mean that hands-on tests will not be used by training departments because the latter are nevertheless concerned with whether or not adequate performance has been achieved and therefore a valid test of performance must still be included.

With regard to the form and content of any test or test battery it is worth differentiating between tests intended to measure component skills, such as discussed above, and those intended as global measures of performance. The latter type of test would probably involve a sample of the end results of training or job requirements. To illustrate this difference, a TV service engineer could be tested on component skills such as reading circuit drawings, identifying parts, fault-finding and repair procedures and so on or, if a global measure was required, by a test in diagnosing and repairing a selected group of faults in which all the component skills are required.

It is evident from the content of the different types of test that the hands-on tests, especially the total job, are more likely to be valid. Since, the content of the test directly reflects the content of the job. However, it must be emphasized that some tests may look valid (ie have face validity) but may not in fact be valid. The subject of validity is discussed further in Chapter 9. From this it is fair to say that all performance tests or test batteries should include some degree of hands-on testing in order to establish that the candidate possesses the necessary manipulative and related skills. Ideally one would always use the total job test to ensure this, but there may be several practical obstacles to this, some of which will be discussed below. The hands-off tests will be brought in when one wants more information about the candidate or where a wider range of skills must be measured in a fairly short time. One clear advantage of hands-off tests is their brevity and cheapness as compared with hands-on tests.

If one is using tests as devices to predict future performance, a different approach may need to be employed. The sample of behaviour comprised by the test will need to be based on those tasks which have been found to discriminate between levels of proficiency in future performance. For selection purposes, those tests may be used which improve the accuracy of our prediction.

One method of testing that enables a detailed monitoring of each trainee's performance is the technique known as 'phased testing' (also known as 'progress testing' in the USA). As the name implies the test is phased, there being one test for each discrete phase or block of training. The philosophy behind this technique is that the trainee's performance can be assessed after each phase of training and any deficiencies in his performance can then be tackled by further training followed by a second attempt at the test and so on. Unfortunately, the system often does not work like this in practice because training programmes are sometimes so tightly scheduled that any remedial training is out of the question. This does not place phased testing completely out of the court because any widespread deficiencies at one phase might point to a weakness in the training itself and this could be remedied in the following years. In this way the training itself can be monitored (see Chapter 8).

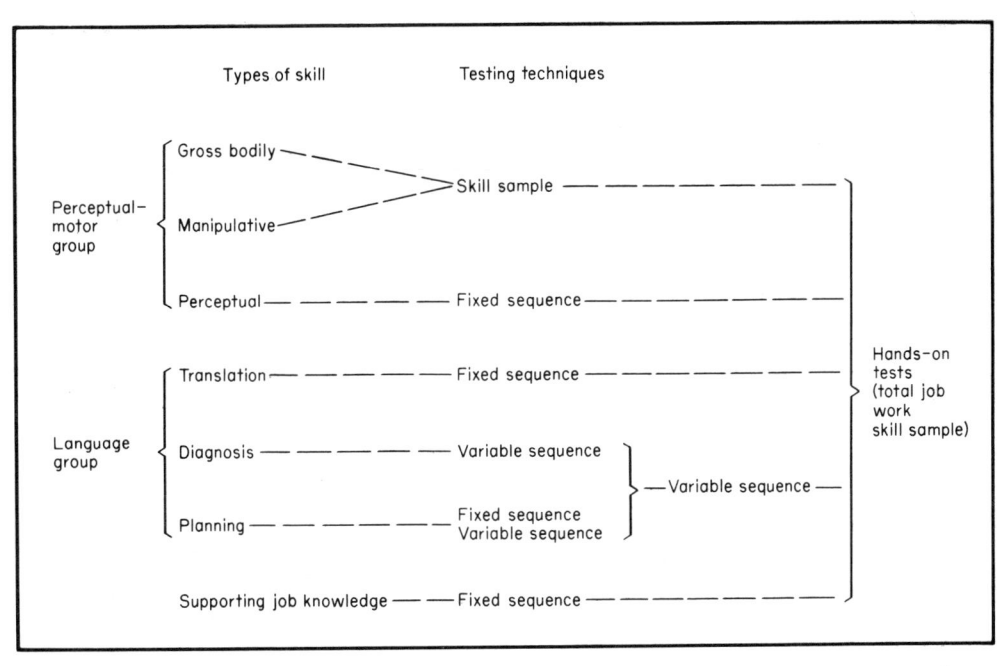

Figure 5.2 Types of skill and associated testing techniques (for full explanation see text)

Another aspect of the purpose of testing is the type of criteria that are being used. It was mentioned earlier that performance tests are not the prerogative of the training department; they are often used to grade personnel in accordance with some sort of salary structure and when this is the case, the ability of the test to discriminate between levels of ability might need to be much greater than a ready-for-works type of test. Frequently the higher grade posts require personnel with a greater knowledge of company 'geography' and procedures or other aspects of job knowledge. At one factory where tests for grading were developed, the criterion for promotion was based on the number of machines of which a person had detailed knowledge. Clearly this type of situation will often be best handled by hands-off tests where objectivity and standard presentation must each be kept at a maximum and the possibility of offending a so-called skilled man by putting him in a situation related to testing his basic manipulative skills is avoided. Test records and actual test performances may need to be kept for a considerable time, and the storage of hands-off test performance is of course easier.

ATTITUDES TOWARDS TESTING

There are many people whose attitude towards testing may influence the type of test that is used. The example described above is equally applicable here and although it dealt with the attitude of the candidate, his case will often be taken up by his trade union. A converse position is likely to arise when developing tests to be accepted as an entry qualification to a particular trade or company. It may be that management or union will not accept a test without considerable hands-on content. As a general rule work sample and skills sample tests should be of a nature to command respect and establish the confidence of tradesmen. It is now possible to see why such attitudes needed to be examined in the original analysis since there would be little point in developing sophisticated hands-off measures that will not be accepted by the customer. Fortunately such dogged attitudes are rare and it is perhaps more important to realize that there are many people such as anxious trade union officials and managers who will be concerned about the method of testing employed and they should be kept informed of the tester's intentions right from the start. Indeed the authors have found that it is not 'new fangled' ideas that are objected to as much as the rudeness of not telling these people what is being done.

TYPE AND LEVEL OF PERSONNEL

To a certain extent the type and level of skills to be tested will ensure that the tests are appropriate to the type and level of personnel to be tested, particularly if testing is related to training. It is, however, worth examining such factors as the articulateness of candidates, age, and so on. Paper and pencil tests may be unsuitable for individuals with a poor academic record; in fact the prospect of such an ordeal may mean candidates are unwilling to be tested. Similarly older personnel may resent paper and pencil tests because it is 'like being back at school'. So such factors as face validity and the applicability of tests to various groups have to be taken into account. For example, the hydraulics course discussed in Chapter 3 was taken by both apprentices and experienced workers, so particular care had to be taken to ensure the form of the test did not upset the latter. In fact, the older personnel seemed to enjoy the rather 'tricky' hands-off test while the apprentices took a blasé 'we have seen it all before' attitude.

ADMINISTRATIVE SITUATION

The administrative situation probably puts the most restricting conditions of all upon the choice of testing technique and it is for this reason that one needs to collect information about this at an early stage in the analysis and it was stated in Chapter 3 that information should be collected regarding:

1 Amount of money available for testing.
2 Availability of equipment for testing.
3 Availability of staff and equipment for testing.

All of these things will obviously influence the type of testing chosen; simple paper and pencil hands-off tests are relatively cheap to produce and run as compared with hands-on tests which usually entail high costs in terms of materials used, possible damage to equipment and personnel, time spent, etc. It should be noted that once the analysis has been carried out, the construction of hands-on tests is usually quite simple, whereas a great deal of thought and experimentation may be needed with hands-off techniques. On the other hand, the running of hands-on tests is usually time consuming while that of hands-off tests is not.

It was mentioned earlier that it is essential to use some hands-on tests since this is the only way to be sure of a person's capabilities, but the use of well designed hands-off tests to extend the area tested was also considered. Thus when testing bench fitters, for example, one might give them a hands-on test which involved the manufacture of an item such as a small vice and this would demand the use of most of the skills and knowledge required of a bench fitter. One might argue, however, that these skills have only been demonstrated in relation to one particular job and that some aspects of the job, particularly reading drawings, planning, choice of tools, etc, would not necessarily carry over to other situations. In such a situation one could develop tests to assess these skills more directly as described in the previous chapter. From a cost point of view the actual development of paper and pencil techniques may be more expensive (in terms of time spent) than the designing of a straightforward test-piece. The running costs will show a complete reverse of this situation; the cost of materials will be low, tools and machines will not be occupied, and fewer examiners or invigilators will be required. Another aspect of cost which is demonstrated here is that the amount of time available to spend on testing is often restricted. If tests are being developed for a fairly short training course, say two weeks, one is unlikely to be given more than a day for testing and production-type hands-on tests may take more time than this.

The availability of staff for testing presents the same sort of problems as the availability of trainees. The type of test as well as the type of marking scheme is also important here. Tests that examine both process and product usually require a fairly high examiner/candidate ratio since the process has to be assessed while the test is actually underway. Again production tests are time-consuming when the test itself is over because a detailed marking scheme is usually essential and this means that a great deal of time will be spent assessing the test pieces. Situations where testing is difficult because of shortage of staff or equipment may be just the situations where testing is necessary to help ensure training is effective and that trainees, despite these difficulties, are in fact acquiring the relevant skills.

Of course, the effect of the attitudes and degree of influence of examiners are important aspects in the administration of tests. Many unsuccessful candidates for driving tests blame the examiner's particular prejudices or behaviour for their failure. The examiner 'breathing down their necks' may make certain candidates nervous and eventually lead them to fail the test. In order to remove such influence, a division of the Singer sewing machine group in the USA is developing an electronic testing system for drivers which removes the need for in-car examiners. The driver is alone in the car and receives instructions by radio from the examiner in a central control tower. The test involves driving around a special driving course performing certain manoeuvres. Electronic sensing and transmitting devices in the car and on the road monitor the driver's performance which is analysed by computer. A hands-off test utilizing colour slides assesses the candidate's knowledge of the Highway Code by showing a series of traffic problems which the candidate has to solve. The weakness in this system is that the high degree of standardization of the test content and removal of examiner bias is achieved at the expense of making the test situation rather unrealistic; there is a complete absence of other traffic on the circuit, yet every driver must learn to cope with other drivers if he is to be a good driver. It would seem therefore that this system is ideal for testing basic driving skills but further assessment is needed of in-traffic driving performance.

Complex simulators have been discussed in relation to cost and it was noted that although they represent a convenient form of testing they are invariably expensive to produce but may be fairly cheap to run. The simpler kinds of variable sequence test are often worth considering when the budget is low for the most important ingredient to the production of this type of test is imagination rather than money.

Another way in which expenditure restrictions and shortage of equipment can be overcome is by using photographic or other representations. This type of material can be particularly useful when testing various aspects of perceptual skill such as recognition of components and machine items, while the technique can be extended to include such things as recognition of faults and wear and the associated diagnosis and service recommendations.

Figure 5.3 illustrates some of the aspects of the administrative situation. From all the factors discussed it can be seen that the choice of testing techniques cannot be laid down exactly but is rather a matter of considering all the relevant factors in relation to each other. Thus although one might prefer a fairly extensive hands-on test, it may be that other factors such as cost and time available will restrict this to the extent that only part of the job situation can be tested by means of a hands-on test and the rest will require the use of one or other of the

Choosing Between Testing Techniques

hands-off techniques. It is possible, however, to give some broad guide-lines and these are shown in Figure 5.4 which also serves as a summary for this and the previous chapter. The table also gives some details of the methods of assessment involved which are discussed in the next chapter.

Technique	Development costs	Cost of materials	Use of materials	Examiner/ Candidate ratio	Testing time
Total job	Low	High	High	Medium to high	Medium to high
Work sample	Low to medium	High	High	High	Medium to high
Skills sample	Medium	High	High	Medium	Medium to high
Hi-Fi	High	Low	Low	Low	Low
Low-Fi	Medium	Low	Low	Low	Low
Hi-Fi	High	Low	Low	Medium	Medium
Low-Fi	Medium	Low	Low	Low	Low

Hands-on: Total job, Work sample, Skills sample
Fixed sequence: Hi-Fi, Low-Fi
Variable sequence: Hi-Fi, Low-Fi

Figure 5.3 Relation between administrative considerations and testing techniques

77

Choosing Between Testing Techniques

Testing techniques	Content	Where most useful	Method of assessment
Total job	Job carried out in work-type situation or on 'exact' simulator	Simple production and maintenance tasks	Checklist marking of product and/or process, error rate etc automatic recording devices
Work sample	Selected part of job assessed in work-type situation, usually part of a battery of tests	More involved production and maintenance tasks	Checklist marking of product and/or process, error rate, etc
Skills sample	Selected skills measured by test piece	'Skilled' personnel and apprentices in production industries	Objective assessment of test piece utilizing measurable dimensions etc
Fixed sequence Low fidelity	Paper and pencil tests: essay type, short answer, oral tests, multiple choice items	Job knowledge	Structured assessment Objective testing techniques
Fixed sequence High fidelity	Simple representation of part of job; photographs, models, tape recordings	Perceptual skill, diagnostic skills. Where actual equipment cannot be used	Error rate, yes/no answers, multiple choice questions etc
Variable sequence Low fidelity	Paper and pencil tests, electronic fault finding	Decision-making aspect of fault finding. Planning	Structured assessment of logicality of approach, speed of fault location, use of correct procedures
Variable sequence High fidelity	Simple and complex simulators representing important aspects of job situation and demands	Fault finding including job knowledge and perceptual skill content. Equivalent to total job or work sample test without being in full job situation (eg flight simulators)	Structured assessment of logicality of approach, speed of fault location, use of correct procedures

Figure 5.4 A summary of testing techniques — their content, use and method of assessment

6

Assessing the Test Performance

MARKING SCHEMES

The whole purpose of testing is to arrive at an assessment of the capabilities of an individual (though this information may also be used for assessing training methods, instructors, and so on). So far the decision as to what to test and how to test it has been looked at, but it has always been borne in mind that ultimately performance in the selected tasks must be assessed in an efficient manner. To carry out this assessment a marking scheme must be utilized. The term marking scheme will be used to cover all methods of scoring a test, even though marks as such will not always be involved. Efficient assessment depends largely on the existence of an efficient marking scheme.

Two questions must now be considered: Just what is meant by 'an efficient marking scheme?' 'What constitutes a good marking scheme?'

The marking scheme must be composed of a good sample of the behaviour or the product that is to be tested. That is, it must include aspects which are indicative of the goodness of the candidate's performance. Since any marking scheme comprises only a sample of the behaviour in which there is interest it must be ensured that this sample is as representative as possible and thereby provides an adequate reflection of the realities of the situation. It can happen that a marking scheme looks impressive but is not efficient since it represents an inappropriate sample of the behaviour under examination.

The point that any marking scheme is only a sample of behaviour and that for any one performance numerous marking schemes are possible is an important one,

Assessing the Test Performance

since a marking scheme can often be accepted on the false assumption that it is the ideal scheme and no other versions are possible. For example, in some training centres the marking scheme for building tests are divided into two halves, one to assess the final product and one the approach to and technique of carrying out the task. The second half of this assessment is unnecessary from a readiness for employment point of view but useful for remedial training.

Marking schemes should be as objective as possible. The objectivity of a marking scheme can be assessed in a number of ways but the most common approaches are:

1. That it looks objective since it specifies what is to be assessed and how marks are to be awarded. In other words there is less room for personal interpretation.
2. By comparing scores given to the same performances by different examiners to see if examiners do in fact agree. The extent of their agreement is often expressed in terms of a correlation coefficient. More will be said about this method and details of some studies that have been carried out will be given in Chapter 9.

An efficient marking scheme should provide the information required (regarding the candidate) and this will vary with the purpose of testing. One way in which tests vary is in the amount of discrimination between levels of performance of candidates required by the test user.

At its most basic level the question will be whether the only information required is if a candidate is acceptable or whether further information is needed. For example, one test user may want to know only if a candidate has reached a given standard of performance; another whether he is merely adequate or very good; another whether he performed so poorly that little is to be gained by giving further training and so on. These three different situations are illustrated in Figure 6.1.

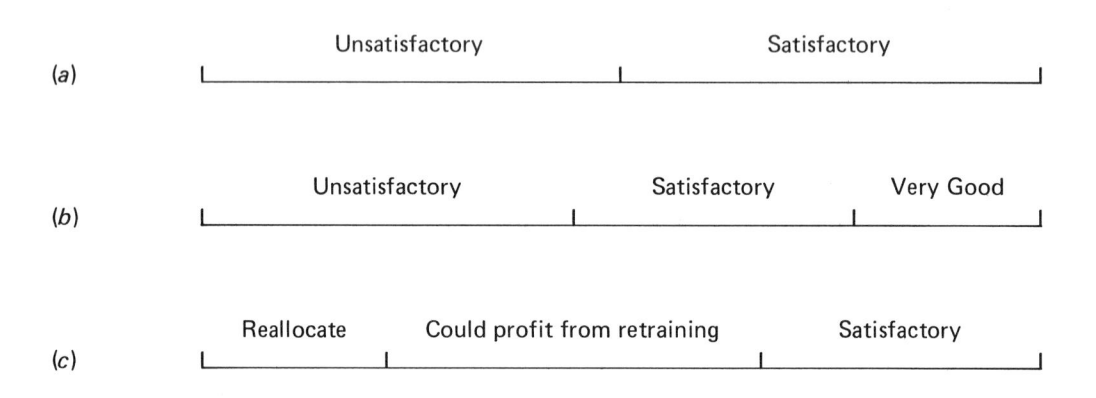

(a) |⎯⎯⎯⎯Unsatisfactory⎯⎯⎯⎯|⎯⎯⎯⎯Satisfactory⎯⎯⎯⎯|

(b) |⎯⎯Unsatisfactory⎯⎯|⎯⎯Satisfactory⎯⎯|⎯⎯Very Good⎯⎯|

(c) |⎯Reallocate⎯|⎯Could profit from retraining⎯|⎯Satisfactory⎯|

Figure 6.1 Different levels of discrimination which may be required in assessment: a simple pass/fail situation (a); pass/fail plus upper discrimination (b); and pass/fail plus lower discrimination (c).

Assessing the Test Performance

An efficient marking scheme should employ the relevant standards of performance. There is a great confusion over the term standards, largely as a result of the misapprehension that standards exist in isolation rather than that they are what any one person is prepared to accept. There may be, for example, quality control standards in operation in the job which is being examined, but it must not be forgotten that these standards will be the result of a previous agreement or compromise.

That is not to say standards are the result of people just sitting round a table and compromising and that analytic work is useless. In fact, quite the reverse is the case; the better the analytic work the better the marking scheme is likely to be. All that is being stated is that at some stage responsible persons have to agree on the standard. They may say 'It's up to you' or 'Standards must be those of the quality control department' or 'All interested parties will have to get together and go over the standards you propose', but in any of the above cases there is a process of agreement. It is a process of decision not of pure discovery.

The four types of standards which most frequently occur in tests are:

1 Quality (of the end-product).
2 Quantity (number of items produced or serviced within a specified time).
3 Process (the way the candidate carries out the task).
4 Speed (time taken for a given task).

These four types of standards can apply equally to hands-on and hands-off tests. For example, in a hands-off test of fault finding, quantity (number of faults found), process (logicality of approach), and speed (in finding faults) might be the aspects of performance that would be considered.

Once it is recognized that the standards embodied in the test are based on decisions (backed up by analytic procedures) then it can be seen that a variety of decisions are called for.

The most important question is 'Are we concerned with training or job standards?'. The meaning of job standards here is actual day to day standards of what is acceptable in the production or other departments. Experienced worker standard (EWS) is one such standard. This is a basic question which needs to be asked by every test developer to clarify the situation. If it is not asked, problems may crop up at later stages. For example, if the standards are based on job requirements and the test is for trainees completing a course which is not supposed to equip them to do the job as efficiently as an experienced worker, one is likely to become unpopular with the training staff since it is probable that many trainees will fail the test.

Suppose, that it has been determined that the test will be based on job standards, the question will arise as to how far one can adopt measures like EWS? It may be that the test user demands the use of EWS and so one has no choice. It is worth noting that in some areas standards are often not cut and dried and so EWS may not be available or appropriate. This point is particularly relevant to fault finding tasks where experienced workers may use wasteful and inefficient strategies that they have picked up trying to solve day-to-day problems. Analysis may show that more efficient strategies are available. Nevertheless on

Assessing the Test Performance

straightforward production work EWS is probably a good starting point in the search for relevant quality, quantity, and speed standards. It will probably be little help as regards process standards.

A marking scheme should reflect the degree of product or process emphasis in the requirements of performance. A major decision which faces the test developer is the relative weight in the marking scheme between the quality of the end-product and the 'correctness' of the procedure or process used to achieve it. This might be characterized as the product orientation versus the process orientation. The product orientation is characterized by the foreman who says 'As long as he produces the goods, I don't care how he does it', while the process orientation stresses the importance of doing things 'the right way'.

The middle view between these two is probably the most accepted, namely that while the quality of the end-product is of great importance, some consideration should be given to how this quality is obtained. Obviously, an aspect such as safety is always important in the assessment of performance, but such factors as care of equipment, amount of scrap, and number of errors before achieving the end-product are worthy of scrutiny.

The relative emphasis of these two elements in the marking scheme will vary with the job and the aims of the test. For example, a test for personnel who lay and have to repair gas mains would constantly stress safety precautions when working with live gas, whereas a test for determining whether a trainee can castrate a pig emphasizes the end product (a castrated pig in good health) since a variety of equally acceptable methods can be used for such things as holding the pig. In some cases the distinction between product and process becomes rather forced and unnatural. For example, if someone's ability in driving is being assessed, what is the product as distinct from the process or way he goes about driving? Here the process is assessed, rather than some 'product' such as 'vehicle driving from A to B without damage'. In other cases it may only be possible to infer the process from the quality of the product.

As a general rule it is probably correct to say that a test based on course standards will place more emphasis on procedures than a test based on production standards, if only because training departments place emphasis on implanting good working habits. Once out on the shop floor, the trainee is of course open to the influence of all the old hands who like to point out that he is doing the job 'all wrong' or can do it quicker if he follows their own, perhaps less safe, practices. However, since the assessment of process usually involves considerable resources in terms of examiners' time, it should always be ascertained that it is really needed, rather than simply including it because it is possible.

The criteria for a good marking scheme can therefore be summarized as follows. It should:

1. Comprise a representative sample of the behaviour under test.
2. Be as objective as possible.
3. Give the type of information required.
4. Embody the relevant standards of performance.
5. Reflect the product or process emphasis in the requirements.

Having considered the general requirements for a good marking scheme the types of marking schemes available will be discussed.

USE OF ON-THE-JOB MEASURES

It may be very tempting to a test developer to make use of data gained from assessing the person doing his job in the normal work environment. Such an assessment situation has the obvious advantage that it is the criterion situation. However, this advantage has to be weighed against other factors, notably the problem of achieving a controlled test environment. If the test situation is not well controlled, then different candidates may perform different tasks or under different conditions or be assessed in a subjective or otherwise unfair manner.

The types of jobs where on-the-job measures may be most useful are those where a definite product is involved (as distinct from a service) particularly short-cycle production-line tasks.

Stead[1], for example, used a more or less normal production situation when assessing packers in a cannery. One conveyor belt was set aside for testing purposes and the candidate was assessed on the basis of the number of cans packed per hour.

However, there are pitfalls in the use of on-the-job measures:

1 The quality of the performance may depend not only on the candidate but also on other people. For example, during World War II an attempt was made to use bombing measures to assess the competence of bomb aimers. These measures were eventually rejected because the way the pilot flew the plane affected the accuracy of the bombing.
2 The conditions of assessment may vary from candidate to candidate. To take an obvious example, the equipment provided to one candidate in a machine-shop may put him at a disadvantage; it may be old, badly maintained, and so on.
3 Our on-the-job measure may only represent a limited sample of the requirements of the job. For example, if in an assessment of secretaries only typing measures were considered, this would omit such important aspects as answering the telephone in a polite manner, making notes of appointments, and so on.
4 Performance as measured by production may be subject to substantial time variations. Rothe and coworkers[2] in a series of studies of output rates among a variety of production-line personnel (eg butter wrapper, coil winder and machine operator) showed that job performance as measured by production data is subject to substantial time variations. Correlation on the reliability of production data ranged from 0.05 to 0.85 with the magnitude being influenced by the length of the time period between measures. However, it is worth emphasizing that personnel did not think they were 'on test'. Rothe was attempting a measure of typical performance, whereas testing aims for a measure of maximum performance. Perhaps if candidates had been told they were being tested, test reliability would have been increased.

Attention is now given to the type of marking schemes that can be used for the four aspects of performance; quality, quantity, speed, and process. For each aspect various types of marking schemes, their advantages and disadvantages, will be discussed and examples of each type given.

Assessing the Test Performance

THE ASSESSMENT OF QUALITY

Dimension-orientated marking schemes

Probably the most common type of performance test is the engineering test piece. Since here the interest is as to whether or not the candidate can work to certain specified tolerances for dimensions and finish, such marking schemes are referred to as dimension-orientated. Measuring instruments such as ruler, vernier scales, micrometers, etc, can of course be used to assess the dimensions of the candidate's test-piece.

In the last chapter the skill sample test involving manufacturing a taper plug was shown (Figure 4.6). Figure 6.2 shows a marking scheme of the type which might be used for this test.

	Total possible marks
30 DIA	10
14 DIA	10
20 DIA	10
Taper	20
21 DIM	10
11.5 DIM	10
10 DIM	10
60 DIM	10
Chamfers	10
Finish	20
	120

Figure 6.2 A marking scheme for the taper plug test piece

The obvious objection to this type of marking scheme is that it leaves too much to the individual examiner's discretion so that examiners may vary in the marks they give to a candidate. In order to help make marking more objective one could specify more precisely the way in which marks are to be awarded. Figure 6.3 is an example of this.

With such a marking scheme an increase in interexaminer (or interrater) reliability should be expected: Interexaminer reliability being the extent to which examiners agree or disagree on how many marks to give to a candidate. With high interexaminer reliability a candidate would receive (more or less) the same marks irrespective of which examiner marked the test piece which he produced. With low interexaminer reliability the marks given might depend more on the examiner than on the actual piece of work.

Within specified tolerance	Full marks
Outside specified tolerance	No marks
30 DIA	1 or 0
14 DIA	1 or 0
20 DIA	1 or 0
Taper	3 or 0
21 DIM	1 or 0
11.5 DIM	1 or 0
10 DIM	1 or 0
60 DIM	1 or 0
Chamfers (2)	1 or 0
Surface finish of Taper	1 or 0
Form of Knurl	1 or 0
Surface finish of remaining areas	1 or 0
Total possible marks	15

Figure 6.3 A more objective marking scheme for the taper plug test piece

However, even with an objective looking marking scheme such as the one above it may be that examiners disagree. The use of measuring instruments requires relatively precise readings which may be difficult when a large number of test-pieces are being assessed. It is worth noting that Lawshe and Tiffin[3] found the use of precision measuring instruments in industrial plants very inaccurate. In one study[4] it was reported that the correlations between examiners' ratings of machine work varied from 0.11 to 0.55. These assessments were based on the marking of dimensions, yet there was still considerable disagreement between examiners. However, the use of specially made go/no go gauges increased the correlations between the same examiners to 0.93 and 0.94. When the same examiners marked the test-pieces ten days later, the correlation between first and second marks was 0.97.

It is therefore always worthwhile considering the introduction of such devices to improve the objectivity of marking and often they also considerably speed up the marking process. Figures 6.4 to 6.7 show examples of specially constructed gauges and dial test indicator in use.

McPherson[5] applied a similar technique to a wood-working test comprising a model-like wood block. A plastic pattern was imposed on the test piece to check dimensions. Other techniques can be used such as testing a soldered joint for its conductivity using special types of galvanometers or special apparatus to determine the strength of a joint and so on.

Assessing the Test Performance

Figure 6.4 Taper plug test piece and specially constructed go/no go gauge for measuring the taper

Figure 6.5 The go/no go gauge in use

Assessing the Test Performance

Figure 6.6 Another go/no go gauge — this time for the 10 DIM — note the minimum and maximum dimensions

Figure 6.7 Using the dial test indicator (DTI) for measuring the taper plug test-piece

Assessing the Test Performance

Another variation on the marking of test-pieces is to examine the test pieces to see whether they fit together, function or whatever (note: this obviously will not be possible in all cases). If the piece passes this inspection it is marked using a marking scheme such as Figure 6.3; if it does not pass the inspection, then it is automatically failed and no time is wasted marking it. This is in line with the philosophy outlined previously where it was argued that one should always consider the amount of discrimination required before designing a marking scheme. In this case, only upper-discrimination (ie in the 'pass' part of the spectrum) is contemplated.

Finish can also be defined in an objective way and assessed in terms of whether or not it is acceptable to the standard defined on the drawing or test specification. The use of graded comparison standards (see below) can further help here and perhaps provide greater objectivity.

If possible, where a number of test-pieces are marked it is preferable to mark the same dimension on every article, then move onto another dimension rather than marking all dimensions on one test-piece and then moving onto another. This procedure helps to reduce the 'halo effect' mentioned elsewhere.

Bemetel, a Dutch organization concerned with both training and testing, run yearly tests for many industrial trades which involve a highly developed marking system[6]. All candidates in a trade make exactly the same test-pieces in the same week from exactly the same blueprints provided by Bemetel. Afterwards all test-pieces are brought together at a central point. Here experts from industry assess, check and measure them according to identical rules. Three hundred or more experts are involved on the assessment for around two weeks and each dimension or aspect to be assessed is marked on every test-piece before going on to the next dimension or aspect. With a turning test, for example, the first of its 91 details is marked on each test-piece before going on to the second detail. Examiners come to work faster and more accurately than if they examined a test-piece for all aspects, then moved on to another test-piece. Where there are specified limits, a test-piece is either within these limits or not (eg one mark or zero; four marks or zero). Other aspects are assessed on a four-point scale (three = excellent; two = good; one = not good; zero = poor), a method selected after finding that scales with more than four points led to an unacceptable degree of subjectivity.

Checklists

A checklist, as its name suggests, consists of a list of items against which the examiner checks the candidate's performance. Each item requires a Yes/No decision on the part of the examiner.

An example of this type of marking scheme as used in harpsichord manufacture is given in Figure 6.8. Figure 4.5 gave an example of a checklist in shipbuilding.

Note that in both cases, each item comprises a description in specific terms of what is required, eg 'spring tied securely to jack'.

Checklists are useful in situations where the dimension-orientated marking schemes are not appropriate; they are usually fairly quick to use and examiners can be trained quite quickly in their use and they are generally well-received. It is of course essential that examiners understand the items on the checklist and are technically competent in the skill under test.

TEST No. 9

JACK ASSEMBLY

In some companies jacks may be preassembled. If they are not, the trainee is required to bore and assemble a premachined jack, preparatory to assembly into the harpsichord.

1. The three small holes for the spring of suitable dimension for the wire used and located correctly.

2. The tapped hole for the torque adjustment screw at the desired angle.

3. The wood not split.

4. Jacks cut to required length.

5. Jacks correctly drilled and tapped for lower adjustment screw.

6. Mould not split.

7. Square torque holes for the leather the correct size for the torque,

8. The bottom surface of the torque hole angled to take the tapered leather.

9. The groove for the torque spring stopped and smoothed to receive the spring.

10. Leather screwed at correct angle under face of the torque.

11. Spring tied securely to the jack.

12. Torque fits squarely into the jack slot.

13. Bushing is out flush to sides of torques.

14. Torque centred to jack so that
    (a) There is no side play.
    (b) It does not foul the sides of the torque slot.

15. Damper felt fitted to 1mm above the top surface of the leather (or to company specification).

Time: 10 minutes

Test to be stopped after 10 minutes

Figure 6.8   A test in assembling jacks for a harpsichord

Assessing the Test Performance

Rating scales

Rating scales, are used in other industrial contexts besides testing, notably in staff appraisal schemes. They are therefore quite familiar to many people in industry.

In fact, simple go/no go checklists are rating scales with only two-points, but the use of the term will be restricted to scales with three or more points. Rating scales of between three and five points are most suitable for performance tests, since rarely is there interest in more discrimination than this, and also the introduction of more points leads to decrease in interrater reliability[7]. Rating scales should always be used with caution since they are open to a number of sources of error particularly with inadequately trained examiners. For example, Dolan and Schulz[8] had an instructor rate a piece of machine-shop work on several different occasions. On each occasion a different rating was obtained ranging from 72 to 90. However, it is arguable that with so many points the rating scale was inherently unreliable. However, Human Factors Research Incorporated[9] reported success in developing reliable rating scales for assessing the performance of electricians and engineers in submarines. The reliability from one rating session to another was 0.88, and the agreement between raters 0.70. Indeed in this case the rating scales yielded information as meaningful as the more specific checklist method of assessment. However, the rating scales compared one man with another rather than measuring absolute performance.

The three major sources of error in rating scales are: errors of leniency, central tendency errors, and the halo effect.

Errors of leniency

Every rater tends to have his own standards or frame of reference which he uses when judging performance. One rater may have low standards and another high ones, the 'true' one being somewhere in between. Figure 6.9 illustrates how this may affect the assessment of candidates' performance.

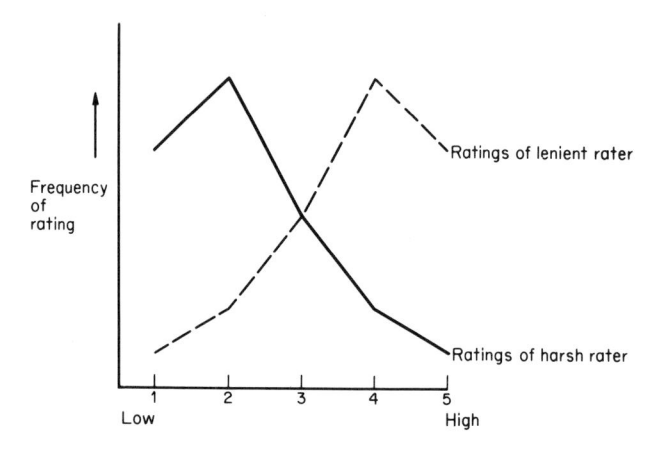

Figure 6.9 Assessment of performance of a number of candidates on a five point rating scale by a harsh and a lenient rater

There are a number of ways to avoid this type of error. In performance testing the best way is to define clearly the categories and provide anchor points on the scale. This, together with detailed instructions or training sessions, goes some way to establishing a common frame of reference for all raters. Figure 6.10 gives examples of three ratings scales.

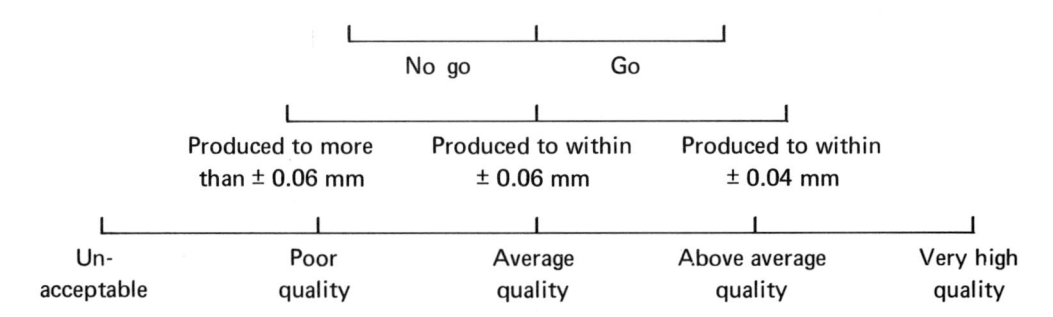

```
              L_____L_____J
                  No go          Go

         L_____L_____J
         Produced to more   Produced to within   Produced to within
         than ± 0.06 mm       ± 0.06 mm            ± 0.04 mm

L_____L_____L_____L_____J
Un-              Poor            Average         Above average   Very high
acceptable       quality         quality         quality         quality
```

Figure 6.10 Three rating scales

Training sessions may involve the rating of a standard object or representation of a task (eg video tape); the ratings of a number of examiners are compared, then shown to the group and the process continued until similar reference levels are established. Seaborne and Thomas[10] suggest that in industry inspectors making quality judgements may often end up using the same standards as a result of working together. No doubt such a process might also work with a group of examiners or instructors.

Examinations of the ratings of several raters over a number of candidates should reveal if any rater is displaying harshness or leniency and this should be used as a follow-up technique to help indicate when more rater training is required.

As part of the project mentioned above, Human Factors Research Incorporated carried out a study, the results of which suggest that when raters know they are judging the performance of someone, the value of poor performance tends to be underestimated and that of good performance greatly overestimated. When raters were not judging a performance but simply an event, judgement of both good and poor performances tended to approach average. Another study showed, not surprisingly, that raters tended to underestimate the performance of individuals whom they disliked. Raters who were less proficient at the task were more influenced by their attitude towards performers than proficient raters. It was concluded that attitudes are more likely to influence less proficient raters, but there is a general tendency to underestimate disliked performers, even though the rater is a sound and objective judge of performance on a given task. Skilled performers are likely to make more accurate and valid raters of the performances of others, particularly of poorer performances.

Central tendency errors

Some raters are often reluctant to make extreme judgements about candidates (i.e. they do not use the high and low categories in the scale) and restrict themselves

Assessing the Test Performance

to the middle categories. This restricts the amount of variability in their judgements. Again, training sessions and anchor points can help reduce this tendency.

The halo effect

This error is a tendency to let one's assessment of a candidate on one part of a performance influence the assessment of him on another separate aspect. For example, if candidate A is judged to be a safe worker, one might be more inclined to judge the quality of his work as good. However, since in performance testing one attempts to define observable behaviours, this type of error is probably less important than in other rating situations, although it is always worth checking to see if it occurs. One study[9] indicated that an unusually good performance had an undue influence on the final rating when it occurred at the beginning or end of a test session, while an unusually poor performance had such an influence only when it occurred at the beginning of the session. It was concluded that 'first impressions' of an individual being rated could significantly bias a judgement and produce invalid ratings. The practice of checking all of one dimension on test-pieces rather than assessing all test-pieces in turn is in part an attempt to reduce any halo effect. A similar practice with rating scales is to have an examiner rate one aspect on all test-pieces, then another aspect and so on.

There are other types of errors in ratings, but since the use of rating scales in performance testing is limited, they will not be dealt with here. Readers are referred to Ghiselli and Brown[11].

Graded comparison scales

Human beings are more accurate at making comparative judgements than absolute judgements. With comparative judgements the individual has a standard with which to compare the object he is judging. Even when an attempt is made to make marking objective, in certain types of work it is difficult to define the standard verbally, but it is possible to demonstrate it by the use of actual objects, photographs, tape-recordings, or whatever. For example, if the performance of a candidate in developing colour prints is being tested, it is impossible to define verbally the correct intensity and balance of colours involved but it is relatively easy to demonstrate if by the use of a series of prints from the same negative which show a range of colour intensities and balances, ranging from the totally unacceptable to the acceptable. This type of scale is referred to as a graded comparison scale, since then objects are used which serve as a comparison against which to judge the quality of a candidates' work, and the comparisons are graded as to their degree of acceptability. Machined blocks are available for the assessment of surface finish etc, in terms of the relevant British Standards.

The development of graded comparison scales (or 'bench marks' as they are sometimes referred to) involves firstly the utilization of the opinions of experts as to the degree of goodness of a product. To do this experts can be asked individually to rate a number of products; these ratings are then pooled. If there are any disagreements, these should be examined and if possible resolved. If this is not possible then new comparison objects must be introduced. As far as possible, the number of points or the scale should be kept small. This should help interexaminer reliability and usually no more than five discriminations are needed anyway. Wherever possible the test developer should run an experiment to determine whether examiners do agree when using the scale.

MEASURING QUANTITY

If one is concerned with a task where the rate of production of work is important, then obviously part of the assessment must cover the number of items produced, handled or whatever. This will probably only be the case with short-cycle tasks. From the point of view of the objectivity of the assessment, this poses no problem since the items can be counted either by the examiner or an automatic recording device such as the Veeder counter.

The problem here is probably in the definition of the acceptable rate of production, and it may be possible to make use of work-study data. Another point to be borne in mind is that if the candidate is to be assessed on his rate of production, every attempt should be made to eliminate extraneous factors which may restrict it, eg machines which do not work at optimum rate.

Baldwin[12] describes a Truing Test where rate of work is taken as an index of ability. The test involves placing a plug in a four-jaw chuck mounted in an engine lathe. Before the test session the plug is offset to 1/16 inch, and the candidate has to true the plug to within ± 0.0005, then to offset the plug to within ± 0.0005 and so on, returning the equipment to its original setting. The score is the time taken to perform the set of tasks. This assumes that a candidate's ability is inversely related to the time he needs to perform the tasks.

THE ASSESSMENT OF SPEED OF WORK

In all test situations, irrespective of whether one is concerned with the quality or quantity a nominal time has to be derived for the test. This nominal time is the time within which an acceptable candidate should be able to finish the task. With hands-on tests this should be established in the same way as with other standards; that is by analysis and consultation to find out what is acceptable. However, the time arrived at in this way should be checked by pilot-testing the test on a small group of individuals of the same level as those on whom the test will ultimately be used.

With hands-off tests, more attention has to be paid to the results of pilot-testing as the test is something of an unknown quantity to all concerned. Unless there is some reason to emphasize speed of answering questions, then the nominal time should be adequate to allow the great majority (90—95%) of candidates to answer all questions. This is particularly important if the test is divided into separate sections and one wants to know the candidate's attainment in each. Too strict a time might result in a slow candidate answering only some of the sections, which would give no indication of how good he was in the other section. It should be remembered that with performance testing, the interest is in what a

Assessing the Test Performance

person can do and in any knowledge which helps him to do it; the hands-off test is only a way of measuring it and such outside factors as verbal fluency should not be allowed to contaminate the assessment.

Once a nominal time has been established, special attention should be paid to ensuring that:

1. It is clear what happens if the standard or nominal time is overrun. That is; is the candidate stopped or is he allowed to continue?
2. Speed records are not confused with other factors. As far as possible the assessment of quality, quantity, speed, and process should be such that information on each is readily retrievable and not lost in some lumping-together process.

The assessment of speed of work can be handled in a number of ways:

Firstly, to stop the test at the nominal time, and mark the candidate on work completed. This holds the time factor constant for all candidates and so inspection of the amount and/or quality of the work completed should tell whether he is a quick or slow worker.

Alternatively there can be a separate grade for speed of work. An example is given in Figure 6.11.

The nominal time could be included as a factor on a checklist. Here time is treated as just another aspect of performance. This method is particularly suitable in tests where the criterion is completing all aspects of the task (as defined on the checklist) in a given time. An example of this is given in Figure 6.12.

Finally, we might have a composite time and end-product grade which nevertheless retains the basic information about speed and quality separately. How this can be done is illustrated in the matrix shown in Figure 6.13.

Thus a grade of A indicates a quick, efficient performance, B a performance acceptable from the quality point of view but slow, C a quick but unsatisfactory performance and D a performance which is unsatisfactory from the point of view of both time and quality. Figure 6.14 gives an example of such a system.

It goes without saying that an accurate time-piece should be used for testing sessions, and it may be useful to have a timekeeper to record the time taken so that the examiner can concentrate on assessment of other factors.

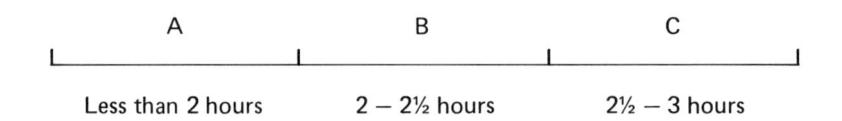

```
         A                  B                  C
 L_____|_____|_____J
   Less than 2 hours    2 – 2½ hours       2½ – 3 hours
```

A   Less than nominal time band (in this case 2 hours)
B   Within nominal time band (2 to 2½ hours)
C   More than nominal time band, up to the maximum time allowed (2½ to 3 hours)

Figure 6.11   A scheme for the assessment of speed of work

Assessing the Test Performance

Centre instructions	Test 1 Common brickwork
Materials required	126 Local Commons Sand and lime mortar Suitable profiles (Method 1 or 2)
Preparation work	Erect profiles and prepare mortar. Deliver bricks
Special instructions	Profiles must be left in place throughout the test
Standard required	Standard B face and rear
Marking	Assessment points

Face plane ranging
— Use long edge
— — or short edge

X = Plumbing points

Plumb to standard at all four points indicated ☐

Face plane as shown on   *Face* ☐

and *Rear* ☐

Gauge to standard ☐

Facework to standard on   *Face* ☐

and *Rear* ☐

Speed test finished in $2\frac{1}{2}$ hours ☐

Total marks: 7

Figure 6.12 A skill sample test in basic bricklaying

95

Assessing the Test Performance

	Within time	Over time
End-product to manufacturers standards ...	A	B
End-product not to manufacturers standards ...	C	D

Figure 6.13   Matrix illustrated a combined speed and quality assessment

Test No.   A 19

Time: 30 minutes

TIMING FUEL INJECTOR PUMP

It is important that the components and timing marks are reasonably accessible. Where necessary, assistance (under the candidate's direction) may be given to turn the engine to the appropriate timing mark. The pump should be in position on the engine, spill-timed and the coupling appropriately marked, but with the high-pressure pipe lines disconnected.

PROCEDURE

Time pump to appropriate mark.
Connect high-pressure pipes.
Bleed and run engine.

SIGNIFICANT POINTS

Check made that reference cylinder is on compression stroke.
Check made that engine crankshaft is required number of degrees before t.d.c.
Check position of timing mark with timing gauge.
New joint washer fitted under pump mounting flange.
Timing mark and pointer accurately aligned.
High-pressure pipe lines connected in proper firing order.
Full range of movement controls checked.

RESULTS

Satisfactorily running engine, with adequate response.

SCORE: A, B, C, D   SCORE | 7 |

Figure 6.14   A work sample test for motor mechanics

Assessing the Test Performance

THE ASSESSMENT OF PROCESS

It was noted earlier that, particularly in the training situation, the interest may be not only in the end-product but also in the way in which the candidate achieves it. The interest may stem from a variety of reasons such as safety, care of equipment, economical use of materials, and the fact that the way a candidate does a job is often a good indication of whether the end-product is barely adequate or of a high standard. For example, a motor mechanic can repair a car so that it can drive out of the garage, but it should be considered whether this is really the criterion. It is more likely that the criterion is that the car will run for a certain length of time without further repair and an examination of the mechanic's method of repair can provide a good indication of this. A poorly assembled engine may run well at first but will soon require further attention.

It is worth noting that assessing the process tends to be more difficult than assessing the product, since the product is a physical object whereas process is comprised of fleeting actions which must be noted during the testing session.

If it is decided that it is important to assess process then a number of marking techniques are available.

Checklists

This type of marking scheme was discussed when looking at the assessment of quality, and the layout of the checklist here is largely the same; those aspects of performance which are considered important or critical are listed and allocated a go/no go criterion for each aspect.

Figure 6.14 gives an example of this — see list of significant points — and Figures 6.15 and 6.16 show a test underway.

Figure 6.15 View of a candidate timing a fuel injector pump—a

Assessing the Test Performance

Figure 6.16 View of a candidate timing a fuel injector pump—b

Often in practice product and process aspects are mixed together on a checklist, as shown in Figure 6.17. (Note that even though in this example quality, quantity, speed, and process factors are all included on the checklist, information about each is easily retrievable.)

Rating scales

Whenever possible, the use of rating scales should be avoided in the assessment of process since it is usually more difficult to provide the necessary anchor points for judgement. Even with anchor points interrater agreement may not be high. Miller[13] reports reliabilities ranging from 0.35 to 0.89 even when behavioural descriptions were used to anchor the high and low ends of the scale. Miller concluded that in many cases the level of agreement was inflated as the result of halo effects, due to knowledge of previous assessments and classroom performance of trainees. Since a checklist is usually more suitable for discrete aspects of performance, ratings will probably only be used for overall impressions or to sum up certain aspects of the candidates performance that have shown themselves in the course of the test. Therefore the rating scale would be completed at the end of the test rather than in the course of it as with checklists. The more use is made of rating scales, the further one moves from a test situation and nearer to an informal appraisal situation. Figure 6.18 shows a rating scale for the assessment of the use of tools and equipment.

Assessing the Test Performance

Test No. IMS/2

SETTING CONDITIONS

PROCEDURE

Candidate sets conditions on machine for given material and mould (as specified on job card) until optimum moulding conditions are reached. Candidate to announce when he is satisfied with quality of moulding.

MATERIALS

1 Polypropylene or Polythene
2 Nylon

ASSESSMENT POINTS

	Material 1	Material 2
Ensures hopper is clean before material is put in	☐	☐
Ensures water flowing correctly	☐	☐
Uses correct material	☐	☐
Locking pressure satisfactory, injection pressure, cooling time, back pressure, injection time set as per job card	☐	☐
Checks second-off moulding for faults	☐	☐
Mouldings produced in first 10/15 minutes of operation put aside for granulating	☐	☐
Sufficient mouldings made to allow changes in settings to have effect on moulding	☐	☐
Machine operated in safe fashion	☐	☐
Good quality moulding at maximum shots per hour as specified	☐	☐
Within time	☐	☐

Figure 6.17 A work sample test in plastic injection moulding

Assessing the Test Performance

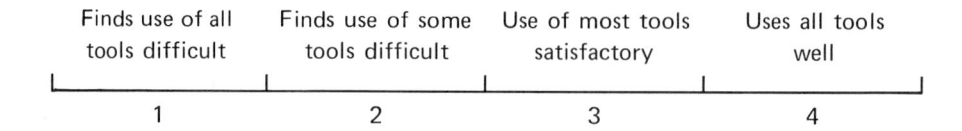

```
Finds use of all      Finds use of some    Use of most tools     Uses all tools
 tools difficult        tools difficult       satisfactory             well
|_____|_____|_____|
         1                    2                    3                    4
```

Figure 6.18 A rating scale for use of tools

To illustrate how the transitory nature of process assessment makes for difficulties, one study may be quoted where a group of trained examiners assessed the filmed performance of a candidate sharpening a drill point. They were provided with an 'objective' checklist of go/no go items and assessed the performance on two separate occasions. The examiners' responses on the checklist on the first occasion corresponded to those on the second occasion in 82% of the cases, rather than the 100% which might have been expected. On the other hand, a checklist used to assess pilot performance[13] showed a relatively high level of agreement with an interexaminer reliability of 0.88, using such items as cruising speed, throttle setting, and degrees of turn which could be scored by reference to control settings.

One final word; it is pointless to have examiners marking process if they have too many candidates to assess. They will not be able to cope and will make either hurried judgements or complete the marking afterwards from memory (a very fallible process open to all kinds of distortions).

SCORING FAULT-FINDING AND SIMILAR DIAGNOSTIC TESTS

The following types of marking schemes apply to both hands-on and hands-off test of fault-finding where the candidates may tackle the task in a number of ways. In fact the task encountered by the candidate depends upon the way he sets about finding the fault.

Several scoring methods can be used to measure the fault diagnosis performance of a candidate, each method using a different criterion of proficiency. Each criterion is based upon one or a number of assumptions which try to outline the characteristic of proficient fault diagnosis. The adequacy of any scoring method therefore depends upon the extent to which its assumption regarding proficient fault diagnosis are valid.

The most obvious criterion is that the fault is found, or in a modified version, diagnosis time. This considers the time taken to locate the fault to be an adequate basis for assessment of proficiency. However, such a criterion is not related to the way in which the fault-finder tackles the problem, except possibly in an implied way. It assumes that the efficiency of a fault-finder can be defined in terms of the time taken to carry out fault diagnosis. Thus, the quicker the candidate locates the fault, the more proficient he is, according to this criterion. However a candidate may guess at a fault and happen to be correct; a fault-finder may locate a fault very efficiently but take longer to do so than an inefficient fault-finder. This criterion would not seem therefore totally valid.

Assessing the Test Performance

Another approach is to relate fault diagnosis efficiency to the number of checks performed in locating a fault and it is possible to develop another criterion on this basis. Unfortunately, this criterion does not take into account the fact that a candidate might be guessing the solution and thereby reduce the number of checks performed. Checks may be recorded by the examiner observing the candidate, or the candidate recording his checks, or by an automatic recording device (eg tabs test, simulators, etc). An efficient fault-finder is assumed to be one who will detect the source of a system malfunctioning with a minimum of activity. Therefore in diagnosing a fault, he will select a minimum number of relevant checks and proceed immediately to the correct solution. The more proficient a troubleshooter is, the fewer checks he will find it necessary to carry out. A candidate's score is calculated by totalling the number of checks that the candidate has carried out.

A criterion that takes into account guessing (in terms of incorrect diagnoses and omissions of relevant checks) on the part of the candidate considers the number of errors that a fault-finder makes in the process of locating a fault. The underlying assumption for this criterion is that an inefficient fault-finder may be considered to be one who performs many errors, in the form of the performance of non-essential checks, the omission of relevant checks, and the making of erroneous diagnoses. The use of non-essential checks can be considered to be inefficient whereas the omission of relevant checks and the making of erroneous diagnoses can be interpreted as guesswork. Each of these behaviours is undesirable for proficient fault diagnosis. An efficient fault-finder is therefore considered to be one who performs only the relevant checks, as defined by the algorithm, and makes no erroneous diagnoses.

Scores are calculated by pooling the number of omissions of relevant checks, the number of non-essential checks performed, and the number of erroneous diagnoses that the candidate makes within the diagnosis of a fault. This would seem a more adequate criterion in terms of efficiency of fault diagnosis, except for the fact that a third type of error is pooled with the other two guessing errors to make a composite score so it is possible that a criterion using such a combined score may not adequately discriminate between performances.

It may be assumed that the amount of information a candidate must apply to obtain the correct diagnosis is exactly equal to the amount of uncertainty introduced into the test. It is therefore possible to obtain the amount of uncertainty present in each of the fault-finding situations presented to the candidate. The technical calculation of information or uncertainty is a highly complex technique and will not be discussed here. Interested readers are referred to Fitts and Posner[15] and Glaser and Schwarz[16]. Each score is calculated by determining the degree of uncertainty in the situation and then dividing by the number of checks needed to diagnose that fault.

Although this criterion would seem more comprehensive than the three already mentioned it does not take into account the diagnosis time. Diagnosis time, although not a particularly adequate criterion alone, is an important factor of efficient fault diagnosis which should not be ignored. Thus a fifth criterion 'efficient use of information' has been developed, which considers the fourth criterion, information per check, in relation to diagnosis time. This criterion defines efficient fault diagnosis as the greatest quantity of information obtained per check per minute of diagnosis time.

All the above criteria, except the finding of the fault and diagnosis time, attempt to assess the logicality of the candidate's approach. The last two methods mentioned are highly complex and probably most test developers will feel that other simpler criteria are adequate, at least in the early days of a test! After a period in use it may become evident that more sophisticated criteria are required. It is further worth commenting that in some cases with hands-off tests, the time to make the check on the test will be unrelated to the time required to make the check in the actual situation. For example, with a hydraulic circuit to check a meter may only take five seconds whereas a check involving stripping down a system may take a considerable length of time. On say a tab-test, however, the time to carry out these two checks will be the same. The test developer may often have to give extra weight to longer checks or give each check a theoretical time required to carry out the check on the job. Bearing in mind these different criterion discussed above, some tests of fault-finding skills will be considered.

Injection-moulding

This relatively simple hands-on test in diagnosing and rectifying faults when producing plastic mouldings is shown in Figure 6.19. The candidate is observed by the examiner and records on the fault cards what is wrong with the moulding, what he thinks has caused it, and how he would rectify the fault. Candidates are given three from a selection of nine faults. Obviously here the criteria are that the fault is rectified and that the candidate diagnoses the fault correctly.

Fault-finding in a simple hydraulic circuit

This test was discussed in Chapter 4. The candidate has to trace a fault in a simple hydraulic circuit; he is given a circuit diagram and a specially prepared sheet of paper giving possible checks. Results of checks are obtained by rubbing out the covering film in the appropriate box. The candidate is also required to record his final diagnosis and remedial action on a separate sheet. The marking instructions for this test are shown in Figure 6.20.

The above system takes into account the finding of the fault, the logicality of approach (errors in checking and diagnosis) and the theoretical time needed to carry out the check in real-life.

An envelopes test for fault diagnosis on an alternator charging system)

A method of hands-off testing which is easy to produce but relatively cumbersome to administer was used by Welborn[17]. Candidates received the results of checks by opening an envelope. The task was to trace faults in an alternator charging system. Welborn compared the use of this method with testing on a simulator (shown in Figure 4.19) and found that it was as acceptable in assessing fault diagnosis ability although not as sensitive in some ways. He compared the two testing methods using the five different types of marking system discussed above. The Figure 6.21 gives a summary of his results.

Assessing the Test Performance

FAULT DIAGNOSIS

Tester introduces three of the following selection of faults in turn.
Candidates to be marked on each fault.

PROCEDURE

For each fault introduced, the candidate is to write down the fault or faults, possible cause or causes, and possible remedy before beginning to rectify the faults. Mouldings to be brought back to optimum conditions after each fault.

FAULTS WHICH MAY BE USED

Short moulding	No moulding	Flashing
Sinks in moulding	Splashing	Burns
Weld lines	Machine not ejecting	Machine not injecting

ASSESSMENT POINTS

	Fault 1	Fault 2	Fault 3
Answers on faults cards (all three answers correct)	☐	☐	☐
Sufficient mouldings made to allow changes in settings to have effect on moulding	☐	☐	☐
Machine operated in safe fashion	☐	☐	☐
Moulding brought back to optimum conditions after each fault	☐	☐	☐

FAULTS CARD

Candidate ....

Fault No. 1

State in your own words:

1 What has gone wrong with the moulding?
2 What do you think caused the fault?
3 How would you set about putting this fault right?

To be completed by the instructor

Correct

Figure 6.19 A marking scheme for a fault diagnosis test in injection moulding

103

Assessing the Test Performance

This test is designed to assess the candidates ability to diagnose a fault in a logical manner when given a particular symptom, to state why the fault is producing the symptom, and to recommend correct remedial action.

The identification of the fault, the drawing of a conclusion, and recommending remedial action can each be objectively assessed. There is, however, in practice considerable variation in the sequence of checks which can be made to arrive at the correct identification of a fault, all of which can be logically justified.

Marks should be allocated as follows:

Assessment A: For the way in which the candidate has attempted to logically identify the fault through the sequence of checks he has made
40 Marks

Assessment B: Whether the candidate has correctly identified the fault.
20 Marks

Assessment C: Whether the candidate has stated correctly why the fault is causing the particular symptom.
20 Marks

Assessment D: Whether the candidate has recommended the correct remedial action to eliminate the fault.
20 Marks

Assessments B, C, and D should be marked as either correct or incorrect and the appropriate marks allocated in total only for a correct answer.

In the answer sheet provided all the checks which could logically be made are identified by a green square, and classified as either P or S.

P = a primary check — should be carried out before any secondary checks are made.

S = a secondary check — should only be made after an appropriate primary check.

For each illogical check a penalty is imposed which is weighted in relation to the time the particular check would take in practice. The appropriate penalty points for each illogical check are shown on the answer sheet.

The marking for Assessment A is then:

Where logical checks only have been used and with P and S checks made in the correct order where applicable
40 Marks

Where a Secondary check has been made without an appropriate primary check
20 points penalty

Where illogical steps have been made, subtract the appropriate penalty points.

The total mark is the sum of the marks obtained for assessment B, C, and D.

Figure 6.20 Examiners notes for marking a test in fault finding — continued on next page

Assessing the Test Performance

EXAMPLE

The candidate identifies the correct fault using a logical sequence of checks but also includes two illogical steps with a penalty of 25 points, he states correctly how the fault is causing the symptom, but recommends the incorrect remedial action.

Marks:	For assessment A 40 − 25 =	15
	For assessment B	20
	For assessment C	20
	For assessment D	0
		55

NOTE:

It is essential that the assessment for this section is made by an experienced hydraulics instructor.

This is necessary because within the constraints outlined above some interpretation of answers is required when making Assessment A.

Figure 6.20   Examiner's notes for marking a test in fault-finding

Criterion	Simulator versus envelope tests
Diagnosis time	Longer time needed to find faults on envelope tests.
Number of checks	No difference.
Number of incorrect diagnoses	Candidates before training make more errors with envelope tests but no difference with candidate after training.
Amount of information per check	More efficient diagnosis on envelope test.
Efficient use of information	Envelope test underestimated improvement in performance due to training but still discriminated between candidates before and after training.

Figure 6.21   A comparison of two methods of testing faults diagnosis

Assessing the Test Performance

As regards time required to administer the test, the envelope test required one and a half hours to test ten subjects, whereas the simulator took five hours for the same number of subjects and faults.

The presence or absence of a photograph (of system components and terminals) did not seem to affect the effectiveness of the envelope test. The author nevertheless suggested that the development of a test with a photograph might make the testing situation more realistic.

The efficient use of information (information per check in terms of diagnosis time) turned out to be the most sensitive scoring technique which discriminated well between good and poor fault-finders.

SCORING TESTS FOR PLANNING AND SIMILAR SKILLS

Having discussed fault-finding tests, it will be found that similar systems can be applied to planning skills. Again the correctness and logicality of approach is what is of interest. Some illustrative examples are given below.

A hands-off test on testing an electrical circuit after installation

Figure 6.22 shows a test to assess how well the candidate knows how to go about the testing of an electrical circuit after installation.

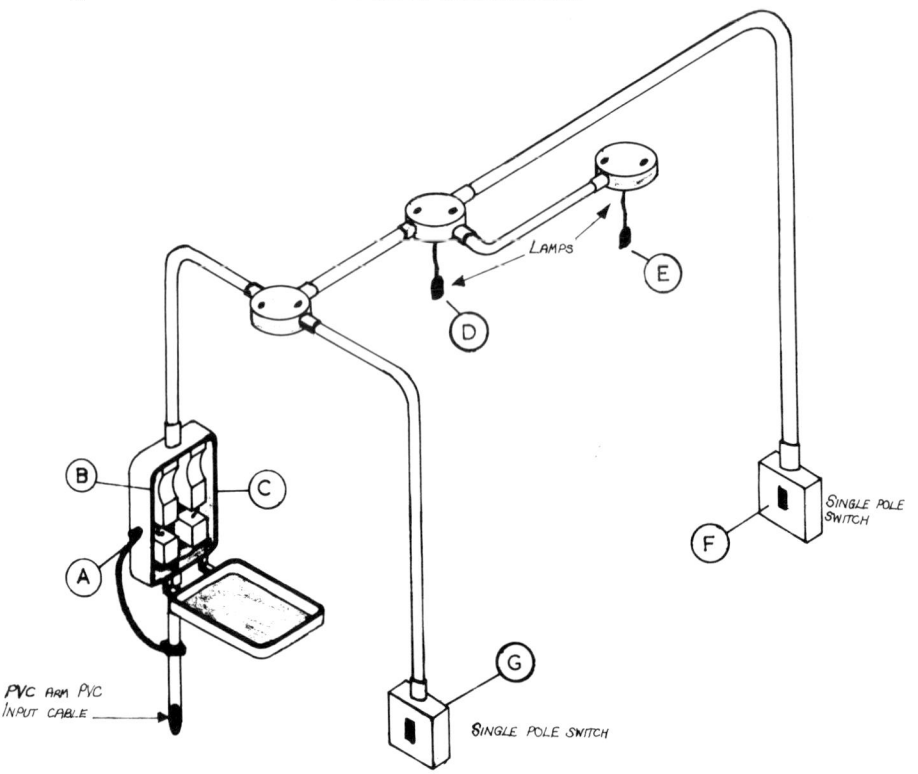

Figure 6.22 A hands-off test for planning skills

Assessing the Test Performance

SECTION 2(b)

You have installed the circuit shown in the diagram. Indicate in the power panel:

(a) The tests you would carry out (IN ORDER).

(b) The instrument you would use.

(c) Between which indicated points you would connect the instrument.

(d) The scale used on the instrument if any.

(e) The expected reading if circuit is functioning correctly.

Test	Testing for	Instrument used	Scale used	Testing between points	Lamp position	Switch position	Expected reading
1							
2							
3							
4							

MARKING 2(b)

One mark for each correct entry

Figure 6.22 A hands-off test for planning skills continued

Assessing the Test Performance

Ability to plan the wiring-up of an electrical circuit

In the test illustrated in Figure 6.23 candidates are required to draw the connections they would make in connecting up the circuit.

Candidates receive one mark for each correct interconnection and one mark for each line with the correct colour code.

Connect components to give direct-on-line reversing.

Push-button control with Electrical Interlocks.

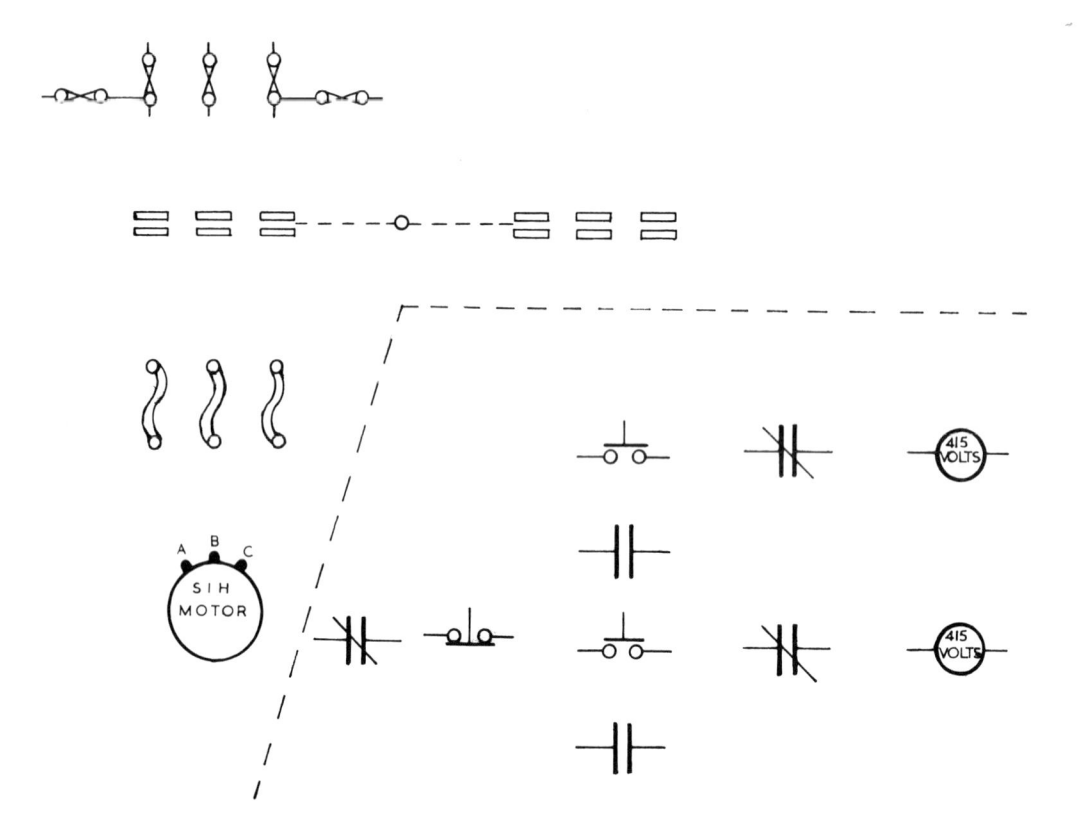

Figure 6.23 Another hands-off test for planning skills

Assessing the Test Performance

Planning a job involving bench fitting

In this test mentioned in Chapter 4, the candidate is provided with a drawing of a piece of work (in the example a 'C' spanner) which has to be produced. He is told that the job has already been marked out and that he has to give the sequence of operations for completing it. He is given a set of cards describing the necessary operations (Figure 6.24(a)) and an answer sheet (Figure 6.24(b)). He is then given the instructions shown in Figure 6.24(c). He fills in the answer sheet which is marked on the following basis. For each job, there is a critical sequence. This is the sequence in which the job must be tackled if it is to be done properly. The critical sequence in this example is given below.

Card	
E – C	Must be done in that order before the rest.
H	Must be done after C.
J.A.D.	Can be done in any order after H.
F	Must be done after the series J.A.D.
B	Must be done after F.
G	Must be done last.

If the candidate arranges the operations within the definition of the critical sequence given above, then he receives full marks. Otherwise he receives no marks, since the definition of the critical sequence says what must happen to turn out a successful job.

The candidate next lists what tools he would use for each operation. To assess his performance his answers here are compared with the specimen correct list given in Figure 6.24(d).

SUMMARY

1. Wherever possible dimensions or defined standards should be used for the assessment of quality. Tailor-made gauges, templates, graded comparison scales, etc, can often make marking more objective as well as speeding it up.
2. It should be insured that the time for the test is fair and that the speed scores are not confused with quality marks.
3. In the assessment of process, one should have, if possible, go/no go checklists.
4. Detailed instructions for marking and if possible training sessions should always be given to examiners.
5. The examiners should not be given more to do than they can do without rushing.
6. With tests for fault-finding and planning skills, what is meant by a good performance on such a task should be examined and the marking scheme constructed accordingly. One should try as far as possible to break down such concepts as 'logicality of approach', 'correct planning', and so on.
7. After a period in operation marking schemes should be reviewed to ensure that they are being used properly and that relevant items have been included.

Assessing the Test Performance

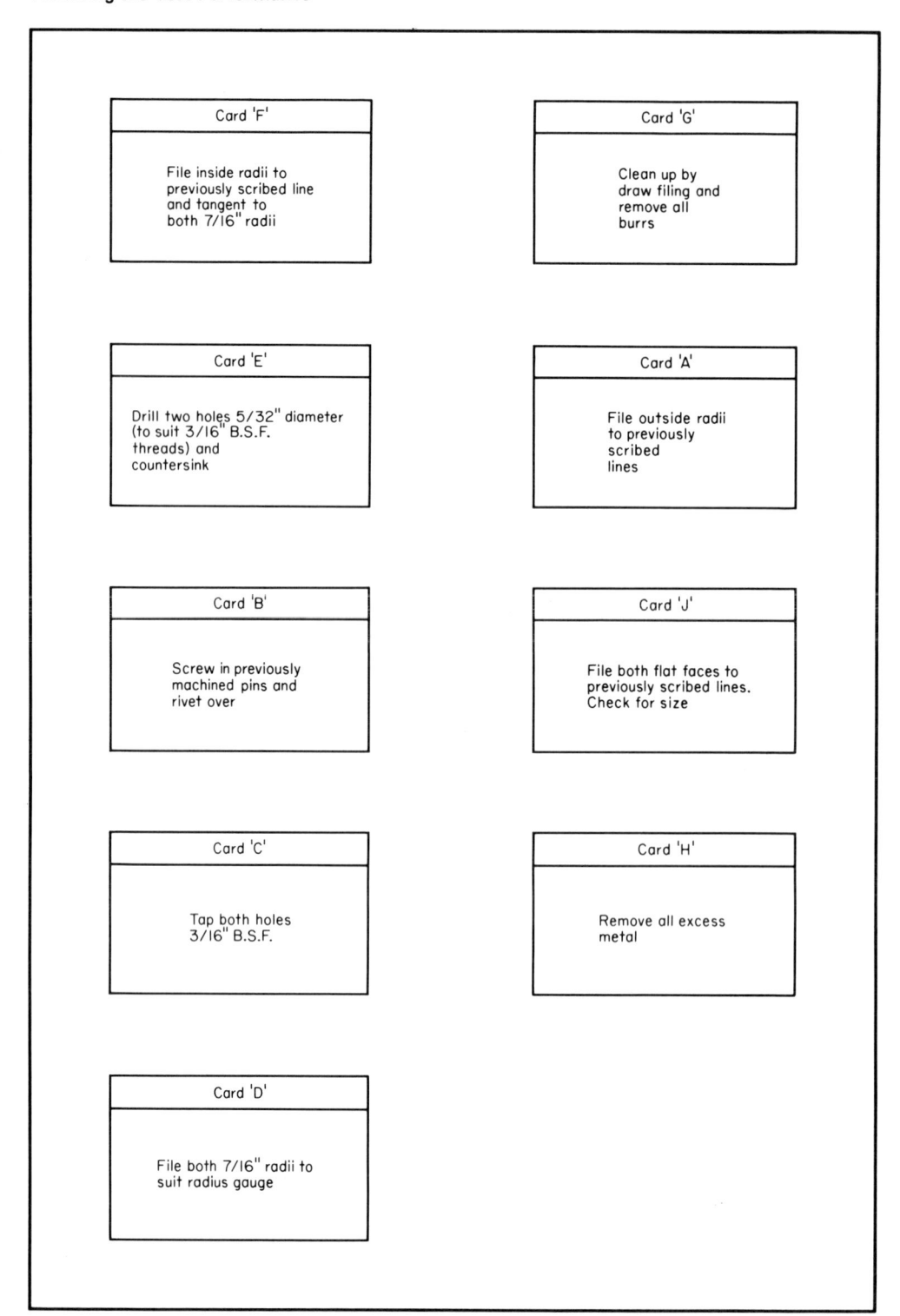

Card 'F'

File inside radii to previously scribed line and tangent to both 7/16" radii

Card 'G'

Clean up by draw filing and remove all burrs

Card 'E'

Drill two holes 5/32" diameter (to suit 3/16" B.S.F. threads) and countersink

Card 'A'

File outside radii to previously scribed lines

Card 'B'

Screw in previously machined pins and rivet over

Card 'J'

File both flat faces to previously scribed lines. Check for size

Card 'C'

Tap both holes 3/16" B.S.F.

Card 'H'

Remove all excess metal

Card 'D'

File both 7/16" radii to suit radius gauge

Figure 6.24(a)   Cards used in the test planning test described in text

Assessing the Test Performance

Sequence of cards		Tools used (including sizes where necessary) for operation
1st		
2nd		
3rd		
4th		
5th		
6th		
7th		
8th		
9th		
Correct ☐ Incorrect ☐		Correct tools used $\overline{17}$

Answer sheet

Figure 6.24(b)   Answer sheet for planning test

Assessing the Test Performance

This section is designed to assess how well you can *plan* out the completion of a job once you have marked it out. You are provided with a drawing, a set of cards on which the various essential operations are described, and an answer sheet.

Study the drawing and decide how you would complete the job, ie in what order and with what tools. Look through the cards until you find the card with the operation you think should be carried out first, then the card with the second operation and so on. Carry on until you have placed all the cards in the correct sequence.

Now complete the first column on the answer sheet by entering the letters of the cards in the sequence you have selected. For example, if you think Card 'B' is the first operation, put B in the 1st box.

When you have done this, complete the next column by giving details of the tools you would use (including sizes where necessary) for each operation.

You have 15 minutes to answer this question.

Figure 6.24(c) Candidates instructions for planning test

Card	Operation	Tools used
E	Drill two holes 5/32" dia. To suit 3/16" BSF threads and C/SK	5/32" drill 1/4" drill
C	Tap both holes 3/16" BSF	1-set 3/16" BSF Taps 1 tap wrench
H	Hacksaw all excess metal	Hacksaw
J	File both flat faces to previously scribed lines. Check for size	10" rough file 10" smooth file 12" rule
A	File outside radii to previously scribed lines	10" rough file 10" smooth file
D	File both 7/16" radii to suit radius gauge	6" rough file 6" smooth file 7/16" rad. gauge
F	File inside radius to previously scribed line and tangent to both. 7/16" radii.	10" ½ round file
B	Screw in previously machined pins and rivet over	1lb ball pein Hammer
G	Clean up by draw filing and remove all burrs	10" smooth file

Figure 6.24(d) Specimen correct list for planning tests

112

REFERENCES

1. Stead W.H. et al, *Occupational Counseling Technique*, American Book, New York, 1940.
2. The work of Rothe is to be found in the Journal of Applied Psychology, 1946, 1957, 1958, 1959, and 1961.
3. Lawshe C.H. and Tiffin J., 'The Accuracy of Precision Instrument Measurement in Industrial Inspection', *Journal of Applied Psychology*, 29, 413–19, 1945.
4. Stuit D.B., (Ed.,) *Personnel Research and Test Development in the Bureau of Naval Personnel*, Princeton University Press, Princeton, 1947.
5. McPherson M.W., 'A method of objectively measuring shop performance', *J. Appl. Psychol.*, 29, 22–26, 1945.
6. Hardebeck G.C.M., *Trade Testing and the Assessment of Training*, BACIE Journal, March 1966.
7. Helmstadter G.C., *Principles of Psychological Measurement*, Methuen and Co. Ltd., London, 1966, Chap.8, 'Scales and Inventories'.
8. Dolan F.D. and Schultz H.A., *Machine Shop Grading in Ordnance School*, Industrial Arts and Vocational Education, 33, pp.403–405, 1944.
9. Human Factors Research Incorporated; *Research on the Development of Shipboard Performance Measures and Performance Judgements*, Santa Barbara, 1965.
10. Seaborne A.E.M. and Thomas L.F., *Subjective Standards in Industrial Inspection*, Her Majesty's Stationery Office, London, 1964
11. Ghiselli E.E. and Brown C.W., *Personnel and Industrial Psychology*, McGraw Hill Book Company, New York, 1965, Chap.3 'The Measurement of Job Proficiency' and Chap.4 'Rating Methods'.
12. Baldwin T.S., *Evaluation of Learning in Industrial Education* in Handbook on Formative and Summative Evaluation of Student Learning, Bloom B.S., Hasting J.T., and Mandaus G.F., Eds., McGraw Hill Book Company, 1971.
13. Miller N.E., (Ed.,) *Psychological Research on Pilot Training*, Government Printing Office, Washington D.C., 1957.
14. Siegel A.I., 'Retest Reliability of a Movie Technique of Test Administrators Judgement of Performance of Process', *J. Appl. Psychol.*, 38, 390–392, 1954.
15. Fitts P.M. and Posner M.I., *Human Performance*, Brooks/Cole Publishing Company, Belmont, California, 1967, Chap.5 'The Measurement of Skills'.
16. Glaser R. and Schwartz P.A., *Scoring problem solving test items by measuring information*. Educational and Psychological Measurement, 14, 665–670, 1954.
17. Welborn I.W.B., 'The Development and Validation of an Envelopes Test as Proficiency Measurement of Fault Diagnosis on an Alternator Charging System', unpublished M.Sc., thesis, University of Hull, 1970.

SUGGESTED FURTHER READING

Boyd J.L. and Shimberg B., *Handbook of Performance Testing*, Educational Testing Service, Princeton, New Jersey, 1970, Chap.4 'Grading the Performance Test'.

Dunnette M.A. and Kirchner W.K., *Psychology Applied to Industry*, pp.19–24 'Studying Job Performance'.

Jessup G. et al; *Manual of Trade Proficiency Testing*, Ministry of Defence, 1968, Chap.8 'Designing the Practical Test'.

Jones A., *Performance Tests for Industrial Skills*, Industrial and Commercial Training, Volume 3, Number 10, October, 1971.

Ryans D.G. and Frederiksen N., 'Performance Tests of Educational Achievement', in *Educational Measurement*, Lindquist E.F., Ed., American Council on Education, Washington, D.C., 1951.

Fitzpatrick R. and Morrison E.J., in Educational Management, Thorndike R.L., Ed., American Council on Education, 1971, [*Performance and Product Evaluation*].

7

Implementing and Administering the Test

Although this chapter deals chiefly with the problems of administering the test to candidates, it also discusses some general points regarding developing and running a testing system. The necessary additions to a test after its content and marking scheme have been determined will therefore be discussed.

The conditions under which a test is taken and the instructions given to the candidate are important in obtaining a valid and reliable assessment of performance. One of the requirements of a test is that the tasks or problems set to a group of candidates should be the same whenever and wherever the test is taken. This not only allows a direct comparison between test centres or training groups but also ensures that all candidates have an equal opportunity of success apart from any differences in ability.

As a general guide then one can say that all administration should aim for standardization of procedures. To this end one can draw up standard requirements for all tests by listing the information that must accompany each test. This information is given below but it is worth noting that standardization also requires uniformity or equality in test equipment; it is obviously unfair, for example, to have some candidates using machinery which is inadequate in some way.

TASK SPECIFICATION

This is a specification of the task and the conditions under which it should be performed; it includes details such as material and equipment which is needed or should be available.

The specification of the task to be performed must aim to indicate what the candidate is required to do. If written instructions are being used, they must be clear, concise, and unambiguous. In many hands-on tests it will be appropriate to use production drawings; these must be clearly reproduced and should reflect a realistic standard of draughtmanship, (clarity, appropriate conventions, etc).

The test conditions must be defined for the benefit of the test organizers and examiners. Conditions will depend a great deal upon the type of test involved but some guidance will come from the original analysis where some record was made of actual working conditions. A hands-on test should reflect these as far as possible. With a hands-off test a more classical 'examination' setting may often be appropriate. The main requirement is to specify the conditions to ensure that they are standard.

CANDIDATE INSTRUCTIONS

Candidate instructions must include (where relevant):

1 Task specification.
2 Time allowed.
3 Tools and equipment allowed.
4 Any part of the test that is not to be completed.
5 A reminder that safety is important.
6 The conditions of the test.

In very simple situations, directions to candidates may be given orally. For example, in a test for motor mechanics, the candidates may be told to 'adjust the fan belt'. Insofar as this is a straightforward task that the candidate might be faced with in the normal course of his work these directions are probably sufficient. However, such informality may lead to unstandardized testing conditions; the examiner may inadvertently give more details than he should or he might omit something important from his instructions.

It is obviously a sensible precaution to prevent such possibilities by providing written instructions which the candidate may read himself or which are read to him. If necessary one should allow a briefing session and permit the candidate to keep a copy of the instructions so he can refer to them during the test.

Instructions should state the purpose of the test ('This test is intended to test your ability in ......'), any time limits which are operating, any materials or equipment that are needed or should be available to the candidate ('The appropriate service manual is available'), any special safety precautions ('Do not switch on until the examiner has inspected your work'), and what is expected of him ('The fuel injector should be correctly fitted so that there are no fuel or gas leaks'). It is often advisable to indicate how the test is scored, although such information should obviously not violate any necessary security requirements. For example, if the candidate is making a test-piece such as the tray discussed in Chapter 4 (Figure 4.8) it is often useful to let him see the marksheet before starting the test (Figure 7.1). He can then see how marks are apportioned and satisfy himself that the marking scheme is a fair one.

SERVICE TRAY

Time allowed — 6 hours

Name ....

Operation	Marking scale	Possible marks	Marks deducted	Marks rec'd
Applying plastic to plywood top	− 1 mark for each corner not hard down or any other fault	4		
Trimming off plastic ready for lipping	− 1 mark for each edge not square to 1 mm	4		
Mitring lippings by hand mitre machine	4 marks for each mitre joint, − 1 mark for each 1 mm + or −	18		
Glueing and nailing lippings and flushing off	2 marks for each lipping, − 1 mark for each nail not neat and punched or lipping not flush	8		
Marking off base for mortice and tenon joints	3 marks for marking off each tenon, − 1 mark for each 1 mm discrepancy	6		
	3 marks for marking off each mortice, − 1 mark for each 1 mm discrepancy	6		
	3 marks for both mortices being in centre − 1 mark for each 1 mm discrepancy	3		
Machining mortice joints	3 marks for each mortice, − 1 mark for each 1 mm + or −	6		
Cutting tenon joints	3 marks for each tenon, − 1 mark for each 1 mm + or −	6		
Glueing up base	2 marks for each joint being up and square	4		
Drilling and counter-sinking base and screwing up	1 mark for each of 5 screws	5		
Cleaning up		2		
	Total marks for practical test	70		

Figure 7.1 Mark sheet for joiners and woodcutting machinists phased test

Implementing and Administering the Test

However, in cases (eg Figure 6.14) where a knowledge of the marking scheme would provide 'clues' or other forms of unwanted help to candidates, the actual details of the marking scheme should be kept secret, although there is no harm in informing the trainee (in broad terms) how he will be assessed ('You will receive marks not only for the end product but also for how you go about the job').

An example of a set of instructions to trainees (for a testing in terminating, harnessing, and soldering) is given in Figure 7.2.

INSTRUCTIONS TO TRAINEES

1 You are required to mount the 12-way connector and tag board on the piece of hardboard supplied; fixing holes are already drilled. Mark run of cables in pencil, and wire accordingly between connector and tag board, all details for which are given in the attached drawing.

2 You may take up to 3 hours to complete the testpiece, after which time you will be stopped and your testpiece marked.

3 One length of each type of wire is supplied and this is ample to complete the testpiece. If you run short of wire you must inform the instructor.

MATERIALS
- 1 — piece of hardboard
- 1 — 12 way connector strip
- 1 — 12 way tag board
- 4 — No. 4BA screws
- 4 — No. 4B nuts
- 1 — Length 14/0076 single PVC
- 1 — Length 1/044 single PVC
- 1 — Length whip cord
- 1 — Length fuse wire
- 1 — Length resin-cored solder

TOOLS AND EQUIPMENT

Pliers, sidecutters, screwdrivers, knife, and small electric soldering iron.

Figure 7.2 Candidate instructions for an electrical test

A major benefit of having written instructions is that each candidate receives exactly the same information about what he is required to do. Naturally this makes for a more highly standardized test situation. It also ensures that the candidate is not penalized if he happens to forget instructions once the test has started or if he becomes confused. There is also the point that a candidate cannot accuse the examiner of omitting to tell him something that is important to the successful completion of the task. But one must be very careful to ensure that the written instructions are clear to the candidate. It must be remembered that his grasp of the language may not be as complete as one's own and that trade terms may vary from area to area.

If some or all of the test is in paper and pencil form, then it should be made clear to the candidate how the questions should be answered. ('Put a tick in the box against which alternative you think is correct'). It may be a good idea (particularly if the test is a timed one) to give the candidate an example or a number of examples to complete before the test itself. Not only does this help to insure that he has understood the instructions but he may also gain confidence (examples should be made easy) and possible practice effects are reduced. If relevant some advice on the best test strategy should be given ('Work through each question. If you find you cannot answer a question, leave it and go on to the next question.')

Figure 7.3 shows the candidates instructions for the test in fault finding in hydraulic circuits discussed in Chapter 4 (Figure 4.18).

INSTRUCTIONS TO EXAMINERS

These should outline the procedure to be followed, list the equipment needed, point out especially hazardous aspects and emphasize safety precautions that are applicable, and tell the examiner how to set up any equipment for the test. Details of how the test is to be scored should also be given. The instructions should be sufficiently detailed so that an examiner who is competent in the area covered by the tests should be able to set the test, run through the tasks himself, and administer the test to candidates in a standardized manner. Figure 7.4 shows examiners instructions for a battery of tests in setting plastic injection moulding machinery. In addition to this, special instructions about how the test should be introduced to the candidate may be necessary to indicate whether or not a briefing session is allowed and what information may be brought out during discussion.

It should be ensured that all examiners understand the marking system and can use it in a consistent manner. With simple systems, well written instructions will suffice but for more complex set-ups a briefing may have to be held or even training sessions (see Chapter 6).

Uniformity should be stressed; it is essential that all examiners follow the marking schemes strictly.

MARKING SCHEMES

The development of a marking scheme has already been discussed in Chapter 6 but there are some points worth bearing in mind when it comes to its presentation. Firstly it should be neatly and logically laid out so the examiner can abstract any information almost at a glance.

Implementing and Administering the Test

BASIC HYDRAULIC TESTS

SECTION 9

The following question will assess your ability to trace a fault in a hydraulic circuit in a logical manner. You are given the circuit diagram, the sequence of operation of the circuit, and the fault symptoms which have occurred. You have to trace the fault using a logical approach. It is important that you use a logical approach and do not guess what the fault is. You will be severely penalized for guessing.

Now look at the Information Sheet provided. In the columns headed Circuit Reference are the various components of the circuit, and in the spaces on the right of each component reference, under the column heading Condition, are comments relating to the condition of each component. These Condition columns have been covered over.

When you start to trace the fault, decide which component you wish to check first, then using the eraser supplied, rub out the covering over the box in which you are interested. There you will find a comment regarding the condition of the component. By using this information you should then make your next check in a similar way. Number the checks in the order you make them on the sheet.

When you think you have found the fault, put your answer in the space marked Conclusion and state why the fault is causing the particular symptom, then alongside Remedial Action write down what action you think need be taken to make the circuit operable.

You will be assessed on:

1 The way in which you attempt to logically identify the fault through the sequence of checks you make.

2 Whether you correctly identify the fault.

3 Whether you can state why the fault is causing the particular symptom, ie draw the correct conclusion from the fault discovered.

4 Whether you recommend the correct remedial action to eliminate the fault.

Figure 7.3 Instructions for a test in faults diagnosis

Implementing and Administering the Test

PRACTICAL TESTS

INTRODUCTION

1   These tests have been designed to assess a candidate's practical ability at various operations in injection moulding setting.

2   The Procedure Section of the test indicates what the candidate is required to do and should be presented to him (orally or in writing) as his instructions.

3   In order to make the assessment of success or failure as objective as possible, a list of assessment points is provided for each test. The examiner should place a tick or a cross against each assessment point depending on whether the candidate's performance is satisfactory on this point.

4   The value of this objective approach depends on the examiner *recording the candidate's performance as the test proceeds*. An assessment point is either correct or incorrect; there are no 'half-marks'.

5   The list of assessment points is not necessarily comprehensive; it is intended to cover the main aspects of the task and is arranged as far as possible in a logical sequence. Thus at the end of the test it provides the examiner with an objective measure of the quality of the candidate's work and how methodically he has performed the required task.

6   *In order to pass the test the candidate must perform satisfactorily on all assessment points.*

7   The tests are designed to encourage safe practices as well as competence in the particular tasks, and safety is mentioned in the assessment points of all tests. The examiner should stop the test immediately and disqualify the candidate in either of the following circumstances:

   (a)   The candidate's action is endangering his own safety or that of others.
   (b)   The candidate's action is causing permanent damage to any equipment.

8   The candidate must not be allowed to see actual test sheets. He should be informed only of the 'Procedure' for the test.

9   The examiner must enter the candidate's name on the front of each test booklet, explain what the candidate has to do for each test and record the candidate's performance on the assessment points as the test proceeds.

10 The result (pass/fail) for each test should be recorded on the marksheet provided.

Figure 7.4   Examiners' instructions for a hands-on test battery

Implementing and Administering the Test

All examiners should be familiar with the layout of the marking scheme and if possible have been briefed beforehand so that they can appreciate the workings of the system. The marking scheme should, of course, have been made as objective, as possible, but any additions which can be made to increase objectivity are worth doing. For example, we saw that the use of templates, jigs, special gauges, or standard work-pieces in marking test-pieces can help in increasing objectivity.

Where rating scales are used it is particularly important that examiners should be briefed in the meaning of the scale and its various gradations. After the test it may be useful to compare examiners ratings to see if there is any evidence of errors of leniency, harshness, central tendency or any of the other types of error associated with rating scales.

The actual allocation of marks should be laid down in the marking schemes but it is often possible to improve the lot of the examiners by putting some thought into the design of answer sheets and marking keys. For example, multiple-choice questions are quite easy to mark since there is only one correct solution, but one can speed up the marking procedure by making sure that the alternative chosen will be easily recognized and scored clerically or even mechanically. A similar method can also be used for tabular and many other objective techniques.

Closely related to the type of marking scheme used is the correct examiner/candidate ratio. It should always be ensured that the examiner/candidate ratio is sufficient to allow for effective administration of the tests, particularly with regard to ease of marking a candidate's performance. If an examiner has too many candidates and cannot observe each candidate in sufficient detail, then even the most objective marking scheme will prove unreliable.

Clearly this is related to the type of test being administered. Hands-off paper and pencil tests will only need a low ratio of say one examiner to 20 candidates but a hands-on test where process is assessed will need a much higher ratio, often up to 1:1. The actual ratio required may not be determined until the test has been pilot tested but as a general rule, tests which involve the assessment of process will need a high ratio, whereas product-orientated and hands-off tests may need only a low ratio which puts emphasis on invigilation rather than assessment during the testing session itself.

MARK SHEETS

These can record other useful information not just test results, and should be kept even when the person leaves the organization.

This information can then be used at a later date to contribute to any or all of the following:

1. Making a final assessment of the candidate.
2. Providing references and information for other parts of the organization (eg those planning follow up on the job training).
3. Marks from mark sheets can be combined with other data either on the mark sheet or on other personnel records.
4. Validating and evaluating the training system.
5. Validating and evaluating the testing system.

Implementing and Administering the Test

By keeping a careful record of the results of in-plant testing or supervisor ratings it may also be possible to see how off-the-job testing is related to on-the-job performance and thereby if the testing system and/or the training is adequate.

In general one should look for obvious groupings and trends within the data — this can show where correlations may exist and one can then go on to verify one's suspicions by a careful analysis.

The mark sheet may be the same layout as the marking scheme (eg Figure 7.1) or different such as the mark sheet shown in Figure 7.5 for a battery of work sample tests for motor mechanics.

Again, the layout should be clear, neat, and logical so that the examiner is in no doubt what should be recorded and where it should be entered.

Mark sheets may be for an individual or for a group. For most purposes it is better if the original mark sheet contains the score of one person only. If required individual's scores can later be transferred to a group mark sheet.

PILOT TESTING

After the development of the test in its initial form it should be thoroughly tested to eliminate inconsistencies, errors, vague wording, and omissions. To begin with, one can let technical experts inspect it and try it out. This will provide many useful comments for improving the test and will detect most of the major errors. After making any necessary changes the next step is a trial run or pilot test using actual candidates.

Normally it is sufficient to try out each test or subtest with a small number of subjects (examiners and candidates), taking particular note of any comments they have. The pilot test sample should be from the same sort of population(s) which will eventually be involved in testing.

Pilot testing will be useful in determining whether the time allowed is reasonable. With hands-on tests a time should already have been estimated on the basis of analysis but this may need to be modified in the light of test conditions. With hands-off tests sufficient time should be allocated to enable 90–95% of the candidates to complete the tests within the stated time.

A typical group can be selected at random. By trying out the test on a sample of candidates an accurate reaction can be obtained from the type of people who will be taking the test. Candidates will detect most of the errors on the drawings instructions, etc, and too long or too short time allotments will be noted. Each of these can then be easily adjusted. When the trial group has completed the test they should be invited to make comments and suggestions. The major reason for pilot testing the performance test is to improve the test before its implementation. If the changes made after the trial are reasonably minor the tests can be put into operation. If major changes are required, they should be made on the draft and then the test should be administered to a second group before it is produced in its final form.

Five questions can be answered by a pilot test:

1 Do candidates understand the instructions given?
2 Are instructions adequate for the candidates to complete the test?

Implementing and Administering the Test

Figure 7.5 A mark sheet for a test battery on motor mechanics

3 Do examiners go about scoring in the same way?
4 Are the test equipment, tools, and general setting and arrangement of the test layout adequate?
5 Are the items on the marking scheme or the test questions measuring the relevant abilities?

One example of the more unexpected sort of problems that can arise comes from a batch of farming tests; one test required the candidate to remove young pigs from a pen (where they are kept with the sow) so that various holding techniques could be demonstrated.

It will be seen from Figure 7.6 (the prototype form of the test) that the first operation to be carried out is to isolate the sow from the litter for obvious safety reasons and it was decided during early development that the candidate should be aware of this, as indeed he should. But pilot testing showed that practically all candidates failed to do this. The cause of this failure seemed to be the candidate instructions which simply said 'Catch a pig and hold for earmarking' and this rather specific instruction coupled with the candidate's nervousness caused him to rush in and grab a piglet without really thinking. To avoid this one simply had to add an earlier instruction 'Isolate the litter.'

The pilot test can also be used to estimate how objectively examiners can mark the test. This is particularly important if process is involved or ratings are being used. Although the problem of test reliability will be discussed in more detail in Chapter 9, it is worth noting here that a rough estimate can be arrived at by having two or more examiners mark the same test performances independently. Areas of disagreement can then be identified and appropriate action taken; this may be simply rewording the item on the marking scheme, or developing tailor-made devices to help assessment, or even arranging training sessions for examiners.

With hands-off tests it may also be appropriate to use one of the internal consistency methods discussed in Chapter 9 to estimate the reliability of a candidate's performance. This should of course only be done if there is reason for supposing the test is internally consistent, eg measures the same thing throughout its length.

In short, pilot testing should be used to provide as much information as possible in order to iron out any faults before the tests are put into operation.

TIMETABLING AND LAYOUT OF TESTS

Timetabling of tests should aim for the optimum utilization of examiners, candidates, equipment, and time. Special tactics, for example, may need to be adopted where equipment is limited so that only a few candidates may be tested on a piece of equipment at a time. Unless there is some reason why tests must be tackled in a given order, candidates can be rotated from one piece of equipment to another.

Obviously, no hard and fast rules can be laid down since so much will depend on the particular testing situation. However, to indicate the tactics which can be adopted, the timetabling of three tests is given as an example[1], one a 30 minutes hands-on test where the assessment of process was important, one a written test

Implementing and Administering the Test

C/E/I

Test No: PI

Time: 10 minutes

HANDLING YOUNG PIGS

CATCHING AND HOLDING YOUNG PIGS

Section (c) and (d) are designed to test the candidate's ability to select a pig of a particular number as well as his ability to hold the pig in an appropriate way. It is necessary, therefore, to quote an appropriate number for the candidate to select (eg 'Catch pig number 276 and hold it ready for earmarking').

PROCEDURE

Prepare the litter for earmarking and weighing etc.

Catch and hold as appropriate:

(a) One pig for castration
(b) One *gilt* for earmarking
(c) Pig number .... for dosing
(d) Pig number .... for iron injection

SIGNIFICANT POINTS

General points
1   Isolates litter from sow
2   Pigs caught by gripping the hind legs just above the knuckle*
3   Pigs not handled by the ears*

Castration
4   Correct sex
5   Candidates hands well out of way
6   Pigs legs not held too far apart
7   Scrotum easily accessible

Earmarking
8   Correct sex (as instructed)
9   Head secured and ear easily accessible

Dosing
10 Correct (number) pig selected (as directed)
11 Head secured and mouth held open without obstruction

Injecting
12 Correct (number) pig selected
13 Ham easily accessible

RESULT

Pigs selected, caught and held in appropriate positions for the intended operations. All holds effective in that the animal cannot move excessively. All pigs returned to pen without escape, and marked to show that the task has been completed.

SCORE   A, B, C

Score

13

* One point per pig

© Copyright Skills Testing Service

Figure 7.6 A work sample test used in the agricultural industry

Implementing and Administering the Test

(short answer) which lasted one and three quarter hours, the third a test requiring identification of components, etc which lasted 45 minutes. The timetable is shown in Figure 7.7.

Fifty men had to be tested and it was possible to test ten candidates at once on the hands-on test (bearing in mind availability of examiners and equipment) and 25 at a time on the identification test. The written paper required only invigilation. The fifty candidates were split into five groups, labelled I to V on the diagram. Although each candidate took the hands-on and identification tests without interruption, groups II, III, and IV had to be interrupted during the written tests. This was not considered a serious problem as short-answer items (rather than essays) were involved and strict invigilation minimized opportunities for candidates discussing the test while moving between testing areas.

Note that timetabling could have been such that all candidates took the written test first, and this would then involve a queue for the other tests, and the test session would not have finished until 11 45 am instead of 10 30 am.

Similarly with the layout of the test area, the plan must try to optimize the fit between the resources and the demands of the tests. A major aspect of layout is the question of ensuring it does not jeopardize any security requirements of the test; for example, that candidates cannot copy off one another. With proper invigilation and design of the test area, utilizing devices such as movable screens, this can usually be achieved.

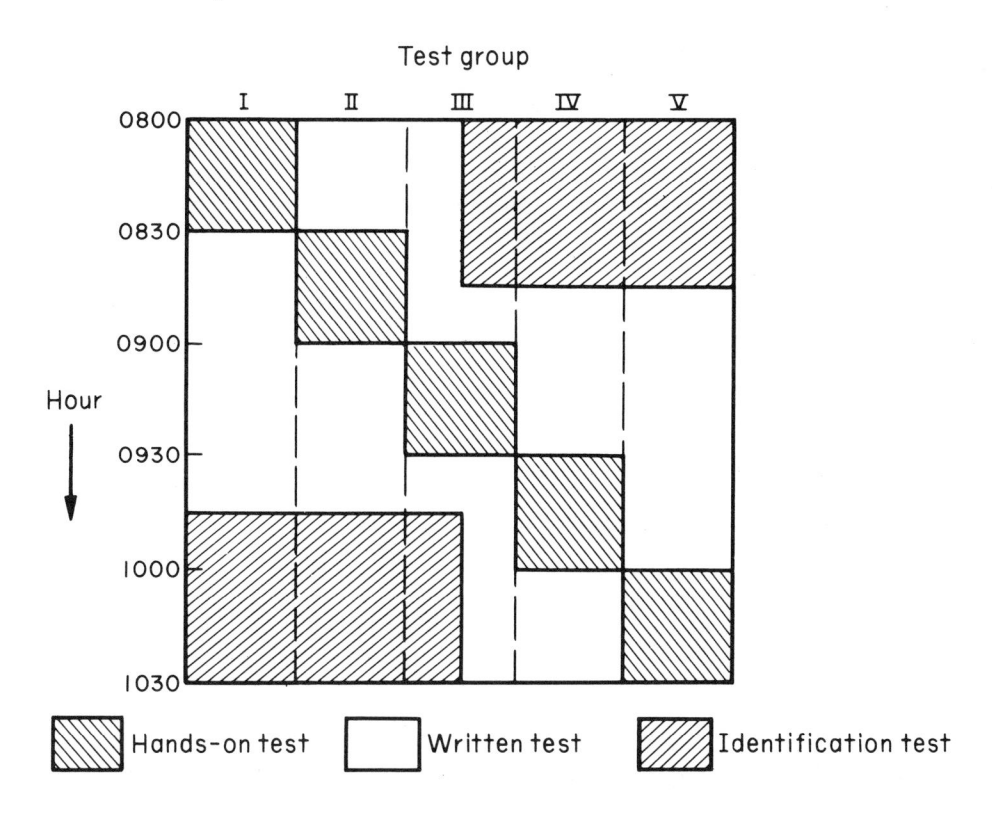

Figure 7.7 Timetable for a battery of tests *(by courtesy of Princeton University Press)*

Implementing and Administering the Test

Figure 7.8 gives a possible layout for the tests in stripping down hydraulic valves discussed in Chapter 3. Six different examples of a single vane pump and six of an in-line Axial Piston Pump are required. Any trainee works on only *one* of each type (ie two pumps in all). So, if there were 12 trainees, each would work on one pump, then change over to another. Trainees simply change benches when they have dealt with one type of pump.

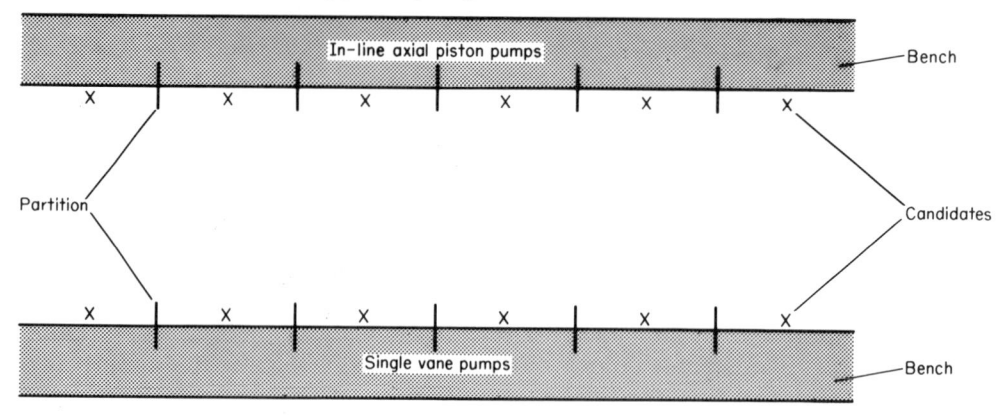

Figure 7.8 Possible layout for the tests in stripping down hydraulic valves

With hands-off tests special presentation devices may be used.

The Colchester Lathe Training Centre utilizes a 'feedback classroom' which can be used for testing as well as instruction. Thirty-two trainees can be tested at a time.

Test material can be projected onto a screen at the front of the classroom. Trainees can respond to multiple-choice questions by use of a specially designed response unit, incorporating a four-position switch hidden from the view of other trainees. The response units (Figure 7.9(b)) are wired up to the instructor's main control where the instructor can mark correct answers and record them by means of a digital response counter (Figure 7.9(c)). Test items can be presented in a number of ways:

1 Chalk board
2 Magnetic board
3 Flip charts
4 Overhead projector
5 Remote controlled slide projector and/or tape recorder
6 Film
7 Xerox or similar duplicated handouts
8 Cassette loaded projectors

Such a system can bring about considerable saving in testing time. Sharpe[2] reports that a 50-item test was administered, marked and feedback given to 30 trainees in one hour using this system, as against two hours testing and eight hours of instructors' time involved in marking a written test covering the same material. In the latter case results were not available until seven days later.

Implementing and Administering the Test

Figure 7.9(a) General view of the feedback classroom

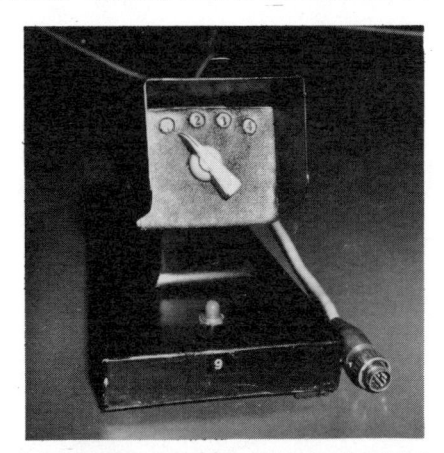

Figure 7.9(b) Response unit used in the feedback classroom

Figure 7.9(c) Digital response computer used in the feedback classroom to record trainees' responses

129

Implementing and Administering the Test

SECURITY

If one is in the position of using tests repeatedly or wants to give candidates an idea of the areas and standards involved, one is faced with the question 'How security conscious should I be?' 'Should tests be top secret or should I allow trainees to see them?'

The chief guideline is whether the test covers all or most of the area in question; if so there is no reason, particularly with hands-on tests, why candidates cannot know what they are up against. If on the other hand, tests are a sample, as they often are, test validity is obviously lowered if candidates know the test before hand. Note that with hands-off tests it is usually advisable for candidates to see and preferably answer a specimen item which is not included in the test paper itself.

THE TEST MANUAL

Tests are usually gathered together in a manual which should provide all the necessary details to administer the test and in most cases to interpret test results. Below is a checklist which can be used to assess the adequacy of the manual and some aspects of the tests themselves whether the tests are provided by an outside body or home-grown.

Check the test manual against the following questions:

1. What is the name of the test?
2. Who are its authors/publishers?
3. What is the cost of the manual, entering for the test and certification (if offered)?
4. Are all relevant documents included in the test manual ie test specification, candidates' instructions, examiners' instructions, marking scheme, mark sheet, etc?
5. Does the manual provide a clear statement of the purposes and applications for which the test is intended?
6. How long does the test take to administer?
7. Are there any restrictions about where and when testing can take place?
8. What (analytic) techniques were used in developing the tests?
9. When was the test last revised?
10. Does the manual provide a clear statement of the qualifications and/or experience needed to administer or mark the test?
11. Are the directions for administration sufficiently full and clear to ensure acceptably uniform conditions?
12. Are the procedures for marking/scoring set forth clearly and in detail so as to maximize scoring efficiency and objectivity?
13. Do the test manual, records forms etc guide test users towards sound and correct interpretations of the test results?
14. If scales or profiles are used for reporting scores are they clearly defined and carefully described so that the test user can understand them?

REFERENCES

1. Sharpe P.H., *Feedback Classroom Techniques.* The Training Officer Volume 7, Number 3, 1971.
2. Stuit D.B., Ed., *Personnel Research and Test Development in the Bureau of Naval Personnel*, Princeton University Press, Princeton, 1947.

8

Interpreting and Utilizing Test Results

In this chapter the authors deal with what is normally termed results determination and also attempt to show that a test can be used for more than simply arriving at pass/fail decisions.

The ultimate object of any test or set of tests is to allow the test-user to make a decision or decisions; the better the testing system the more clear-cut the decision should be. The purpose of tests is to determine whether trainee X should be allowed out on the shopfloor or whether trainee Y needs any remedial training, and so on. However, many test developers seem to forget that making a decision is ultimately what testing is all about and during the development of tests they neglect the problem of utilization of test scores so that a post hoc system has to be developed. It is important to bear in mind that test scores must be capable of interpretation and utilization.

The question of determining results in a pass/fail type situation will be discussed first.

DETERMINATION OF RESULTS IN A PASS/FAIL TYPE SITUATION

Criterion-referenced versus norm-referenced results determination

Most readers will have had experience of norm-referenced results determination in schools and educational examinations. Norm-referenced results determination means that the standard, or cut-off point(s), is set in relation to the performance of the whole group on the test. For example, if 60% of candidates achieve a

Interpreting and Utilizing Test Results

score of X or above, X may be set as the 'pass mark' (assuming one wants 60% of the candidates to pass). What is interesting about this system is that it is rarely explained to candidates in this way, and so somebody who achieves less than 'X' probably believes he has failed to come up to some standard of intrinsic value. However, the pass marks often vary from year to year in order to obtain the same pass rate (the proportion of 'successful' candidates). Such a system is based on the assumption that 60% (or whatever) of candidates are satisfactory and the others are not each year. This assumption is obviously open to criticism; suppose some years candidates are better taught, for example. The whole point about the type of normative results determination outlined above is that it is not based on the content of the test itself but on the performance of candidates and one's own assumptions.

Lewis Carol in Alice's Adventures in Wonderland describes this sort of situation very well:

'... how can you possibly award prizes when everybody missed the target?' said Alice.

'Well' said the Queen, 'Some missed by more than others, and we have a fine normal distribution of misses, which means we can forget the target.'

There is another system of normative standards for tests based on the same system as used in aptitude testing etc. It is different from the above approach in that a study is undertaken to establish a set of norms before testing takes place. Such norms are derived from testing a representative sample of the population in which there is interest and then transforming raw scores into norms. There are two classes of norms, reference norms and statistical norms. Reference norms translate raw scores into directly meaningful terms such as 'Scores above 35 are typically scored by competent craftsmen'. Statistical norms, on the other hand, report scores in terms of the relative performance of the sample and are therefore not directly meaningful, such as 'Scores above 35 are obtained by 25% of the population'.

Criterion standards, on the other hand, involve setting the standard in relation to the quality of the product or acceptable performance on the task; that is the content of the test forms the basis for decisions not the performance of the group of candidates. An example of a criterion standard is 'job passes quality control department inspection', or in Alice's terms hitting the target.

Figure 8.1 contrasts norm-referenced and criterion-referenced standards.

Normative standards have been and are often used in performance testing when criterion standards are not clear. As more criterion standards are specified so the use of normative standards should decrease, although some organizations may use them for the relative grading of personnel. It must, however, be admitted that in some cases it is much more difficult to define the criterion cut-off point for a test rather than simply give a normative report such as 'the candidate is in the top 20% of candidates'. This is a particular problem when there are a number of points in a checklist or number of marks achieved by a candidate.

It is apparent from the above discussion that criterion standards are more relevant to performance testing than normative standards. The chief reasons for the latter's use are:

Interpreting and Utilizing Test Results

1. Criterion standards are not clear.
2. Influence of educational examinations and psychological tests.
3. They can be used for grading when based on a proportional pass rate system.
4. When tests are used to predict later performance (see Chapter 9).

To sum up the difference between these two types of standards: Normative standards are for discriminating between individuals and not in the first instance for discriminating between levels of performance. Criterion standards are for discriminating between levels of performance and therefore as a secondary result can discriminate between individuals to a certain extent.

	Norm-referenced	Criterion-referenced
Quality	To standard achieved by 70% of candidates	+ or − 0.04 mm
Quantity	Number of items achieved by 70% of candidates	4 in 1 hour
Speed	In time achieved by 70% of candidates	1 hour
Product	Number of significant points achieved by 70% of candidates	Observing all significant points

Figure 8.1 Norm-referenced and criterion-referenced standards

Defining adequate performance for criterion-referenced tests

The possible differences between training standards and job standards were discussed earlier (Chapter 6). But often, particularly with hands-off test, the test task will be in a form far removed from the job situation.

Three kinds of test standard can therefore be distinguished.

1. Job standards
2. Training standards
3. Intrinsic test standards.

In any given testing situation the three may be the same as or different from one another. Whatever training or job standards have been agreed on must now be used in interpreting results, or if there are 'intrinsic' standards (eg in a multiple-choice test) the meaning of performance on the test must be ascertained (eg 'on a test sampling the symbols used in basic electronic maintenance work, a score of at least 90% is required'). Note that the method of presentation of hands-off tests should be borne in mind when deciding what is satisfactory, eg on a multiple-choice test the candidate may obtain a considerable score through guessing whereas in other types of tests the likelihood of this is much less.

Suppose there is a checklist or a set of rating scales, the problem is 'How do we determine what constitutes satisfactory or unsatisfactory performance on the test?'. Obviously information from analysis of the task and the requirements of the test user determine this, but the form of the marking scheme means that there is in practice the question 'What proportion of ticks on the checklist are we prepared to accept?'.

Consider the checklist shown in Figure 8.2. Three systems are possible:

1 The candidate has to achieve a given number of points (eg 8/10). This is often an adequate, although rough system. It also takes into account that it may be unreasonable to expect a perfect performance on any one test. Often however the marking schemes have been developed on the basis that the points on the checklist define adequate performance. Therefore, another system is given in 2 below.
2 The candidate has to achieve all checkpoints. This may sound harsh, but the marking scheme points may represent the basic minimum level of performance, so it is not logical to go below this. For example, during World War II the US Navy developed a test for its amphibious training bases in which trainees had to recognize perfectly all beachmarker signals indicating where certain types of cargo were to be unloaded, signals identifying different kinds of craft, and so on. Since this was truly a key area mastery on the test was required. The only argument against this is that even 'competent' candidates may make one error which in no way reflects on their overall performance. Therefore an error allowance of say one or two points may be made. However it must be considered what the position would be if the candidate were to perform badly on the one or two really essential points.
3 To get round this difficulty a parallel marking system may be used, such as the one illustrated in Figure 8.4. To be successful the candidate must achieve the full number of ticks, in the essential ('must do') column and a certain number in the other ('nice to do') column. Alternatively the number of ticks in the 'nice to do' column can be used to give upper discrimination, so that candidates can be further classed as 'adequate' or 'superior'. Of course, these different systems are more suitable for different situations. The first one for a phased test during training, the second for an end test with a minimum acceptable level of performance, and the third for grading and for situations requiring upper discrimination.

The test battery: the profile or multiple cut-off method

If there is a battery of tests, it must be decided how an overall decision about the candidate's performance is to be achieved. A decision may have to be made, for example, as to when the overall performance is considered adequate enough to go on to the next bit of training or the shop floor. Since presumably the test areas have been chosen for their relevance and importance and appropriate standards have been set for each test as in the previous section, the logical thing to do is to 'pass' the candidate only if the performance is up to the minimum on each test. This is the concept of the MAPP or minimum acceptable performance profile, as illustrated in Figure 8.3.

Interpreting and Utilizing Test Results

TEST No. 1

STRINGING

The trainee is required to prepare a single manual harpsichord for subsequent operations by fitting the strings.

Examiner should check:

1. Back is blocked up firmly on trestles and wrest plant.
2. Listing, hitch pin washer and wrest pin washer fitted correctly.
3. Correct stringing scale selected.
4. String eyes made correctly, ie coils wound evenly and tightly, and neatly with the tags pointing in a uniform direction.
5. Strings free of kinks, ie no kinked wire to be fitted.
6. Coils knocked down tight with eye at base of pin.
7. Wrest pins levelled to specified height.
8. Wrest pins to be firm in the lock. Bit to turn smoothly with jumping when tuned.
9. Strings threaded through spring correctly.
10. If there are any adjustable spaces, these should be directly under the appropriate strings (to be checked after chipping up).

Figure 8.2 **A checklist for a test in stringing a harpsichord**

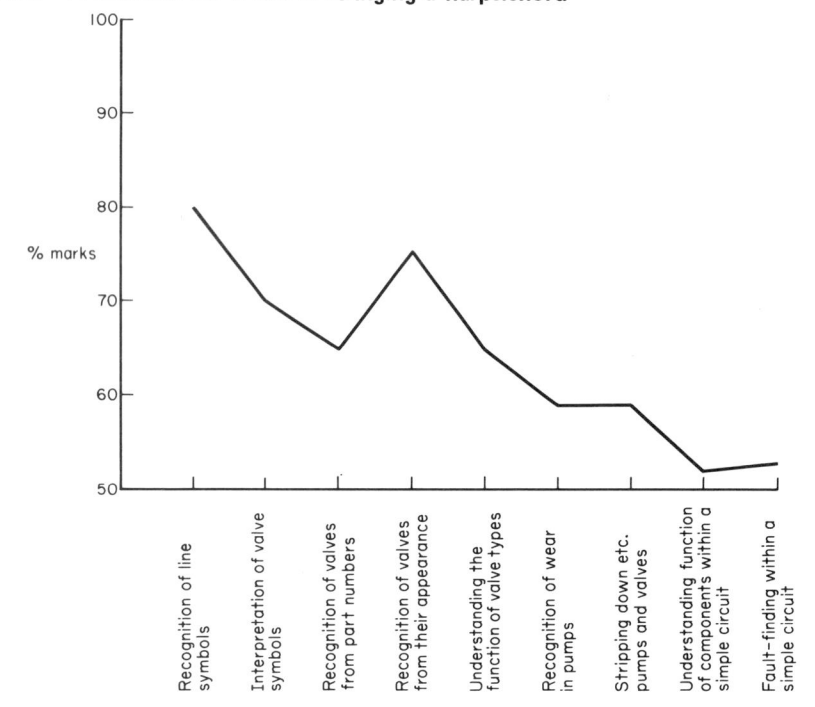

Figure 8.3 **A minimum acceptable performance profile**

Interpreting and Utilizing Test Results

Test P103 — Castrating young pigs

Standard time: 10 minutes
Maximum time: 12 minutes

Requirements

A group of pigs between one and six weeks of age to be castrated. Scalpel and sterile blade. Dry cotton wool and antiseptic solution. Paint stick marker. Competent assistant to catch and hold pigs as instructed by the candidate

Procedure

Candidate to castrate two pigs giving necessary instruction on holding and marking to assistant

Significant points

		Start
		Finish
		Time
Must do	Nice to do	

1. Equipment prepared before any pig is caught
2. Blade safely fitted to scalpel
3. Clear and concise instructions given to assistant
4. Scrotum checked for any abnormality, eg hernia. If any found, pig marked and reported*
5. Area of skin to be cut cleaned with antiseptic*
6. Each testicle gripped firmly before cut is made*
7. Both cuts made parallel to centre line of body, and at base of scrotum (to assist draining)*
8. Testicles removed with minimum loss of body wall (peritoneum)*
9. Spermatic cords pulled or scraped, NOT CUT*
10. Antiseptic administered*
11. Pig marked (by assistant)*
12. Scalpel blade removed safely at end of task

*One point per pig

Figure 8.4 A work sample test illustrating parallel marking systems

Interpreting and Utilizing Test Results

Figure 8.3, gives a graphical illustration of the levels of performance acceptable on each test. Any candidate's performance can then be compared with this profile, and one may discover, for example, that he is not satisfactory on area four but above the minimum standard on area five (assuming upper discrimination in the test).

Norm-referenced results determination

When in the position of having to determine results normatively, it is important to understand the reasons for the situation. There may be an interest in the relative performance of individuals or centres and not in absolute judgements. The Manuals of First Year Engineering Tests discussed below are an example of this. Another reason may be that one just cannot get an adequate definition of criterion standards.

If the test developer or user is faced with norm-referenced result determination, then the following comments are in order:

1. The simplest case is probably where one is told 60% of the candidates must pass. The immediate reaction is 'Why?' and it is worthwhile asking this — perhaps no one has ever really thought about it.
2. In a normative results determination situation dealing with the results of more than one test, the profile or the weighting methods can be used. The profile method has been discussed above. In the case of the weighting method the contribution of tests is altered by giving scores on them different mathematical weights (see Figure 8.5). Often tests scores are added in together 'without weighting' so that each test has equal weighting. This method involves a non-statistical combination of scores. In psychological testing, multiple correlation is used to arrive at a statistical weighting of tests. However, in such cases this method is being used to obtain the best correlation between test scores and what one wants to predict. This is a very different situation from most performance testing so such a technique is usually an irrelevant complication.

Test No.	Mark obtained	Weighting	Weighted score
1	56	0.10	5.6
2	65	0.10	6.5
3	70	0.10	7.0
4	48	0.10	4.8
5	60	0.15	9.0
6	55	0.20	11.0
7	72	0.25	18.0
		Total	61.9

Final score: 61.9

Figure 8.5 A specimen weighting system

3   Often the norm-referenced system is hidden by a system such as 'the pass mark is 50%', here the pass mark is 50% because say 60% of candidates achieve 50% of marks or above. Often pass marks such as 40%, 50%, or 60% are a combination of the normative and criterion approach ('a trainee ought to be able to manage 50%').

Ready-made tests with norms

It was noted in Chapter 4 that there are on the market, particularly in the USA, sets of tests which are designed to measure trade knowledge or skills. A set of reference norms is usually provided with each test.

One reason for this is that such tests are often short of low fidelity or cover only a small portion of the job; the normative data are an attempt to relate performance on the test with performance on the job.

This is a predictive or more usually a concurrent validity situation. For example, a series of short (18 or 22 items) occupational knowledge tests for such occupations as plumber, welder, truck driver, were designed by Science Research Associates Incorporated of Chicago to provide an index of an individual's familiarity with the current content and concepts of the occupational area. Tests were validated by taking a group of specialists and non-specialists in an area and comparing their performance. As the test developers point out there is little point in having a validity study of carpentry tests which compares carpenters and say secretaries. What is needed is a test which differentiates between competent carpenters and handymen with only a low level of competence. Groups for the study were chosen on this basis. The tests give only three scores: pass, fail and unclassifiable, the latter being the result of an overlap in the scores of specialist and non-specialist groups.

Having carried out the study the test developers then attempted to predict from test results alone whether a candidate was a specialist or non-specialist. How successful they were is given as a 'percentage Hit' figure, that is the percentage of accurate predictions made after removing unclassifiable subjects.

For examples, with truck drivers they obtained a percentage hit of 89.2%, with 17.2% of candidates unclassifiable. With draftsmen 92.2% hit and 17.9% unclassifiable.

TROUBLE-SHOOTING WITH RESULTS DETERMINATION METHODS

Reference should be made to Figure 8.6, which shows the major steps in result determination. So far the discussion has gone as far as the second level (profile or weighting method). Once results have been subjected to whatever method has been chosen, the result provided need to be examined. It must be considered whether they look right or whether they look 'funny'. If they do look funny, one must then decide the reason for this. There are a variety of possible reasons for incongruous results:

1   Misjudgement of the level of the population. For example, perhaps the training does not teach them a certain skill after all.

Interpreting and Utilizing Test Results

2. The test administration is not as it should be — candidates' instructions are insufficient, administration is not uniform, and so on.
3. The test content is inappropriate.
4. The test marking scheme is concentrating on irrelevant aspects of performance or is too subjective, thus giving unreliable scores.

The problem of 'funny' results is particularly serious with norm-referenced determination of results, because unlike the criterion-referenced system, there are no landmarks to suggest in just what way or why they are funny (one may have hunches) unless a related validity study has been carried out.

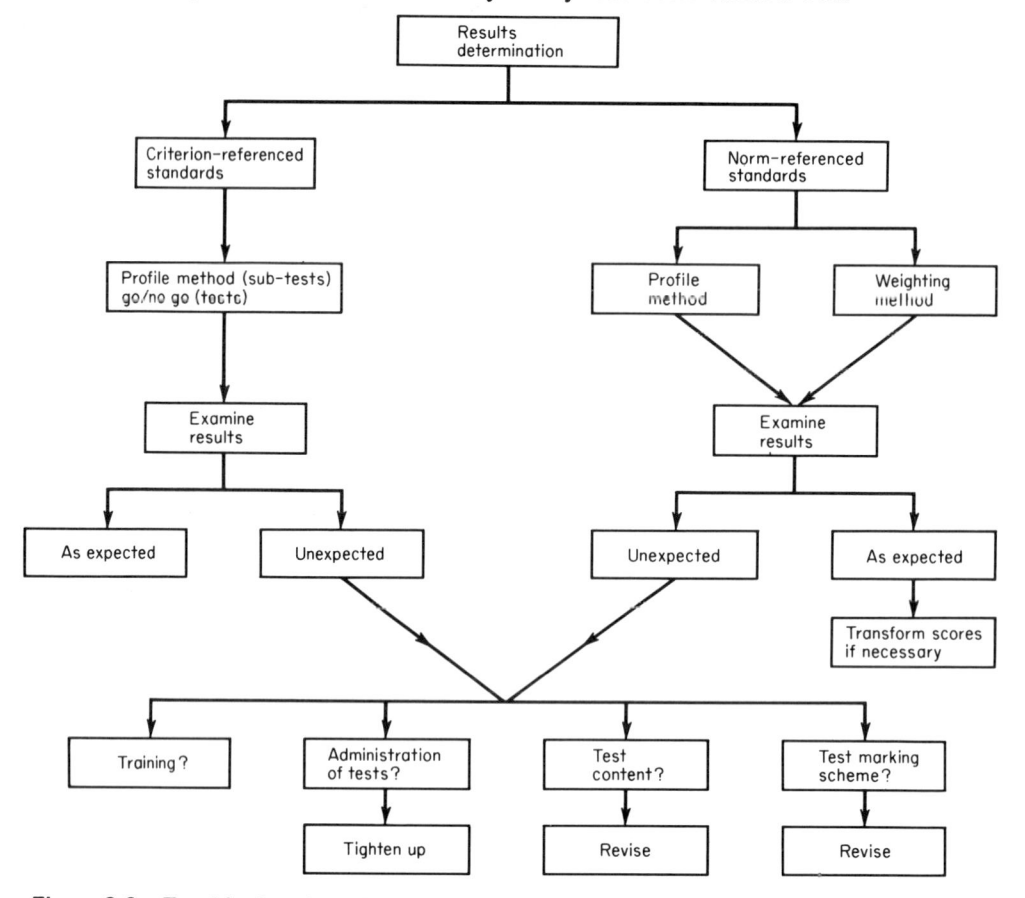

Figure 8.6 Trouble shooting with results determination methods

UTILIZING TESTS AND RESULTS

Some of the ways in which scores can be treated in order to allow decision about the candidate to be made were discussed above. These decisions may be simply how to describe the performance ('adequate', 'very good', etc) or how the candidate should proceed in his training or career. This section expands the concept of interpreting test results to the assessment of other areas.

Interpreting and Utilizing Test Results

Classifying candidates

The first purpose of testing is to classify candidates. However, it is worth emphasizing that tests are not perfect measuring instruments. No test can measure only the relevant behaviour and measure it with perfect consistency, so it should always take into account that any score is only an estimate or sample of the candidate's true ability. This will be discussed more fully in Chapter 9, but it is worthwhile introducing the concept of the 'zone of uncertainty' in a test score.

The zone of uncertainty can be regarded as a range of scores within which one is not sufficiently confident to say that different scores are in fact truly different. Take for example a test with a maximum score of 50 with a zone of uncertainty of four marks on either side of the score. This would mean that the true score of a person scoring 30 will probably lie within the zone 26 to 34.

Often in criterion-reference measurement the only requirement is a pass/fail decision so the interest will be in the zone of uncertainty around the criterion. This point is discussed more fully when test reliability is discussed. Obviously the zone of uncertainty will vary from test to test, but from first principles it would appear that the better the sample of skills and/or knowledge tested and the more objective the marking scheme the smaller the zone of uncertainty will be. For example, a hands-on test of milling involving several milling tasks would have a smaller zone of uncertainty than a few tests sampling the whole of a motor mechanic's work. Perhaps in future, where necessary, test results will be presented in such a way as to enable the interpreter to take into account the uncertainty or unreliability in scores.

If a test classifies candidates into pass or fail, then the test user would like to know what the likelihood is that such a classification is reliable or consistent. Again this would have to be determined empirically so that a question such as 'What is the likelihood that a candidate passing this test on one occasion would pass it on another?' can be answered.

Of course before such an approach can be implemented considerable research would be needed to estimate the reliability and 'zone of uncertainty' for each test.

Tests as sources of information for remedial training etc

All testing, but particularly phased testing, can provide interested parties with information about a candidate's strengths and weaknesses. Phased testing is usually superior only in that it tests a specific chunk of skills and ensures the trainee possesses them before he moves onto the next chunk. If the timetable is well designed it will also have taken into account the possible need for remedial training after the testing session.

As an example of this Figure 8.7 shows the performance of five trainees at a large shipbuilding training centre on a fitting test. It will be noticed that across the top of the table there are various groups of operations such as 'relief hole drilling', 'cutting to squareness' and so on. It is therefore possible to highlight any particular weakness in a trainee's performance. For example, Trainee A is poor on 'edge square to square', 'corner radius', and 'cut to squareness'.

Interpreting and Utilizing Test Results

At this particular centre trainees who failed the test were asked to give their comments on the test (Figure 8.8). Not only does this provide instructors with information it also allows trainees to analyse and assess their own performance, therefore providing a form of intrinsic feedback.

Name		Square corners	Edge square to surface	Corner radius	Relief hole drilling	Cut out squareness	Dimensional accuracy	Quality of finish	Total mark
	Possible	12	16	8	4	16	30	14	100
Trainee A		12	(6)	(2)	4	(2)	20	10	56
Trainee B		10	(8)	(4)	4	8	(12½)	6	52½
Trainee C		(6)	(9)	6	4	(4)	(15)	8	52
Trainee D		(4)	(7)	6	4	(0)	27½	10	58½
Trainee E		8	11	(0)	3	14	(12½)	8	56½

Figure 8.7 Performance of trainees who received less than 60% marks on a fitting test.
Circles indicate that a trainee received less than 60% marks on a particular area.

Trainee A
Problems filing square and hacksawing — time for test seemed tight.

Trainee B
Tried to finish both parts first before checking for dimensional accuracy. Problems hacksawing to a line and filing square. Time for test tight.

Trainee C
Slight problems reading micrometer. Forgot to radius corners until last 4 minutes.
Problems filing square.

Trainee D
Time for test tight. Problems hacksawing to a line and filing.

Trainee E
Hurried job at start when he saw time allowance — problems in filing edge square to surface.

Trainee F
Problems in filing edge square to surface — more practice with vernier required.

Trainee G
Problems hacksawing to a line and filing square. Tried to get both parts to fit together right from the start rather than making each individual part to the required standard.

Figure 8.8 Some trainees' reactions to a phased test

Interpreting and Utilizing Test Results

Although the method described above provides a very comprehensive system for feeding back results to trainees, other methods of displaying results are possible:

1. Displaying top and bottom marks of the group and the average mark obtained by the group.
2. Displaying the marks of all trainees.
3. Giving each trainee his mark and position in the group.

Such methods are more concerned with the motivational effects of test results. However, in assessing the effects of phased testing it is somewhat difficult to disentangle the effects of motivation and of outcome feedback. It must be considered whether the trainee's performance improves because he knows his strengths and weaknesses or whether the competitive situation spurs him on to greater efforts.

Self-testing

Tests administered by trainees themselves can provide the trainee with feedback on his level of proficiency and reinforce skills and knowledge. For example, in a training programme for the conversion of bus conductors to bus drivers it was decided that knowledge of road signs was a key area. To help trainees to learn signs, a self-testing pack of 45 cards was designed. One side of the card showed a road sign, the other the official Highway Code definition of its meaning. Trainees worked through the pack giving their answers and then marking their answers themselves. This method was repeated over the four-week course. Trainees using this technique were compared with trainees using traditional methods and trainees were also divided into groups of 30 years of age or less. To do this all trainees were tested on all 45 road signs. The results are shown in Figure 8.9.

Clearly, both age-groups but particularly the older group benefitted from self-testing, one probable reason for this being that older learners like to pace themselves, which they could do with the pack of cards.

	Aged 20–29 years average score	Aged 30 years and over average score
Group 1 before training	55	45
Group 2 traditional techniques: lectures, visual aids, Highway Code etc	66	56
Group 3 traditional techniques plus 40 minutes of extra practice on self-testing pack	77	75

Maximum possible score: 90

Figure 8.9 Results on self-testing in recognition of road signs

Interpreting and Utilizing Test Results

Self-testing, or at any rate, self marking is also used in other situations. For example, in some shipbuilding training centres, trainees mark their own test pieces. It is argued that trainees can in this way get an idea of the standards towards which they are being taught.

Trainability tests and assessments

Trainability tests are an attempt to provide an estimation of the suitability of a candidate for training. The candidate is given a short training session followed by a test. The test attempts to predict success at training by his behaviour on a number of areas. For example, a trainability test for fork-truck operators involves the candidate driving the truck around a course and lifting a pallet and so on (see Figure 8.10). He is assessed using the marking scheme illustrated in Figure 8.11. Each error is noted as the test takes place; errors are expected as candidates are novices.

Immediately after the test the instructor makes a rating of the candidates' approach. The gradings are defined as follows:

A   Stands out as having exceptional potential, above nearly all other applicants.
B   Markedly better than most applicants without being positively outstanding.
C   No serious difficulties, but not having markedly more potential than most.
D   Certain weaknesses suggest he has less potential than most, but may be good enough to 'get by'.
E   Would need a great deal of help to reach even a passable standard.

A study using 164 trainees showed that performance on the trainability test was a good predictor of success on a competence test at the end of the training period. The table given in Figure 8.12 shows what percentage of trainees obtaining each grading received scores of good, average, and unacceptable on the final competence test. The table in fact provides a set of reference norms.

It was also found that the following relationship held between total errors and overall gradings, thereby giving a guide to help instructors in their grading in future.

Total errors	Trainability grading
0–4	A
5–8	B
9–12	C
13–14	D
15 or more	E

Trainability tests can be seen as a type of performance test where the candidate's approach and his score (expected to be well below acceptable performance levels) are used as predictors for success at training. As such they must be validated using a predictive validity method. Trainability tests are being developed by the Industrial Training Research Unit for a variety of skills.

Interpreting and Utilizing Test Results

The circuit is laid out as in the diagram.

The trainee is told that he must drive the truck round the drum to pick up the pallet and transfer it to the square. He must then reverse round the drum back to the starting position and park the truck.

The instructor 'walks' the trainee through the course and makes sure that he understands what he has to do. If the trainee wishes to ask any questions he is urged to do so at this point.

The test takes place without the intervention of the instructor, unless a dangerous situation occurs or the trainee needs to be prompted to complete the course.

If faults occur such as hitting the drum or incorrectly depositing the pallet the trainee should be encouraged to carry on.

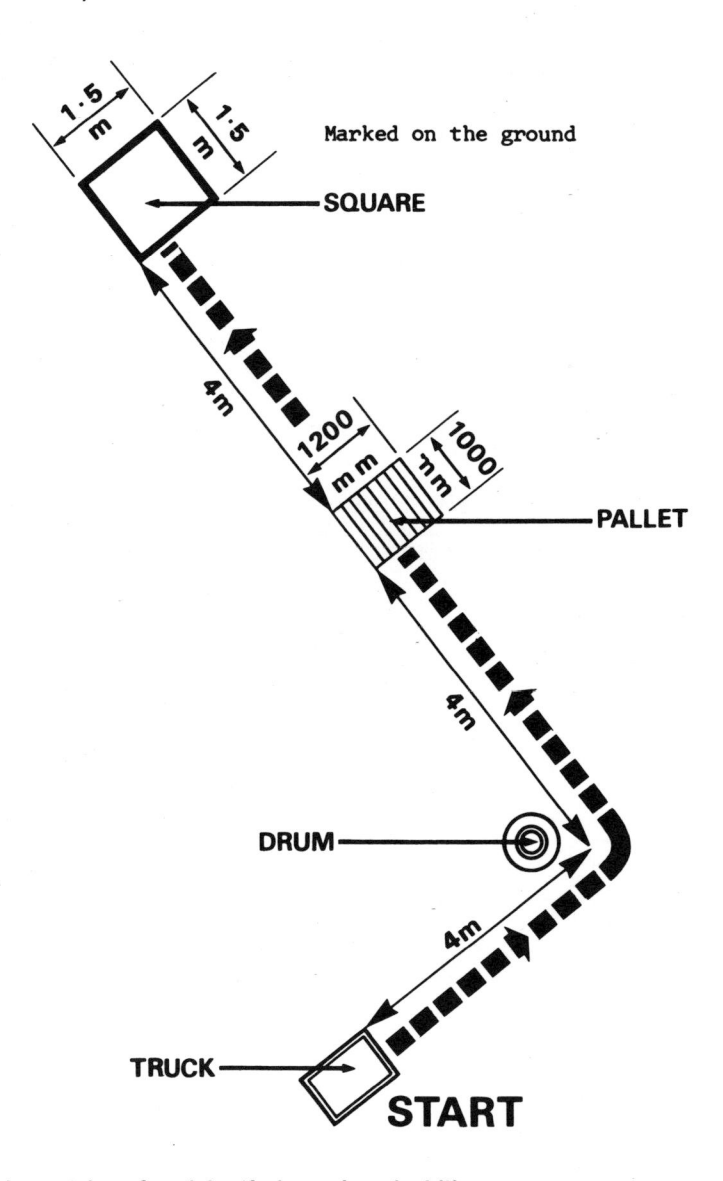

Figure 8.10 Instructions for giving fork truck trainability assessment test

Interpreting and Utilizing Test Results

FORK TRUCKS

Name .... Age .... Date .... Assessor ....

Previous experience: Car .... Fork Truck .... Other Vehicle (specify) ....

Errors (to be noted as they occur)　　　X = error　　　X √ = corrected error

General	Uses brakes incorrectly	
	Selects wrong position with hydraulic/direction controls	
	Uses tilt and hoist controls roughly	
	Accelerates and brakes erratically	
	Fails to look in direction of travel (forward or backward)	
	Fails to check for rear end swing	
Starting	Holds wheel to climb on to truck	
	Fails to hold driving wheel prior to moving	
	Fails to tilt mast to get forks clear of ground	
Drum	Fails to line up on drum correctly for turning	
	Hits drum	
	Steers more than a truck width from drum	
	Leaves lock on too long	
	Corrects steering too soon	
Pallett	Fails to stop and hits pallet	
	Stops too close to pallet	
	Fails to approach pallet square and central	
	Fails to tilt forks sufficiently	
	Tilts forks too far forward	
	Over-run pallet by an inch or more	
	Tilts mast back before raising pallet clear of ground	
	Raises pallet too high	
Box	Fails to position pallet within box	
	Lowers pallet before returning mast to vertical	
	Tilts mast too far forward	
	Fails to ensure forks are clear of pallet before withdrawal	
	Fails to glance forward when reversing from pallet	
	Fails to stop before re-positioning masts for travelling	
	Fails to position mast for travelling	
	Fails to reverse round drum	
Parking	Fails to apply parking brake	
	Fails to lower forks flat to floor	
	Fails to remove key when leaving truck	
Other errors		
	Total errors	

This assessment to be made *immediately* the test drive is completed.
Please ring appropriate letter. Definitions are on the instruction sheet.

　　　　　Likely to be a good trainee　　　　Unlikely to be a good trainee

　　　　　　Exceptional　　A　　　　　　　Below average　D
　　　　　　Above Average　B　　　　　　　Unsuitable　　E
　　　　　　Average　　　　C

Figure 8.11　Trainability assessment test sheet

Interpreting and Utilizing Test Results

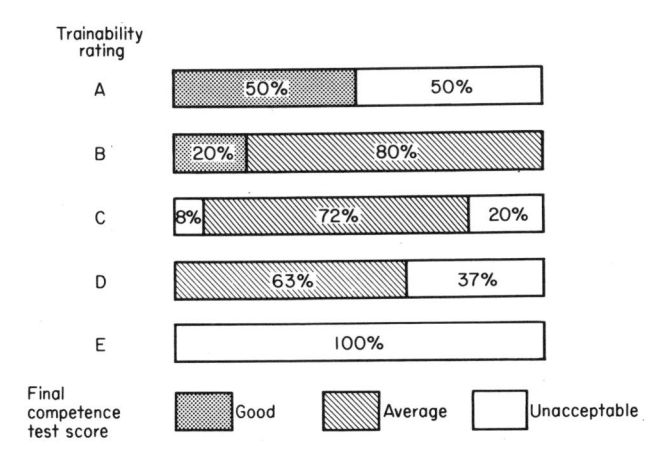

Trainability rating			
A	50%	50%	
B	20%	80%	
C	8%	72%	20%
D	63%	37%	
E		100%	

Final competence test score: ▓ Good ▨ Average ☐ Unacceptable

Figure 8.12 Table of reference norms for trainability grading

Assessing the performance of instructors

Particularly in large training centres and organizations there is a need to monitor the effectiveness of different instructors who may vary in instructional ability or range of technical experience. To do this, the test scores of the groups taught by different instructors can be compared. This can be done by looking at the average score and variation of scores of the group on the test as a whole and on various groups of operations. The proportion of trainees passing the criterion for each instructor can also be seen. An example of this is given in Figure 8.13 below.

OPERATION

Instructors	A	B	C	D
1	0.75	0.80	0.90	0.50
2	0.80	0.90	0.75	0.65
3	0.70	0.45	0.75	0.70
4	0.80	0.75	0.60	0.80
5	0.80	0.75	0.95	0.65

Figure 8.13 Proportion of candidates achieving criteria on various operations

Interpreting and Utilizing Test Results

It can be seen in the example that Instructor 1 is relatively unsuccessful on area D as is Instructor 3 on B, Area A is relatively well taught by all instructors, and so on.

Assessing overall centre performance

In most cases those responsible for training will want some quantitative index of how effective their training is, test scores are ideal for this purpose. An obvious measure of success is how many trainees reach the criterion on how many tests.

Suppose, however, the training centre is taking part in a widespread training scheme involving national objectives. Often in such cases training managers like to see how well their centre is doing compared with other centres in the scheme. In first year off-the-job training for the engineering industry a testing scheme is available which compares each centre with all other centres taking part in the scheme. Centres may take phased tests or end tests. Centre performance is given in the form of a stanine scale. The stanine scale has nine points, ranging from one to nine. The highest stanine score is nine and the lowest is one, and stanine five is located precisely in the middle of the distribution of scores. Two examples are given in Figures 8.14(a) and 14(b).

In the first example, the centre has performed reasonably well on the mechanical specialization but falls below the average on fabrication and electrical. This would tend to indicate that the level of training for electrical and fabrication is below that for mechanical, although the centre may have been brought down by a few poor candidates. This can be checked by referring to the results list provided which gives details of individual candidates performance. In the second example, this centre taking phased tests is above average on phases five and seven and average on phase six. However, its performance on phases one and three is below average. The overall stanine for this centre is four which is slightly below average. The inference here is that the training content or method is at fault on phases one and three since the candidates' performance as a group was poor and it is unlikely that the whole group would be comprised of candidates who were of below average ability. It may be that this centre does not consider fitting and heat treatment to be of great importance and would not be unduly worried by these results.

Comparing different training methods

It was seen in Chapter 1 how the US Army used tests to assess the effectiveness of two methods of training tank crews. The same kind of comparison is possible in industry if one has two or more groups of trainees undergoing different courses of training with the same objectives. The tests are used as a measure of how far the training objectives have been met.

In one study a group of trainees on a course comprised of one year off-the-job plus one year on-the-job training (Group A) were compared with trainees undergoing two years of on-the-job training (Group B).

Figure 8.15 shows their relative performance on a number of hands-on tests. Only on two tests were there any statistically significant difference between the two groups.

Interpreting and Utilizing Test Results

Example 1: An end test centre
Confidential not for publication

CENTRE STATISTICS

First year engineering end test

Albert Technical College   000010

Phase/section	Stanine	Candidates
Mechanical	5	6
Fabrication	3	9
Electrical	3	4

Figure 8.14(a)   Centre statistics for an End Test Centre

Example 2: A phased test centre
Confidential not for publication

CENTRE STATISTICS

First year engineering phased tests

O'Nottagain College, Knotty Ash, Notts   007050

Phase/section	Stanine	Candidates
Phase 1	2	11
Phase 2	4	11
Phase 3	3	11
Phase 4	4	11
Phase 5	7	11
Phase 6	5	11
Phase 7	7	11
Phase 10	5	11
Overall	4	11

Figure 8.14(b)   Centre statistics for a Phased Test Centre

Interpreting and Utilizing Test Results

Test area	Median score Group A	Median score Group B	Maximum possible score	Result of statistical test (if applied)	Critical points
1 Fitting	3	3	5	Not applied	Not applied
2 Jumpering	3	3	4	Not significant	—
3 Auto construction	8	7	10	Not significant	Not significant
4 Faulting (a)	3	1	3	Significant at 5% level	Not significant
Faulting (b)	—	—	—	—	Not significant
5 Relay adjustment	4	4	5	Not applied	Not significant
6 Test desk	1	2	3	Not significant	Difference significant at 0.1% level in Group B's favour
7 Cable jointing	6	5	10	Not significant	Not significant
8 Terminal block	4	4	4	Not significant	Not significant

Figure 8.15 **Table showing relative performance of two groups of trainees**

What is worth noting is that in some areas both groups performed reasonably well whereas except for Test 4, if one group did poorly the other group tended to do so also, suggesting the training of both groups fell short in these areas.

It is important when designing such experiments to pay attention to the selection of groups (to ensure their equivalence) and to the statistical treatment of data. Since decisions will probably be made on the basis of the results, it is particularly important to ensure that any differences represent 'real' differences and not to assume that a difference in the average score necessarily represents a difference between the groups' scores. As with all test development, care must be taken that the marking schemes are objective and the tests reliable.

SUGGESTED FURTHER READING

Belbin E., *Self-Testing as a Learning Motivator*, Industrial and Commercial Training, Volume 3, Number 5, May 1971.

Selection and Basic Training of Fork Truck Operators, Road Transport Industry Training Board, 1972.

'The Nature and Interpretation of Employee Merit Ratings', Hawthorne Works, Western Electric Company in Whisler T.L. and Harper S.F., Ed., *Performance Appraisal*, Holt, Rinehart and Winston, New York, 1962.

Jones A., *The Use of Performance Tests in Monitoring and Validating Training*, The Training Officer, Volume 8, Number 4, 1972.

Science Research Associates Inc. Chicago, Illinois, 'Short Occupational Knowledge Tests'.

Stead W.H. et al., *Occupational Counselling Technique*, American Book, New York, 1940, quoted on p.283 of Cronbach, *Essentials of Psychological Testing*.

Fitzpatrick R. and Morrison E.J., *Performance and Product Evaluation*, in 'Education Measurement', Thorndike R.L. Ed., American Council for Education, 1971.

Thorndike R.L. and Hagen E.P., *Measurement and Evaluation in Psychology and Education*, John Wiley and Sons, New York, 1969, Chap.17 'Marks and Marking' — a discussion of normative marking.

Phased Test and End Test Manuals, Skills Testing Service, City and Guilds of London Institute, 1971.

9

The Process of Validation

A test is a measurement of a standard sample of human behaviour, which should allow one to draw meaningful conclusions about an individual's attainments. To do this, the test should be measuring the relevant skills — generally known as validity — and measuring them consistently — generally known as reliability.

Validation refers to the process of ensuring that a test is valid for a given purpose. It is worth noting that a test may be reliable without being valid, that is it may be measuring skills and knowledge consistently, but the wrong skills and knowledge. However, to be valid a test must be reliable; if a test were unreliable it might be measuring different skills or knowledge at different times so it obviously could not be measuring only the relevant skills and knowledge. Therefore, validation must also take account of the consistency of measurements. So far the authors have talked about ensuring objectivity, which in performance testing is usually the most important aspect of consistency.

It is unfortunate that because of the needs of presenting the subject of test development, the discussion of 'validation' as such has been left until near the end of the book. This may suggest that validation is something to be tacked on to the end of test development whereas the concept of test validity is the prime one at each stage of constructing a test (see Figure 9.1). When the job or course is analysed in order to select the correct skills to test, or to decide on the most appropriate way to test them, or to try to assess performance on the test in an objective way and so on, we are attempting to increase the validity of the test. Not only is validation a continuing process, it should also be an empirical one. The test developer or user should not rely on opinions and guesses; he should base the process of validation on facts.

The Process of Validation

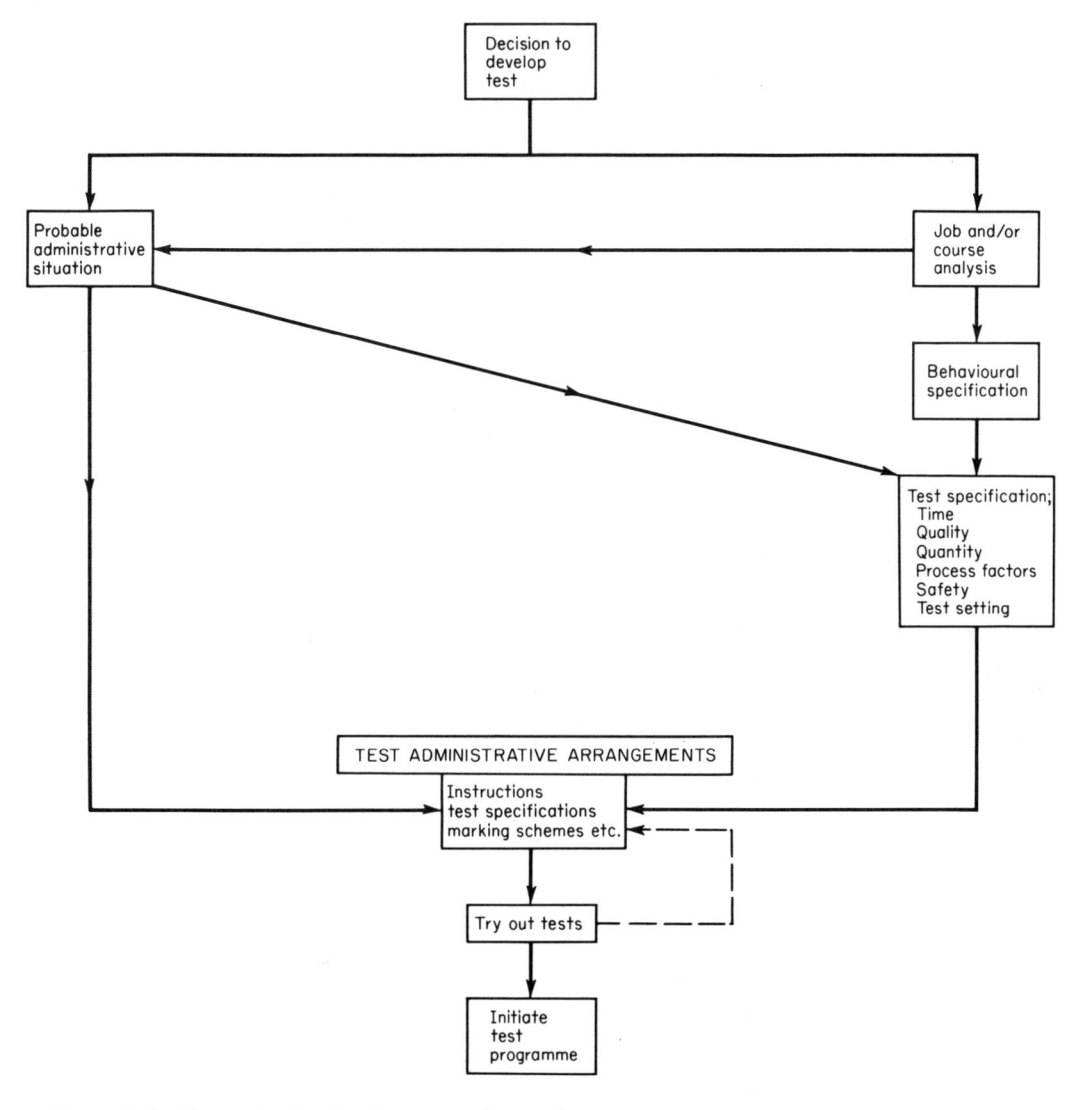

Figure 9.1 Stages in the development of a performance test

THE VALIDATION OF PERFORMANCE TESTS

Many readers will be familiar with the concept of 'validity' from intelligence testing, aptitude testing, and so on, where the usual approach to determining validity is to check the test score against some other observation that serves as a criterion. This method is adopted because in such cases the interest is in using the test score to predict how well an individual will perform the criterion behaviour; the merit of the test is judged by the accuracy of prediction it offers. This type of validity is known as predictive validity. An example might be a test designed to help in the selection of personnel for a certain kind of training and ultimately a certain kind of job

The Process of Validation

The authors will argue that this approach to the problem of validity is usually inappropriate in performance testing and that the uncritical adoption of its concepts and methods leads not only to confusion but also sometimes to nonsense.

The validity of performance tests designed to measure the acquisition of skills is usually expressed in terms of 'content validity' which can be described as the extent to which the content of the test reflects the content of the area of proficiency in which one is interested. For example, a typing test may be considered valid if it contains examples of typical typing material and the assessment of performance takes into account realistic speed and error rates. However the concept of validity in performance testing is still a cloudy one. Panitz and Olivo[1] surveying competence testing in the USA concluded that the problems of validity and reliability had been 'barely scratched'. This situation was equally true in industry, the military, and special test agencies. Content validity was generally based on the authority of recognized experts, such as experienced tradesmen and teachers. Unfortunately content validity is sometimes no better than face validity; that is assuming the test is valid because superficially it looks valid. Baldwin[2] points out that face validity, although generally desirable, does have its disadvantages, notably a tendency on the part of the test developer to ignore such factors as test reliability.

Elsewhere in test literature many types of validity are discussed, but the authors have restricted themselves to talking about content validity, predictive validity, concurrent validity, and construct validity. Figure 9.2 sets out the characteristics of these types of validity. The approach chosen should reflect the purpose of the test.

The reader may have come across references to 'construct validity' this approach is often found in psychological research and is closely related to theories and the design of experiments. Here one proposes that a test measures a given type of behaviour or ability and adduces evidence to support this contention. In a sense every approach to validity may be seen as 'construct validity', since the latter involves putting forward a proposition about a test ('this test measures such-and-such') and then trying to show that the proposition is correct. However, construct validity is usually thought of as relating to situations where the form or content of the test may raise doubts. For example does that rather impressive battery of hands-off tests really assess fault-finding skills which are used on-the-job? If it does then certain conclusions can be drawn (eg trainees should score higher after ten weeks training than after five weeks) and one can check to see if these conclusions are correct.

The predictive validity method is used when attempting to validate a test intended to predict future performance from test scores. The method requires that test scores, or predictions made from them, be compared with an independent measure of the performance in which there is interest. Although this method is the usual one with aptitude tests, it is difficult to apply to performance tests since the development of a suitable independent criterion measure usually poses the same problems (including validation) as the development of the performance test itself.

Suppose, for example, one is dealing with a battery of work-sample tests for motor mechanics. The test battery is intended to sample adequately motor mechanics' work. It might therefore be argued that people who do well on the test would in future also do well on some measure of on-the-job performance, and that people who perform poorly on the test would perform poorly on-the-job. It would be necessary to devise an independent measure of proficient on-the-job performance. However, any such measure of performance would have to be validated before its results could be relied upon. Since the test battery was originally intended as a measure of proficiency in motor mechanics' work one ends up in a viscious circle.

Type	Question asked	Procedure	Example
Content validity	How good a sample is the test?	Determine whether the test gives a representative and fair measure of performance on some set of tasks by comparing content of test with the content of the area it is supposed to measure.	A set of tasks for motor mechanics is examined to see if it measures typical and important aspects of a mechanics work.
Predictive validity	How well does the test predict a certain future performance?	Determine whether test scores predict the future score in which there is interest by giving it and using scores to predict outcome. Some time later obtain a measure of the outcome. Compare the prediction with the outcome.	A trainability assessment for motor mechanics is developed and results compared with performance at the end of the training course.
Concurrent validity	How well does the test discriminate between present levels of ability?	Determine whether the test assesses the performance in which there is interest by giving the test and obtaining a 'direct' measure of performance. Compare the two.	As a substitute for a lengthy selection procedure, a short trade knowledge test for motor mechanics is introduced. Scores on the test are compared with supervisers ratings or other performance criteria.
Construct validity	What evidence is there that the test is in fact measuring what it is supposed to?	Various procedures depending on situation. The experimental procedure is often similar to that used in the concurrent validity situation.	A hands-off fault-finding test for mechanics is given to an experienced and inexperienced group. If the test is valid, then the experienced group should have higher scores.

Figure 9.2 Types of performance test validity

The Process of Validation

Ebel[3] points out that at some stage the test developer must decide what is the best available measure of the ability in which he is interested. One can see that in many cases the performance test which one has developed will appear to be the best measure. It is pointless to then attempt to validate this best measure against an inferior one. In any case performance tests of skills and knowledge are not intended to predict (at least not in the same way as aptitude tests) but to *discriminate* between those who have the necessary skills and those who do not. A more appropriate validation technique is the concurrent validation. (It becomes arguable in some cases whether a concurrent or construct validity approach is involved.)

The concurrent validation approach involves comparing scores on the test with some other measure or index of ability. For example, test scores might be compared with grades given by instructors. However, such measures may themselves be suspect; grades might be affected by a trainees' verbal ability or 'good' behaviour. Again the test might be the best available measure.

The influence of predictive validity studies has been considerable; many people think of validity only in terms of a correlation coefficient. Yet test validation can take a number of forms; the form it takes will depend chiefly on the use that is to be made of the test. What one validates is not the test in isolation but the interpretation that one puts on the candidate's test score. Whatever validation studies the test developer or user carries out simply provide more information to guide interpretation of test scores. Validation refers not to the test as such but to *the interpretation of the test results arising from the specified test procedure*. A single test can be used for a number of purposes, so that, for example, one would probably apply different validity methods to a test when used at the end of a course and when used as a selection device.

From this we can see that in a large number of situations many performance tests may be looked at chiefly from the content validity point of view. Performance tests based on content validation may be looked on as instruments for absolute measurement; the test indicates whether or not a person can perform a certain task or knows a certain fact. If the test content is selected in a valid way, then the test is content valid for persons of all kinds (subject to any limitations related to the form of the test and the cultural background of the candidate). By its nature, content validity is impermanent since how representative a test is of an area may change with the passage of time. Technological change may make certain tasks or standards irrelevant, or new tasks may have emerged. Correlation coefficients have nothing to do with content validity.

It has been seen that in performance testing it is important to distinguish between criterion-referenced and norm-referenced tests; norm-referenced tests are used for distinguishing between individuals whereas criterion-referenced tests are used for distinguishing between levels of performance. Norm-referenced tests should have available a set of norms for the test user. Although norms are a characteristic of psychological tests together with predictive validity, norm-referenced performance tests need not be based on predictive validity. For example, a concurrent validity approach could be used and reference norms developed entirely on the performance of the present set of job incumbents, as with many short tests of trade knowledge.

Once it is recognized that validation refers to the validity of interpretation of test scores, it can see that one equally cannot talk of *the* predictive or *the* concurrent validity of a test. If a criterion-referenced test is used, then the validity of test scores can only be ascertained using a method which involves the examination of scores above and below the criterion. For example, if passing or failing a test is supposed to discriminate between good and poor personnel, then the validity must show the relationship between achieving the criterion and being satisfactory on-the-job. If the criterion is not taken into account then a predictive or concurrent validity study can only validate the content of the test; it may also validate it in a norm-referenced way, but this may well be irrelevant to a criterion-referenced test.

RELIABILITY

Reliability refers to the consistency of measurement of a test. With performance testing, this concept has two facets; first the reliability of the marking of the candidate's performance and secondly the reliability of the candidate's performance itself. If a test were completely reliable then one could be confident that the candidate's result would be the same if tested on another occasion or using a different test measuring the same area. However, no test is ever completely reliable. Below are listed some possible sources of unreliability, some of which are more relevant to hands-on tests, others to hands-off tests.

1. Lack of objectivity in the marking scheme, leading to low interexaminer reliability.
2. Lack of standardization in the administrative situation.
3. General abilities and attitudes of the candidate such as reading skills, ability to comprehend instructions, familiarity with test situations, 'examination technique' attitudes, emotional reactions or habits operating in test situations (eg self confidence).
4. Temporary characteristics of the candidate such as level of health, fatigue, emotional strain, motivation, fluctuations in attention, fluctuations in memory for particular facts, temporary emotional states.
5. Guessing.

Any of these sources may lead to the measure of attainment being contaminated, and it is important to realize that any test has the inherent possibility of inconsistency from these and other sources.

Cronbach[4] argues that low reliability is a characteristic of tests where one error may disturb the entire sequence of the performance, as may be the case with complex performance tests.

It is worth noting that in such cases a perfect or near perfect performance is likely to reflect the true level of ability of the candidate. The difficulty is that a poor performance may not indicate a truly poor level of performance; on another occasion the candidate might achieve a perfect score because the previous small error was avoided.

One remedy is to take several samples of the candidates performance. For example, Gibson[5] used a large number of short, similar items rather than a few

The Process of Validation

complex sequences of performance. Another remedy is to mark the performance at appropriate stages so that such errors can at least be identified as they occur. In a way this procedure involves splitting the test into subtests, although the subtests are not completely independent. In other words, increasing the length of the test or number of assessments can lead to increased test reliability. However, there is obviously a point where increase in cost is not justified by the corresponding increase in reliability.

To determine the reliability of marking, an estimate is obtained of the likely amount of agreement between examiners by comparing the marks awarded by a number of examiners for the same product or process. From such data a number of correlation coefficients can be calculated between pairs of examiners or an average intercorrelation using an analysis of variance technique[6]. Illustrating the use of the correlation coefficient for interexaminer reliability, Mackie and High[7] report a test for machinist repairmen which involved the product of a valve stem and hex fitting (Figure 9.3). The product component was assessed using 33 separate inspections, 16 of them involving the use of rules and calipers and the remaining 17 involving more subjective judgements of fit, finish, and alignment of valve stem and fitting. The agreement between two examiners who both marked 64 test pieces expressed in terms of a correlation coefficient (Spearman's Rho) ranged between 0.70 and 0.98 for the 'objective' measures and between 0.71 and 0.99 for the more subjective measures. Most correlations were above 0.90. Clearly both 'objective' and 'subjective' items may lead to high or low agreement. The correlation coefficient for the total score was 0.98, indicating high reliability between these two examiners in placing candidates in rank order.

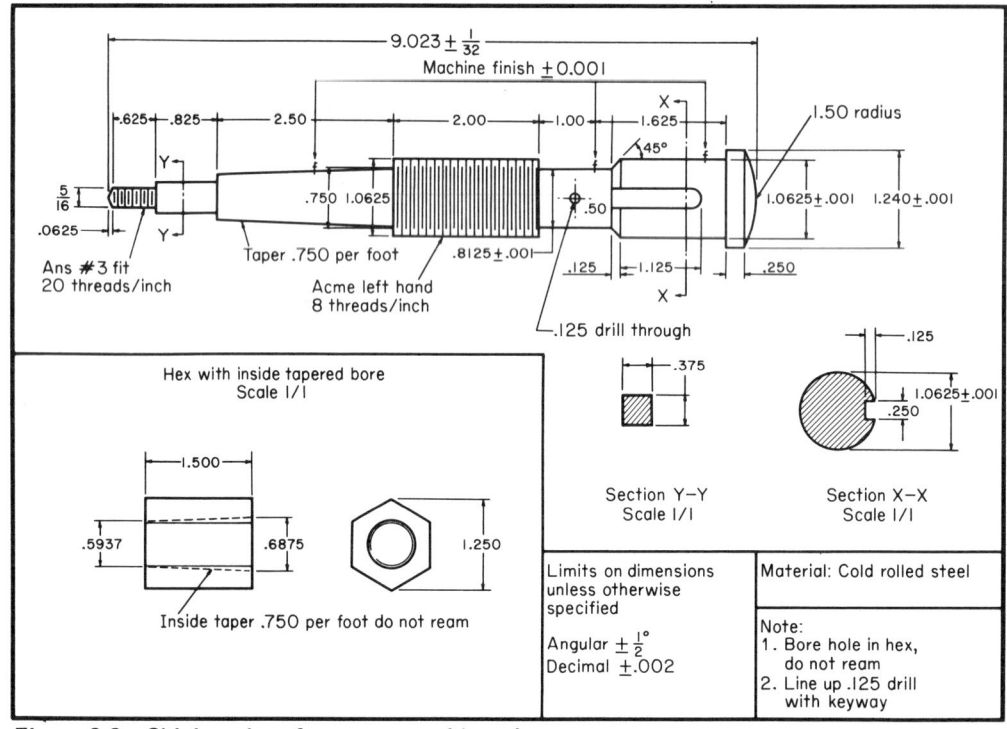

Figure 9.3 Shipboard performance test blueprint

The reliability of examiners assessments can also be expressed in terms of percentage agreement when go/no go decisions or measures of quantity are made. Percentage agreement is calculated by the formula:

$$100 \times \frac{number\ of\ agreements}{(number\ of\ agreements) + (number\ of\ disagreements)}$$

Number of disagreements includes any omissions, since the divisor is the total number of judgements or scores. This technique can be used for overall test results or for individual items in a marking scheme. For example, the use of the specially designed taper gauge shown in Figure 6.4 increased the amount of agreement in marking the taper from 65 to 99% in a study carried out by the authors[17]. To indicate what the index of agreement might mean in practice, 90% agreement would indicate that on average nine examiners out of ten would give the same mark to the test-piece on a particular item in the marking scheme. If interexaminer reliability is calculated and it is found that the intercorrelation is reasonably high (Ryans and Fredericksen[9] suggest around +0.90) or the percentage agreement is reasonably high (around 90%) then it may be decided that this aspect of reliability is satisfactory. Of course, in a practical situation examiners whose marks depart significantly from those of the majority of examiners can be identified and remedial action taken in the form of examiner training sessions and so on.

The procedures which can increase interexaminer reliability are:

1   Selection of better-trained examiners.
2   Training examiners to use the particular marking scheme involved.
3   Defining the standard of performance as objectively as possible.
4   Developing where possible special instruments for marking the product. It was noted in Chapter 6 that the introduction of a set of taper gauges considerably increased interexaminer reliability.

With hands-on tests the determination of interexaminer reliability is usually all that is carried out. This is in part because the estimation of the reliability of candidates' performance poses many practical problems.

It is also worth considering the meaning of the reliability of performance. With a complex task such as a test-piece involving turning and milling, with a functional go/no go criterion such as it being within stated tolerances, there is probably little chance of a candidate meeting the criterion on one occasion and not on another. The situation with a less complex or shorter sequence of behaviour may be different in that chance factors may play a more important role. However, one answer here is to have the candidate perform the task more than once or perform a number of similar tasks. It is unlikely in such a case that the candidates observed performance would not be a true reflection of his level of ability. With hands-off tests, reliability of performance can be increased with a longer test, since a more thorough or representative sample is obtained. The better the sample of items or tasks the more reliable the test should be.

The methods of determining reliability are set out in Figure 9.4. Although they may be used with hands-off tests, their use with hands-on tests is much more restricted.

The Process of Validation

Method	Procedure	Possible restrictions	Example
Interexaminer	Have a number of examiners mark the same end-products or performances and compare marks awarded.	May be difficult to arrange for the assessment of process, unless videotape etc is used.	Marks awarded by a number of examiners marking the same test piece using the same marking scheme.
Test–retest	Test the same group of candidates using same test on two occasions. Calculate correlations between scores on two occasions.	In performance testing candidates may benefit from practice of skills in interval between test sessions or in performing test itself.	A test for high level of skill in fitting is given to a highly experienced group on 2 occasions a month apart.
Equivalent forms method	Give two tests designed to assess the same skills/knowledge to the same group. Calculate correlation between two tests.	Difficult to ensure tests are equivalent.	Two tests in milling given to same group of engineering trainees and scores on two tests compared.
Internal consistency methods	Give a test to a group of candidates. Subdivide test in some way and calculate correlations between these divisions.	Difficult to apply to hands-on tests but can often be used with paper and pencil tests.	A test in reading engineering drawings is given to a group of trainees. Scores on even test items compared with scores on odd test items.

Figure 9.4 Methods of determining reliability

An obvious way to see if a test measures consistently is to give the test to the same group of candidates on two occasions. This is known as the test–retest method. Obviously this method poses problems; for example, it is usually argued that the two occasions should be sufficiently separated so that candidates cannot remember their answers on paper and pencil tests from the previous occasion and simply rewrite them. However, if too long a gap is left, the individual's ability may really change, so that the eventual discrepancy in test scores may represent a real change and not an inconsistency in the test. With a hands-on test the candidates may indeed benefit from practice of the relevant skills whilst performing the tests.

Indeed, with hands-on tests there is an argument for having the two testing sessions as close together as possible, so that real increases in skill cannot take place. The only problem here is that there may be specific (memory) carry-overs from one sessions to another. However, with a skill such a bricklaying such effects are likely to be limited and so to test one day and then repeat the test the next day might be an efficient procedure. However, the test—retest method tends to give a low-estimate of test reliability and can be rather impractical for hands-on tests.

Another approach is to have two equivalent forms of the test and compare scores on the two forms. Of course the problem here is in developing two truly equivalent forms and again an underestimate of reliability tends to result. This method nevertheless is probably a reasonable proposition with many skills.

There are several internal consistency methods. A common one is to split the test into two halves and compare candidates' scores on the two halves. This procedure can only be adopted if the test is intended to measure the 'same thing' throughout all its parts or items. Otherwise, if a low correlation were obtained this might be because measures of different skills were being compared. This is a particular problem with hands-on tests, since it is often difficult to split up a test into parts which are legitimately comparable. A candidate may perform one aspect well because of adequate training and another badly because of short-comings in the training programme. It may, however, be a more feasible method with short-cycle repetitive tasks.

The valve stem and hex fitting test-piece mentioned above was subject to an internal consistency reliability study and it is interesting to note the method employed. The test—retest method was not possible because of shortage of machine time. The split-half reliability estimate for the total performance test score was made by assigning the 33 separate scores derived from the product into two halves such that approximately the same number of scores for lengths, diameters, fits, and finish was represented in each half. In addition an attempt was made to represent each basic type of operation in the two halves (see the table in Figure 9.5). When this was done the resulting reliability (corrected) for the performance test total score was 0.87.

While the authors recognized that the assumptions for split-half reliability estimates could hardly be justified with a test that is known to be complex in terms of the variety of skills involved it was felt that this estimate was better than nothing.

For paper and pencil tests there are a number of techniques available which give an estimate of internal consistency based on correlations between items (for example, the Kuder—Richardson methods).

Internal consistency methods can only be used when the candidate has ample time to finish the test, whereas the other two methods can be used whether or not ample time is available. Each of these methods focuses attention on a possible source of error in the test; with test—retest it is the possible change in scores over time; with equivalent forms it is the possible unrepresentativeness of the sample of behaviour elicited by one test; with internal consistency it is the possible fluctuation in the content of items within the test. The different methods of estimating reliability therefore not only involve different procedures but also involve different interpretations. The test—retest procedure provides an index of the stability of a score over time, whereas the equivalent forms procedure indicates the equivalence of scores representing different samples of test behaviour. The internal consistency methods yield a similar index of how consistent items or combinations of test items are.

The Process of Validation

	A		B
1	ANS thread length	3	ANS thread diameter
2	ANS thread finish		
4	Taper length	6	Taper diameter
5	Taper fit	7	Taper finish
8	Body length		
9	Body finish	10	Body diameter
11	Flat diameter	13	Flat width
12	Flat finish		
14	Undercut diameter	15	Undercut length
		16	Undercut finish
17	Pinhole alignment	18	Pinhole diameter
19	Hex nut diagonal	20	Hex nut fit (inside bore)
		21	Hex nut length
22	Keyway depth	23	Keyway width
		24	Keyway length
25	Square length	26	Square width
27	Acme thread finish		
28	Acme thread diameter	29	Acme thread length
30	Bevel finish	31	Bevel fit
32	Radius fit	33	Radius finish

Figure 9.5 Division of scores into halves for reliability estimate of valve stem and hex fitting test

With paper and pencil tests Kuder–Richardson methods are probably the most popular and the test–retest and alternate forms are little used. In fact in Boyd and Shimberg[10] out of about 140 achievement tests, half used either Kuder–Richardson or split-half methods. Sixty of the tests reported no reliability data at all.

For readers who wish to deal with these methods and their statistics more fully, further references are given at the end of the chapter. For the purposes of the rest of the chapter, it is only necessary to understand the basic concepts outlined above.

It was noted at the beginning of this chapter that the less reliable a test is, the lower its validity will be. The degree of reliability of the test puts a limit to its validity. With a criterion-referenced test, one is concerned with the reliability of scores around the criterion, that is, for example, a candidate who passes the test on one occasion should pass it on another. So unless a test is consistent about placing a candidate in his correct relation to the criterion, it will not be a valid criterion-referenced measure.

RELIABILITY OF CRITERION-REFERENCED TESTS

The concept of test reliability has been defined verbally as the degree of stability or consistency of a test as a measuring instrument.

In 'classical test theory'[11] any score a candidate receives on a test can be conceived as being composed of two components: the true score, or 'real' assessment of a candidate's ability, and the error score resulting from the imperfection of the test as a measuring instrument.

Statistically, reliability is expressed in the theoretical formula

$$Reliability = \frac{True\ Score\ Variance}{Obtained\ Score\ Variance}$$

or, since obtained score variance is composed of true and error variance:

$$Reliability = \frac{Obtained\ Score\ Variance - Error\ Score\ Variance}{Obtained\ Score\ Variance}$$

Where variance is a measure of the spread of scores about the mean of a distribution of scores. Thus error score variance is an estimate of the spread of error scores, and obtained score variance is a measure of the spread of scores actually obtained. It has been seen that in practice reliability must be estimated using one of the traditional methods; test–retest, alternate forms, or an internal consistency method, since only in this way can error score variance be estimated. In a test–retest situation error score variance would be the spread of the discrepancies of candidates' scores on the two occasions.

However, this theory has been developed in situations where the normative grading of test candidates was the prime consideration, that is the placing of a candidate's score in relation to other scores. The mean and deviations from the mean are used as the basis for such calculations. But with criterion-referenced tests this may be inappropriate, since the point of reference is the criterion rather than the average score of the candidates.

The test developer and user is therefore in something of a dilemma when it comes to estimating the reliability of criterion referenced measures, since classical test theory has been developed with norm-referenced procedures. Popham and Husek[12] argue that the traditional theory might lead to an irrelevant or incorrect estimation of reliability. This estimate may be an underestimate since reliability theory is based on the existence of differences among the true scores of candidates while criterion-based measures may be used in situations in which there need be no such differences. According to Baldwin[2] in such circumstances traditional methods of estimating reliability become 'meaningless'. He also points out that if a training course were really meeting its objectives, the more difficult it would be using these methods to demonstrate reliability since differences between trainees would be minimized. In such a situation correlation coefficients will tend to be small since total variance is small.

Livingston[13] therefore proposed the following revision of the theoretical formula:

The Process of Validation

Criterion referenced reliability coefficient =

$$\frac{Obtained\ score\ variance\ -\ error\ variance\ +\ (mean\ -\ criterion)^2}{Obtained\ score\ variance\ +\ (mean\ -\ criterion)^2}$$

In other words, the distance of the criterion from the mean is taken into account in the estimation. In fact it follows that the further the criterion moves from the mean, the greater the criterion-referenced reliability coefficient will be. The problem with Livingston's suggestion is that in practice one still has to estimate the reliability coefficient by a traditional norm-referenced approach since the true and error score variances must be derived from this estimate and the observed score variance, 'correction' is then added to allow for the fact that a criterion-referenced measure is being dealt with.

This correction can give a considerably boosted estimate of test reliability[14]. However, the initial calculation still uses norm-referenced estimation techniques based on deviations from the mean rather than from the criterion. Livingston justifies this procedure by use of mathematical proofs but a procedure taking the criterion into account from the initial stages of the calculation might be more attractive. Moreover, Livingston's techniques would seem limited to situations where the criterion is a cut-off point on some scale involving numerical scores such as a job knowledge test of 50 items. One must, therefore, consider what to do if the test results are classified as pass or fail to begin with.

A technique which can be used to take the criterion into account is the phi coefficient, which can be used in test-retest studies, equivalent form studies, and for estimating the correlation between two examiners. For example, the authors[8] used the phi coefficient to describe the amount of agreement obtained when three examiners marked the same ten test-pieces produced by first-year trainees in an engineering centre. The phi coefficients obtained gave a more realistic index of the amount of agreement present, as regards passing and failing candidates, than did the Pearson's product-moment correlation coefficients calculated for the same data. For example, a phi coefficient of +0.17 as against a Pearson's *r* of +0.57 for a pair of examiners where one failed eight candidates and the other failed only one. A norm-referenced approach may therefore give an under or over estimate in terms of reliability around the criterion which emphasizes the point that it is meaningless to talk in terms of test reliability without reference to the methods and statistics involved.

The index of percentage agreement mentioned earlier can also be calculated from the same data as the phi coefficient. Since results are expressed as go or no go, such an index takes the criterion into account. For example, below is a table describing the results of an imaginary test—retest study for a bricklaying test involving duplicate testing for 100 candidates.

	Fail	Pass
Test session 1	10	75
Test session 2	10	5

It can be seen that 75 candidates passed on both occasions, ten failed on the first occasion but passed on the second, and so on. The percentage agreement would be:

$$100 \times \frac{(\textit{No. candidates passed both times}) + (\textit{No. of candidates failed both times})}{\textit{Total number candidates}}$$

$$100 \times \frac{10 + 75}{100} = 85\%$$

There is then 85% agreement as regards the reliability or stability of candidates' performance on this test. Separate indices could be calculated for the reliability of failures or passes, eg

$$100 \times \frac{\textit{Number of candidates who failed on both sessions}}{\textit{Total number of failures on session 1 and 2}} =$$

$$100 \times \frac{10}{25} = 40\%$$

gives the percentage agreement for unsuccessful candidates, while

$$100 \times \frac{75}{90} = 83\%$$

is the percentage agreement for successful candidates. This indicates that the performance of successful candidates is much more reliable or stable than that of unsuccessful ones. In other words a person who passes on one occasion is likely to pass on another, whereas a person who fails on one occasion may or may not fail on a subsequent one. In some situations it may be necessary to calculate separate reliabilities for different groups, for example a test of trade knowledge to discriminate between journeymen, apprentices, and 'handymen' may need to quote separate reliability data for each group.

Figure 9.6 gives a rough guide to some of the techniques which can be used in the estimation of reliability in both norm-referenced and criterion-referenced situations.

A VALIDATION CHECKLIST

Below are two checklists designed to help readers assess the validity of a test. One checklist is for hands-on and the other for hands-off tests.

Hands-on tests

1 Does the test include the relevant skills as specified by an analysis of the job or course?
2 Does the marking scheme assess the *relevant* aspects of performance?

The Process of Validation

3   Has the marking scheme been designed to achieve optimum objectivity/agreement between examiners?
4   Are the correct standards of performance embodied in the test?
5   Are instructions and other documentation such that administration is as uniform as possible?

Hands-off tests

1   Have test content and marking been developed using sound analytic principles so that the candidate is provided with the same or equivalent information as in the actual situation and so that the questions asked regarding the information are designed to discriminate between different levels of the relevant aspects of the skill?
2   Are candidates' performances on the test reliable?
3   Is marking sufficiently objective?
4   (If it is possible or thought necessary to ascertain this.) Do the tests discriminate between and/or within groups of known ability or between groups which should score differently if the test is measuring the correct skills?
5   Are the instructions readily understood and is administration as uniform as possible?
6   Is the form of the test likely to alienate candidates?

Reliability		Norm-referenced	Criterion-referenced
Interexaminer	Pair of examiners	Pearson's product-moment correlation coefficient Spearman's rank correlation coefficient	Phi coefficient Percentage agreement
	More than two examiners	Analysis of variance Kendall's coefficient of concordance	Percentage agreement
Test–retest		Pearson's product-moment correlation coefficient Spearman's rank correlation coefficient	Phi coefficient Livingston's correction Percentage agreement
Equivalent forms		Pearson's product-moment correlation coefficient Spearman's rank correlation coefficient	Phi coefficient Livingston's correction Percentage agreement
Internal consistency (homogeneous and power tests)		Split half — Pearson's product-moment correlation coefficient Kuder–Richardson	Livingston's correction

Figure 9.6   Statistical techniques for reliability studies

PROCESS OF EVALUATION

Even if one has ascertained that a test is valid, it is worthwhile to ask the questions 'Is the test doing any good?' and 'If the test is doing any good, is the latter sufficient to justify the cost of development and administration?' These and similar questions refer to the process of evaluation.

Evaluation differs from validation in that the former attempts to measure the overall benefit of the testing system and not just whether the test meets the required standards as an instrument of measurement. Evaluation is like validation in one sense; it is a continuing process and not a once and for all event.

The evaluation of any training of personnel system in quantifiable terms is usually a very difficult exercise and the evaluation of a testing system is no exception. However, the fact that it may be difficult to apply precise criteria to the situations does not mean that the attempt should be abandoned, even if more approximate measures have to be used.

Some of the questions we might ask in evaluating a testing system are:

1. Does the testing system fulfil the purpose originally intended? Eg if tests are required to measure proficiency at the end of a training course, do they in fact do this?
2. Has the testing system increased the motivation of trainees?
3. Does the testing system provide information which can be used for remedial training and retraining?
4. Has the introduction of tests led to an examination and possible revision of training objectives, content, or method?
5. Since the introduction of tests, have line managers reported an increase in the standard of working of trainees or job applicants sent to them?
6. Has the introduction of tests generated any administrative or 'political' problems? Eg instructors have to work longer hours preparing for and marking the tests, or there has been a demand for increase in pay from men now certified as qualified in a given area.
7. Are the various persons involved satisfied with the test?
8. Finally (and most important) do the benefits of the type indicated above justify the cost of the development and administration of the system?

It is worthwhile outlining the major areas of cost in a test system:

System development costs

This will be chiefly in terms of time spent by the test developer and any expert advisers or other contacts he has to consult. Pilot testing will involve time spent by candidates and examiners, materials, and equipment.

Running costs

Once testing is introduced, the cost of actual test sessions will be time spent by candidates, examiners, and invigilators and the cost of materials and equipment.

Data processing costs

In this category one has the time spent in determining individual candidates' results, marking paper and pencil tests, recording such data and so on.

System maintenance costs

A testing system must be subjected to validation and evaluation in some form or other. Revisions of tests may need to be carried out. New methods of testing may need to be investigated and so on.

It is worth noting that many testing costs are often hidden. A training centre has instructors on the premises whether instructing or examining, likewise the equipment used may be normally in use in training or actual production. These are nevertheless testing costs and should be considered in the evaluation of a testing system.

EXAMPLES OF ASSESSING THE VALIDITY OF TESTS

A number of case studies will be described in assessing the validity of tests or evaluating the impact of testing systems, which will illustrate some of the methods and criteria which have just been discussed. Some of the studies concentrate exclusively on determining validity while others involve descriptions of both validation and evaluation. It must be emphasized that evaluation is just as essential as validation, or else valid tests may be being used to no purpose.

Study One
Examining the content of tests for machine trades

Since in performance testing so much trust is placed on content validity, one would expect tests covering the same area to be more or less uniform in content in order to cover the requirements of job specifications, etc. Panitz and Olivo[1] found this was far from the case in an analysis of five performance tests from different organizations in the USA covering machine trades. The tests showed an overall emphasis on turning and lathe work. One test involved producing several short test pieces: one, requiring operations such as drilling and other bench work, drill press processes, surface grinding and simple milling machine work and operations. Another test consisted of turning, milling, and universal grinder operations. The other performance tests concentrated on turning processes and lathe work, simple milling operations, and elementary layout work, usually requiring the making of one or more test pieces.

Panitz and Olivo argue that there is no evidence that competence in machining work can be measured simply by acceptable performance on turning and milling processes, bench work and assembly operations. In fact several job specifications and job analyses indicate quite the reverse; a wide range of machine tools, heat treatment, bench and inspection practices are often required. The five tests were further rated on a variety of factors by a panel of tests and technical experts – see Figure 9.7. No one test was judged excellent on all categories, and on only one factor was one test judged excellent.

Factor	Excellent	Average	Poor
Currency of test content	1	2	2
Practicality	–	3	2
Comprehensiveness	–	3	2
Measurement of skills	–	3	2
Measurement of judgement	–	2	3
Measurement of diagnostic skills	–	2	3
Measurement of speed of work	–	3	2
Measurement of planning of procedures	–	3	2

Figure 9.7   Ratings of five performance tests for machine trades on a variety of factors

An examination of 12 paper and pencil tests covering the same area revealed a similar diversity of both content and format (Figure 9.8).

For example, only two of the tests included blueprint reading; three tests attempted to measure competence in the theory of machine sawing and filing operations; seven tests included items on current industrial practices; two tests included problems requiring the use of handbooks as found in the trade; two tests contained problems and processes relating to numerical control or instrumentation applications in the trade.

Within the structure of each of the tests, there was a tremendous variety in the range and number of test items. While all tests included items relating to bench work, turning operations, drilling and drill press operations, grinding practices, and milling machine processes, there was a wide variation in the number of test items supposed to measure competence in the same area as is shown in the table given in Figure 9.9.

All but one of the tests used multiple-choice type test items. Five tests contained only multiple-choice test items. Four tests used multiple-choice and true/false test items. One test utilized multiple-choice, true-false, completion, and short answer types of test items. One test contained true-false and essay-type items.

The sum total of the multiple-choice test items ranged from 65 on the test with the lowest number to 253 on the test with the highest number.

The investigators at first thought that the differences in content were the result of geographic differences in practice, but further examination showed that this was not the case.

This study besides illustrating the content validation of a number of tests demonstrates that different test developers can arrive at strikingly different tests for the same skills. Besides calling into question the analytic techniques employed, the study may also make the reader pause to consider that one superior test rather than a number of poor or mediocre ones might have been produced if resources has been pooled.

The Process of Validation

Factor	Excellent	Average	Poor
Currency of test content	2	4	6
Range of items	2	5	5
Type of items	1	5	6
Distribution of items	3	4	5
Clarity of items	2	3	7
Measurement of trade judgement	2	2	8
Practicality	2	2	8
Comprehensiveness	1	3	8

Figure 9.8   Ratings of 12 written tests for machine trades on a variety of factors

Major areas of the trade	Variation in number of test items
Bench and assembly work	2 to 25
Drilling machines and processes	6 to 22
Turning machines and processes (lathe work)	4 to 78
Grinding machines and processes	3 to 34
Milling machines and processes	4 to 26

Figure 9.9   Disparity in number of test items in major areas covered in all tests

Study Two
Establishing the validity of two hands-off tests

Boyd and Shimberg[15] report a study on the validity of a test comprised of a set of 50 photographs of small automobile parts, most of which were damaged or defective. This test is similar to that described in Chapter 4. The candidate has to identify the part, identify the fault (if any) in the part, and state the most likely cause of the fault. Obviously this was designed to avoid the cumbersome situation of having actual parts presented to the candidate, a procedure which would also have been difficult to standardize across a number of centres.

Since the rationale behind the test was that it should discriminate between good and poor identifiers of faults, three groups were selected which were held to represent different levels of ability in this area. The three groups were motor vehicle instructors, experienced motor mechanics, and storekeepers. The latter group was included since it was argued that storekeepers would be familiar with the appearance of the part but not with fault identification. Analysis of the scores of these three groups did in fact reveal a statistically significant difference between the groups. With instructors scoring highest, mechanics next, and storekeepers lowest. The test was therefore shown to be capable of discriminating between three levels (high, medium, and low) of fault-identification ability.

Similarly Baldwin[2] describes a test for auditory diagnosis of faults in motor vehicles. The test involved the candidate answering a multiple-choice question for each of 45 tape-recordings of malfunctioning parts. To determine the content of the test, instructors and mechanics were interviewed to ascertain the types of sounds important in auditory diagnosis. In order to provide a representative sample of types of vehicles, items were recorded for Chevrolets, Fords, and Plymouths approximately in proportion to the number of these cars on the road, using the most widely used engine for each make. When given to four groups (high school students, first-year mechanics, mechanics at the end of a two-year course, and experienced mechanics) the test discriminated between them, indicating that it was measuring skills associated with job proficiency. One might label the example given above as a 'construct validity' procedure since a hypothesis was put forward and tested out. If these tests were being used as selection devices, a 'concurrent validity procedure' would be adopted, the tests would be given to applicants or potential applicants and scores compared with some other performance criterion (eg previous job performance). The change in design is subtle but is linked to the purpose of the test.

Study Three
Investigating the validity of four batteries of performance tests

Another approach to determining validity is similar to the previous one and involves the comparison of the test scores of trainees at the completion of off-the-job training (for which the test has been devised) with those of a group which has had subsequent on-the-job experience. The assumption behind this method is that if the test is a valid one the score of the latter group should be at least equal to but preferably greater than the former group. If this is not the case then the test would seem to be measuring skills that are not required on the job. It is worth noting that a test may be an adequate measure of training acquisition and still perform poorly when subjected to this method of validation. This is because the technique used validates the test against present on-the-job requirements which may not be the same as training objectives. Using this technique one has to ensure that the off-the-job training content and methods have not changed radically between the two groups and that samples from the groups are selected by the same, preferably random, method. An alternative experimental design is to compare scores of the same group both immediately after off-the-job training and after related on-the-job experience. The latter design has the advantage that selection errors are reduced to a minimum but suffers from the disadvantage in many cases of having to wait several years before results are available. Often it may be appropriate to use the former technique to obtain an immediate estimate

The Process of Validation

of validity and then to follow up the younger group. It should be noted that either technique could be effected by systematic drop-out effects; for example less proficient trainees might leave and so increase the average score of the group anyway. This technique involves 'construct validity' and it is important to understand the logic behind it.

The technique described was applied to four batteries of tests developed for maintenance personnel in a steel plant[16]. These tests were designed to assess the performance of trainees during a specific training course in the following areas:

1   First year fitting
2   Motor control wiring
3   One week hydraulics course (described in Chapter 3)
4   Short electronics course

The tests attempted to identify and measure the various component skills covered by the training programme. The actual areas covered are shown on the graphs (Figure 9.10).

Two groups of approximately fifteen trainees each were selected randomly for each battery of tests. The first group having completed the relevant training course at least two years previously and the second having just completed the course. The tests were administered to these groups and the mean scores of each group on each test are shown in the graphs. The scores of the two groups on each battery of the test were subjected to a Mann Whitney test (White's modification) which is used to test whether two independent groups have been drawn from the same population. Results of this analysis are shown in the graphs (Figure 9.10); the figures 1% and 5% refer to the levels of statistical significance between the scores of the groups. Where no figure is shown, there was no statistically significant difference.

The analysis of scores on the four test batteries showed that the batteries could be divided into two types:

1   Those in which any superiority present was displayed by the group with on-the-job experience, ie fitting and motor control wiring.
2   Those where any superiority present was displayed by the group which had just completed training, ie hydraulics and electronics.

It was found with the fitting tests, that in terms of overall scores the group with the on-the-job experience was distinctly superior, and as regards subtests the latter were superior in the selection, use, and reading of measuring instruments and actual completion of a job involving metal removal using hand tools. It may be that these two areas show a higher score because these skills are practiced more in the on-the-job situation, since these tests involve the use and manipulation of tools and measuring instruments, whereas the other tests concentrate more on planning skills. This may suggest that at least during the two years after completion of training fitters do not practice these skills sufficiently on-the-job to bring about any improvement. As regards the motor control wiring, again the overall score discriminated between the two groups, but only in knowledge of tests and test instruments for new circuits, identification of components on a circuit diagram, and continuity testing did the more experienced group prove to be superior.

The Process of Validation

Surprisingly the less experienced group was superior in the selection of cables and fuses. No real overall pattern emerged, although it may be that electricians did get more practice in the use of test instruments than in the other areas when out in the plant.

Bearing in mind the assumptions behind this method, the possible reasons why no differences emerged in certain areas may be examined.

1. Trainees at the end of the course had a high level of achievement on the test. For example the reading of drawings by these trainees might be good enough to allow them to do the job properly and no further improvement is required.
2. The format and character of the test itself might be foreign to the on-the-job situation. For example, having to verbalize and list the steps in producing a job (see Chapter 4).

The hydraulics and electronics test scores gave a completely different picture. Here the trainees who had just completed the course were the ones who showed any superiority with the exception of one hydraulics test.

Since with these two batteries the results of this validation were at odds with the validity of content derived from an analysis of the training courses, it may be worthwhile to list some of the possible reasons for this:

1. The skills tested were not practiced on the job by the particular group tested. For example, when developing the tests it emerged that only a small proportion of trainees from the electronics course were allowed to deal with electronic equipment in the plant. It would not be surprising therefore if their ability in this area progressively decreased after completion of the course.
2. A related suggestion is that the off-the-job training was not followed up sufficiently on-the-job.
3. The course objectives, although adequately reflected in the tests, were not the correct ones in terms of present job requirements.

From the above discussion the reader will no doubt have realized that one great advantage of the validation technique described here is that not only does it give a quantitative estimate of the ability of the test to discriminate between levels of proficiency but also it provides information for further discussion. This information poses certain questions which necessitate a review of all information collected in the process of test development. In this case, *if* the tests were valid measures of valid training objectives, then test scores should have increased in most cases with on-the-job experience. Since this was not always the case, the test developer and user is forced to reexamine earlier processes and assumptions in an attempt to explain results and eventually improve the test and indeed the training. It should be emphasized that the technique described here attempted to validate the content of the tests against on-the-job requirements; beyond that, it does not validate any particular interpretation of scores. For example, we cannot say that on a given test a score above the criterion of say 70% probably indicates adequate on-the-job performance, or that our criterion of 70% is successful in discriminating between experienced and less experienced personnel. In order to validate these interpretations another study would need to be carried out. The study, however, does show to what extent 'construct validity' involves a sophisticated interpretation of data.

The Process of Validation

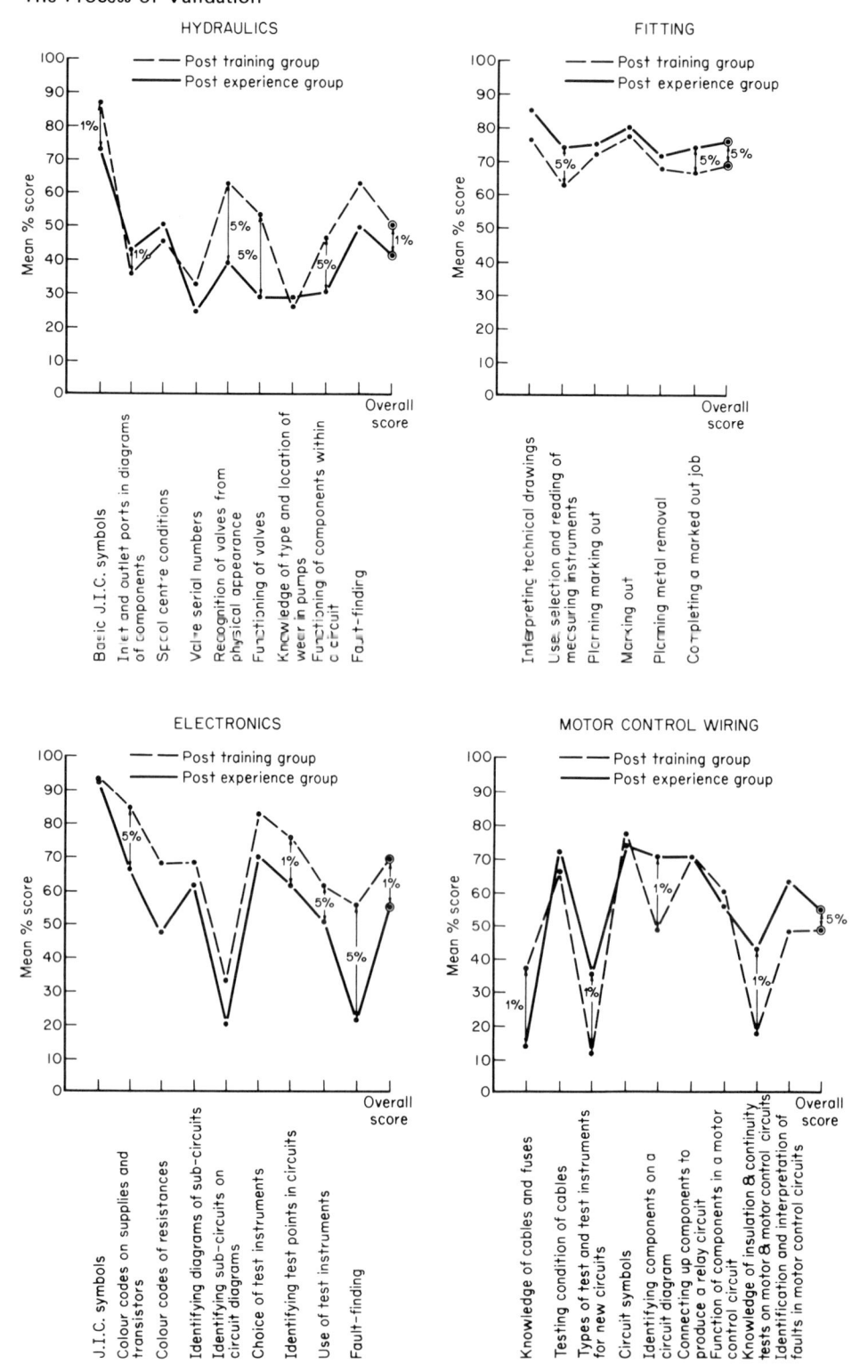

Figure 9.10 Results of past experience group/past training group on four test batteries

Study Four
Developing and evaluating phased testing in the shipbuilding industry

The problem of how to assess the effectiveness of training of ship construction and outfitting trades was encountered by the Shipbuilding Industry Training Board and it was first decided that one way of getting an answer was a system of end tests, taken by the trainee at the end of basic (first year off-the-job) and planned experience (an additional three years on-the-job) training. It was soon recognized, however, that a system of phased testing might prove a more effective method for both basic and planned experience trainees, since the end testing scheme had certain disadvantages. To begin with, some trades such as electricians and shipfitters were not being tested at all. From the trades that were being tested only about one third of trainees were coming forward to be tested and this largely self-selected sample did not perform exceptionally well. Obviously the likelihood of remedial training being carried out after the end test was not very high. A further argument against the end-test system was that by no means every important aspect of the job, particularly installation and other 'on-site' operations, was being tested. For example, aspects such as fitting out a cabin, lining-off pipe work on board ship, or opening up and examining a turbine unit could not be included except at great expense by building mock-ups and with a great increase in testing time. It was therefore decided to introduce two different phased testing schemes for basic and planned experienced training.

In 1970 training centres in the shipbuilding industry were required to develop programmes of phased tests for all the trades taught in the first year off-the-job training period. Tests so developed were vetted with regard to both technical content and testing techniques. After the scheme had been in operation a year a study[18] was undertaken to ascertain the effect it had had on training.

Training staff and trainees at a sample of centres were interviewed with regard to a number of topics, notably:

1. The extent to which tests were used to provide diagnostic information for remedial training.
2. The effect of phased testing on standards of performance achieved by trainees.
3. The effect of phased testing on the motivation of both trainees and instructors.

Other facts emerged, but with regards to the above topics, the conclusion was that phased testing had had a generally beneficial effect on first year off-the-job training; the motivation of both instructors and trainees had improved; attention had been focussed by the demands of developing a test programme on standards and training content. However, it was revealed that many centres had inadequate systems for giving trainees details of their performance and steps were taken to improve this situation. It is also interesting to note that one centre was not aware of the fact that trainees could retake tests (this is usual with phased tests) even though this had been publicized as part of the system. Findings such as this suggest that some kind of enquiry is always necessary if only to ascertain that instructors and other personnel understand the system.

The introduction of phased testing into the off-the-job training was largely welcomed by the industry, which accepted its advantages over end-testing. However, at the beginning of the planned experience project it appeared that its

The Process of Validation

introduction in on-the-job training might not be welcomed. Yet after two years' test development, the system was welcomed in similar warm tones to those which accompanied the basic training tests. To meet the requirements of the situation, it was decided that a rather informal testing situation was required as testing had to be carried out on the job. The test would consist of an actual job completed to production or quality control standards.

The battery of tests was developed by analysing the work of the particular trade and drawing up a comprehensive list of actual jobs. The list had to be comprehensive enough to provide a sufficient number of tests for large and small firms, and for shipbuilding and shiprepair yards. The original study was done in one yard and then vetted by production representatives from two others. Production personnel were called upon to do this task as it was considered that only they could say with any authority what work actually went on. The method was used for all eight trade groupings. Each job gave a specification of the type of work involved and a list of some of the important points in assessing such a job. The latter was to help in ensuring all personnel making assessments were thinking along the same lines and also to give indications of where remedial training might be required. The real criterion was however that the job passed the yard's quality control standards. See Figure 4.5 for an example of a test.

Each battery of tests so developed was then tried out over a period of some three months in around five shipyards and any technical errors ironed out or new tests added. It also emerged that several systems of administration were possible depending chiefly on the size of the yard. For example, in small yards, where trainees tended to be well known to foremen, the former could play a large role in organizing testing, whereas in larger firms the apprentice supervisors could help to coordinate foremen and trainees.

Particularly important was the selling of the scheme and so production supervisors, upper and middle management, and trade unions were all briefed and their cooperation enlisted before each pilot project was put into operation. Trainees were also told how the system would help them and what was involved. In total some 36 production departments in some 18 yards were involved in pilot projects and only in one was the situation such that the project did not get underway. The scheme was welcomed by the production side so long as it did not disturb their job of building and repairing ships, and the pilot project did a lot to dispel any such fears. Another benefit of the system seemed to be an increased interest in training on the part of foremen and front-line supervisors. Involvement in the pilot project for example caused one department manager to make his first visit to the yards training centre, where he was very favourably impressed by the training given and the standards which first-year trainees were achieving. From then on he had more confidence in the quality of trainees he was receiving which he had, by his own admission, previously underestimated.

Study Five
Validating and evaluating phased testing in first year training in the engineering industry

In the engineering industry a phased testing scheme had been in existence for a number of years, which involved first year off-the-job training centres developing

The Process of Validation

their own testing programme. Successful candidates were awarded a certificate issued by a national examining body. However, in this case it was felt that the scheme might not be fulfilling its original purpose. A preliminary survey[19] showed that most training centres entered candidates because they thought the test constituted a 'national standard' against which they would gauge the success of their training. However, since each centre designed their own tests it was unlikely that this was in fact the case. In order to see how comparable programmes were, a questionnaire was applied to each programme by an independent assessor (Figure 9.11).

Figure 9.11 Questionnaire used to assess phased testing schemes

The Process of Validation

It was found that overall there was a wide divergence in the standards (defined in terms of the tolerances employed) used by different centres, specifically that colleges worked to a looser tolerance than industrial training centres for both machining and fabrication work. The two graphs (Figures 9.12 and 9.13) show this difference clearly. A further aspect clarified by the study was that many centres appeared more or less unaware of the fact that phased test results could be used as a diagnostic training aid; centres seemed to prefer to rely on some vague general impression of a trainee's ability. Since the system was not meeting its major objective of providing a yardstick for training, a new system was introduced which could provide the necessary information on the results of training (see Chapter 8).

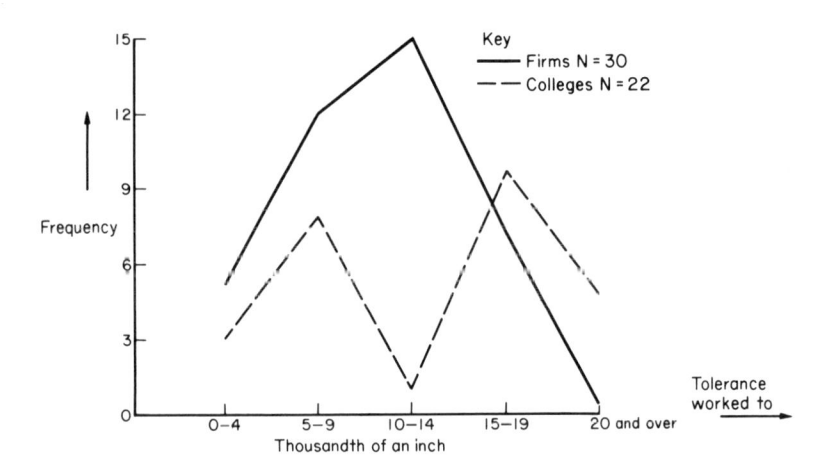

Figure 9.12 Frequency distribution of general tolerance worked to on machining test pieces for firms and colleges

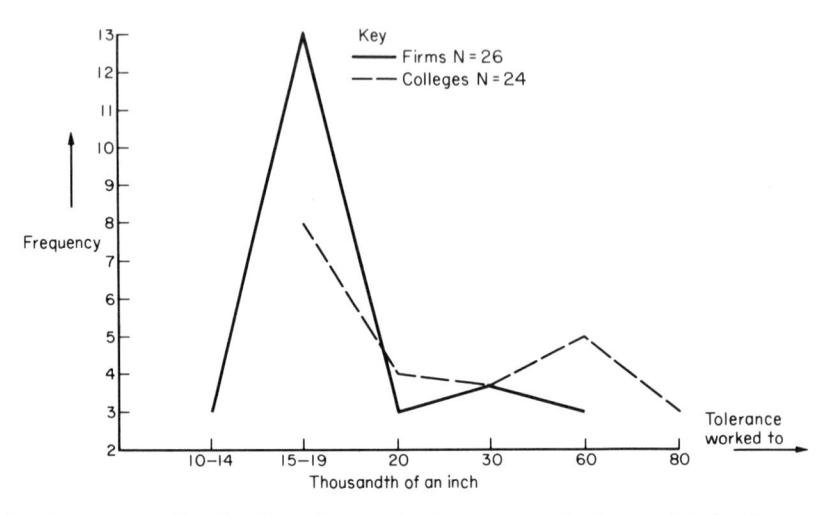

Figure 9.13 Frequency distribution of general tolerances worked to on fabrication test pieces for firms and colleges

SUMMARY

1 Validation and evaluation are continuing processes, which the test developer must bear in mind throughout development and which the test user must examine throughout the 'life' of a test.
2 In most cases validity will rest on the content of the test being representative of the area in which one is interested. In some cases additional procedures must be used to supplement, but not supplant, validity of content.
3 Reliability of performance tests has two main facets; reliability of marking and consistency of the candidate's performance. The former can be estimated by comparing the marks awarded by different examiners for the same performance. The latter is often difficult to estimate because of practical restrictions.
4 With criterion-referenced tests we are interested in the reliability of test results around the criterion. Norm-referenced methods of estimation may be inappropriate or need modification.
5 Besides validating a test, the test developer and user should be concerned with evaluating the impact of testing to ensure that tests are meeting their objectives and serving a useful function.

REFERENCES

1 Panitz A. and Olivo C.T., *The State of the Art of Occupational Competency Testing*, US Department of Health, Education and Welfare, Washington, 1970.
2 Baldwin T.S., *Evaluation of Learning in Industrial Education* in Handbook of Formative and Summative Evaluation of Student Learning, Bloom B.S., Hasting J.T. and Madaus G.F. Eds., McGraw Hill Book Company, New York, 1971.
3 Ebel R.L., *Must all tests be valid?* American Psychologist, 16, 640-647, 1961.
4 Cronbach L.J., *Essentials of Psychological Testing*, Harper and Row, New York, 1966, Chapter 13 'Proficiency Tests'.
5 Gibson J.J., Ed,, *Motion Picture Testing and Research*, Government Printing Office, Washington, 1947.
6 Ebel R.L., *Estimation of the Reliability of Ratings,* Psychometrika 16, 407-424, 1951.
7 Mackie R.R. and High W.A., *Research on the Development of Shipboard Performance Measures, Supervisory Ratings and Practical Performance Tests as Complementary Criteria of Shipboard Performance,* Human Factors Research, ONR Technical Report No.9, Los Angeles 1956.
8 Jones A. and Whittaker P.A., *A Correlational Technique for Criterion-Referenced Reliability Studies,* ETOB Bulletin, Vol.2, No.6, 1973.
9 Ryans D.G. and Frederiksen N , *Performance Tests of Educational Achievement* in Educational Measurement, Lindquist E.F., Ed., American Council on Education, Washington, D.C. 1951.
10 Boyd J.L. and Shimberg B., *Directory of Achievement Tests for Occupational Education*, Educational Testing Service, Princeton, 1971.

11 Stanley J.C., *Reliability* in Educational Measurement, Thorndike R.L., Ed., American Council on Education, Washington D.C. 1971.
12 Popham W.J. and Husek T.R., 'Implications of Criterion-Referenced Measurement', *Journal of Educational Measurement*, 6, 1-9, 1969.
13 Livingston S.A., *The Reliability of Criterion-Referenced Measures*, Report No. 73. The Centre for the Study of Social Organization of Schools — John Hopkins University, July 1970.
14 Jones A. and Whittaker P.A., *The Estimation of the Reliability of Criterion-Based Measures*, ETOB Bulletin, Vol.2, No.3, 1972.
15 Boyd J.L. and Shimberg B., *Handbook of Performance Testing*, Educational Testing Service, Princeton, 1970, Chapter 6 'Variations on a theme'.
16 Jones A. and Whittaker P.A., *A Validation Technique for Performance Tests,* Occupational Psychology, 47, 189-192, 1973.
17 Jones A. and Whittaker P.A., *Inter-Examiner Reliability in the Assessment of Engineering Test Pieces*, Skills Testing Service, City and Guilds of London Institute. Unpublished report, July 1973.
18 Phased Testing in the Shipbuilding Industry, Skills Testing Service, City and Guilds of London Institute, 1971.
19 An Evaluation of a Phased Testing Scheme in the Engineering Industry. Skills Testing Service, City and Guilds of London Institute, 1972.

SUGGESTED FURTHER READING

Guildford J.P., *Fundamental Statistics in Psychology and Education*, McGraw Hill Book Company, New York, 1965, Chapter 6 'Correlation', Chapter 14 'Special correlation methods and problems'.

Siegel S., *Nonparametric Statistics for the Behavioural Sciences*, McGraw Hill Book Co., New York, 1956, Chapter 9 'Measures of Correlation and their Tests of Significance'.

Thorndike R.L. and Hagen E., *Measurement and Evaluation in Psychology and Education*, John Wiley and Sons, New York, 1969, Chapter 5 'Elementary Statistical Concepts'.

Glossary

Achievement Test or Attainment Test
A test to discover what level of skill or knowledge a candidate has reached.

Algorithm
An exact prescription for achieving a given outcome. Often presented in the form of a flow chart where the process of decision-making is reduced to a sequence of yes/no responses to specific questions.

Analysis of Variance
A sophisticated statistical technique which employs means, deviations from means, variances and estimates of error. It can be used to determine whether the effect of various treatments or conditions is statistically significant and also in some cases to estimate correlations within the data.

Aptitude Test
A test to predict what jobs an individual will be capable of or most suitable for.

Competence
The ability to perform a task consistently to an acceptable standard.

Correlation
A correlation coefficient is a measure of the degree of association between two or more sets of data. For example we might calculate the correlation coefficient

Glossary

between the performance on a test and the amount of time spent in training to see whether an increase in training time is associated with an increase in test scores.

There are many kinds of correlation coefficient, which have been developed for use in particular circumstances or with particular types of data. When a correlation coefficient is referred to, it is usually the Pearson product-moment correlation coefficient ('r').

In the case of Pearson product-moment and related coefficients, the value of the coefficient ranges between +1.00 (perfect association) through 0.00 (no association) to −1.00 (perfect disassociation).

There are a number of coefficients derived from the Pearson product-moment formula for use in special situations (biserial, point-biserial, tetrachoric, and phi coefficients).

Other correlation techniques are based on using ranked data (eg Spearman's Rank Correlation coefficient and Kendall's coefficient of concordance).

Criterion Referenced Test
A test designed to measure to what degree the candidate has reached the specified behaviour. A candidate's performance is described in terms of whether or not the criterion has been attained.

Difficulty Value
Used in connection with test items, the difficulty value is an index of how difficult the item is and is calculated by dividing the number of candidates who failed to answer the items correctly by the total number of candidates. Opposite of facility value.

Distractor
An incorrect alternative in a multiple-choice question.

Empirical
An empirical approach to a problem investigates the soundness of a particular solution by experiment and not by reference only to theories, preconceptions, etc.

End-Testing
Testing the trainee at the end of his course of training.

Error Score
A concept recognizing that the score a candidate obtains (observed score) is made up of a true score or true measure of his ability plus an error score caused by the unreliability of the testing situation.

Examiner/Candidate Ratio
The number of examiners needed to administer and/or mark the performance/products of a given number of candidates.

Evaluation
The assessment of the total value of a system. Evaluation differs from validation in that it attempts to measure the overall benefit of the system and not just

Glossary

whether it achieves its laid down objectives. The term is also used in the general judgmental sense of the continuous monitoring of a system.

Face Validity
The degree to which a test *appears* to be a good test. *Not* the same as content validity.

Feedback
The process by which information about the results of an action are communicated to the individual (or systems) making the action.

Fidelity of a Test
The extent to which the test represents the actual job situation.

Frequency Distribution
A group of data that may be displayed in tabular or graphic form showing the number of times different values of variables occur. In testing frequency distributions of scores are often produced, showing the number of candidates who obtained the various scores. See normal distribution.

Graded Comparison Scale
A scoring scale making use of a set of actual objects or representation of objects which have been graded as to their 'goodness'. The examiner compares the candidate's end-product against these standards to arrive at an assessment.

Hands-on Tests
Tests using the actual tools of the job, as opposed to hands-off tests which do not.

Information
That which reduces uncertainty. 'Information theory' sets out to measure such a gain in knowledge in a given situation, the unit of information being the 'bit'. The amount of information potentially available is greater the more uncertainty there is in the situation.

Interrater (or Interexaminer) Reliability
An estimate of the extent to which raters or examiners give the same score for the same performance. Expressed in terms of a correlation coefficient or percentage agreement.

Index of Agreement
An index (usually in the form of a percentage) showing to what extent examiners agree on candidates' scores or the extent to which candidates' performances are reliable (eg using the test–retest method).

$$\textit{Percentage agreement} \ = \ 100 \ \times \ \frac{\textit{Number of agreements}}{\textit{Total number of judgements}}$$

Glossary

Marking Scheme
A specification of how marks are to be awarded.

Mark Sheet
A sheet designed for the recording of marks and other information about the candidate.

Mastery
The achievement of a perfect performance or full score on a test.

Multiple-choice Question or Item
A question where the candidate has a number of possible answers or solutions presented to him, only one of which is correct. The candidate has to select the correct answer.

Matching Item
An item where the candidate has to decide which of one group of words, diagrams or whatever matches up with those of another group.

Mean
The 'Average' — the sum of a series of values divided by the number of values in the series.

Median
The middle score where the number of scores are odd, or the point half-way between the middle scores when the number of scores are even.

Mode
The most frequently occurring score.

Norm
A representative value or pattern, derived from a sample of scores. There are two general classes of norms resulting from the transformation of raw scores:

1. Reference norms in which raw scores have been translated into terms directly significant. For example scores on a trade test might be classified into Novice, Apprentice and Journeyman. Scores between 0 and 19 indicating a novice, between 20 and 35 an apprentice, and above 35 a journeyman.
2. Statistical norms where mathematical transformations are made on the raw score. Unlike reference norms, statistical norms have no meaning in themselves.

Normative Standard
A standard of performance arrived at by examining the relative performance of a group or sample of candidates.

Norm-referenced Test
A test which describes a candidate's score in terms of its relation to the scores of other candidates.

Glossary

Normal Distribution
A mathematical concept (which therefore has certain known properties) of a distribution of values rarely, if ever, occurring in its exact form in practice. A normal distribution curve is bell-shaped and symmetrical about the mean. The figure below illustrates a normal distribution of test scores.

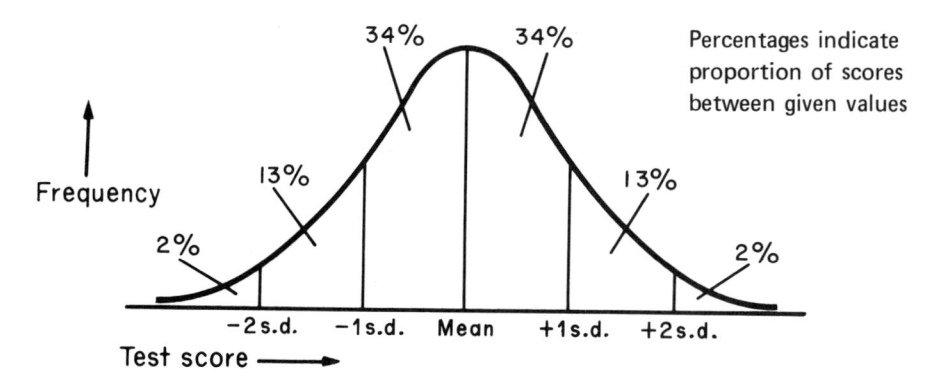

Objective Test or Examination
A test or examination where the marks awarded are independent of who marks the examination.

Objectivity
The objectivity of a test is the extent to which it is free from personal error or bias. Opposite of subjectivity.

Oral Testing
Testing which involves the examiner asking the candidate a set of questions, rather than giving him a paper and pencil test.

Pass Mark
The mark below which candidates are classed as unsuccessful.

Pass Rate
The proportion of candidates who pass an examination or test.

Phased Testing
Testing trainees after specific phases of training, as against end-testing which involves testing only at the end of the course. Also known as progress testing.

Pilot Testing
Trying out a test before putting it into operational use.

Post-test
A test administered at the end of training to ascertain whether the training objectives have been achieved.

Glossary

Pre-test
A test administered before training to ascertain existing levels of proficiency.

Process Orientation
Emphasis in assessment on the *way* in which the end-result is obtained.

Product Orientation
Emphasis in assessment on the end-result or product.

Profile
Graphic representation of a set of scores for an individual, organised so that the high and low scores can be identified.

Range
The difference between the smallest and largest of a set of values.

Rating Scale
A scale on which the rater has to allocate an individual to a given position. These positions may be loosely or strictly defined.

Raw Score
A score or mark which has not been treated or changed in any way.

Recognition/Identification Type Test
A test which involves the candidate naming and/or describing an object or representation of an object.

r_{bis} (the symbol used for biserial correlation)
In multiple-choice and similar items, the correlation between the score on a particular item and total test score of a candidate.

Reliability
The degree of consistency or stability of a test as a measuring instrument. Reliability is usually estimated by test–retest method, equivalent forms method, or an internal consistency method and expressed as a correlation coefficient.

Response Rate
In surveys utilizing a questionnaire approach, the proportion, usually expressed as a percentage, of those people contacted who actually complete and return the questionnaire.

Sample
A selected group from the population in which there is interest.

Significant Difference
Two values are significantly different if the difference between them is so large that it is unlikely to be due to chance. Results of tests of significant are given in terms of the probability of the difference being due to chance.

Glossary

Simulator
A device which represents the individual with a representation of the important features of the real situation and reproduces operational conditions.

Skill
A goal directed, organized sequence of activities which involves extensive utilization of feedback.

Standardization

1 A standardized test is one given under constant conditions and scored in an objective way.

OR

2 A standardized test is one for which a set of norms is available – this is the meaning of the term as used by psychometricians, etc.

Standard Deviation
A measure of how much a group of scores varies around the mean. Often abbreviated to s.d. The standard deviation is the square root of the variance (see below).

Standard Score
A score on a scoring system which has known characteristics. Raw scores from different tests are often converted to standard scores for comparison. Examples are T scores, stanines, etc.

Supporting Job Knowledge
Knowledge about a job or task which is necessary for successful performance of the job or task.

Tabs Test
A hands-off testing technique, particularly useful in testing fault-finding skills, where the candidate receives information by pulling a tab which reveals the results of checks, suggested remedies, etc.

Trainability Tests
Performance tests used to assess whether a person after a short period of training or instruction in an area is likely to benefit from further training in that area.

Test
A test measures a standard sample of behaviour. The sample should be large enough and sufficiently representative to allow us to generalize and predict from the test result.

Test Specification
A specification of the task(s) involved in a test and the conditions under which it is to be performed.

Glossary

True Score
See error score.

Validation
The process of ensuring that the test is measuring the skills and knowledge in which there is interest, and measuring them reliably, so that the test scores can legitimately and meaningfully be used for the purpose intended.

Validity
The extent to which a test measures what it is claimed to measure. Validity may rest on the content of the test, how well it predicts future performance, or how well it differentiates between individuals with known differences. Rather than speaking of a test as valid or invalid, one should specify whether or not its use is valid in a given situation or whether certain interpretations of scores are legitimate.

Variable-sequence Type Test
Tests which allow the candidate to take a variety of routes through the test. Particularly useful in testing fault-finding and planning skills.

Variance (of scores)
Variance is a measure of the spread of scores around the mean of a distribution of scores. Variance is the sum of squared deviations from the mean.

Zone of Uncertainty
The 'zone' of scores within which it cannot be said that two differently obtained scores are truly different.

Index

Administrative details, five important factors on task analysis 18
Administrative situation and choice of testing techniques 75–7
Algorithms 17, 18, 101
Analysing a task, nine points to consider 14
Anonimity in questionnaires, value of 22
Aptitude testing 133
Attitude (candidate's) towards testing 74
Auditory diagnosis tests 69

Behavioural specification in task analysis 26–33
Bench fitting, planning a job for 109
Bench marks 92
British standards and task analysis 20

Candidate, instructions to, prior to carrying out test, importance of 116–19
Candidates, classifying, after tests 141
Cards, packs of, to show sequence of events 61
  for self-testing 143
Central tendency errors by rating examiners 91
Checklists as a marking scheme 88, 97–8
Closed- and open-questions in questionnaire-framing 23
Computers, use of, in tests 76
Conditions (environmental) for testing 116
Confined spaces and task analysis 17
Costs for tests, 167–8
  see also Money, amount of, available for testing
Criticality in task analysis 15

189

Index

Criterion-referenced tests:
  and norm-reference tests, distinguished 4
  themselves 134–5, 166
  process of validation of 165–6

Data collection and questionnaires 22
Data processing costs 168
Decision-making tests 44
Decision trees 17, 61
Diagnostic tests, scoring in 100–2
Difficulty (candidate's) in task analysis 15
Digital response counter 128
Dimension-orientated marking schemes 84–8
Distractors 49, 52–4

Electronic (motor) driving test 76
Engineering drawings, tests on ability to read 59
Envelopes tests for fault diagnosis 102–6
Environment of test to be similar to working conditions 17
Equipment:
  availability of, for testing 75
  care of, assessing extent of, at time of tests 82
Errors:
  assessing number of, at test 82
  in analysis of a task 15
Essay-type questions 45, 61, 62
Evaluation of tests, process of 167–8
Examiner/Candidate ratio 122
Examiners, instructions to, when and before implementing tests 119
Experienced Worker Standard (EWS) 81–2

Fault-finding:
  scoring of tests in 100–2
  tests themselves 44

'Feedback classroom' 128–9
Feedback of results (to candidates) 143
Fidelity of a test 44
Film, use of, in hands-off tests 41
Fixed sequence testing techniques 44–64
Flow diagrams 17
Fork truck trainability test 145–6
Frequency in task analysis 14
Funnel approach in questionnaires 22–3

Goal direction 9
Go/no-go gauge for measuring 85–7, 90
Graded comparison scales 92
Gross bodily skills 10
Group interviews 22
Guessing, elimination of, in fault-finding tests 100–2

Halo effect, when marking essays 45, 91–2
Handbooks, manufacturers' 20
Hands-off testing techniques 41–69, 73, 75, 166:
  differentiated from hands-on tests 35–6
  fixed sequence 44–64
  validation of 166
  variable sequence 44, 64–9
Hands-on testing techniques 36–41, 72, 75, 165–6
  differentiated from hands-off tests 35–6
  by sampling 38–41
  validation of 165–6
Harpsichord jack, test for 89
High-cost tasks 15
High-fidelity tests 44

Illumination, extent of, and task analysis 17

Index

Incongruous results, reasons for 139–40
Information for task analysis: how to collect 18–26
   from colleagues 20
   from interview 20
     who to interview 21–2
     developing a questionnaire 22–4
     direct observation 24–6
   from personal experience 20
   from survey 20
Injection-moulding test 102, 121
Instructions when implementing tests:
   to candidate 116–19
   to examiners 119
Instructors, assessing performance of 147–8
Interexaminer reliability 84, 159–60
Interviews, technique of 20

Job descriptions outlining performance expectancy 13–14, 20, 26, 33
Job-knowledge tests 62–3, 65–6
Job-standards, defined 81

Knowledge, choosing technique to test 72
Kuder-Richardson methods 161–2

Language skills, testing 11
Layout of tests 125–9
Leniency, errors of, by rating examiners 90–1
Low-fidelity variable sequence tests 44, 65–6

Manipulation 9–10
Manual for tests 130
MAPP concept 135–6, 138
Marking of essay-type questions 45
Marking schemes 79–82, 119–22:
   dimension-orientated 84–8
   see also Scoring

Marksheet, candidate to see prior to test 116, 118
   specimen of, for joinery test 117
   when implementing tests 122–3
   see also Scoring
'Matching item' test in multiple choice exercises 54–8
Minimum acceptance performance profile (MAPP) 135–6, 138
Money, amount of, available for testing 75
   see also Costs for tests
Multiple choice items in objective tests 49–51, 61–2

Negative forms of question in multiple choice tests 53
Noise level and task analysis 17
Nominal time in tests involving work-speed 93–4
Normative results 138–9
Normative standards, four chief reasons for using 133–4
Norm-referenced tests:
   and criterion-referenced tests distinguished 4
   results determination 132–4
   themselves 133–4, 166

Objective-type tests, analysing results of 49–53, 53–4
Observation, value of direct, in task analysis 24, 26
On-the-job measures, use of, in assessing performance 83
Open- and closed-questions in questionnaire-framing 23
Oral tests 63–4
Output in analysis of task 16
Overlapping choices in multiple choice tests 53
Overstatements and task analysis 26–7

Packers, testing 83
Parallel marking systems 135

191

Index

Pass/fail situation, assessing and interpreting results of   132–4
Pass mark   133
Perceptual skills, definition of   11
Performance, standard of, in task analysis   16
Performance and written tests discussed   2–3
Performance tests, validation of   153–7
Personnel, type of and level of, when choosing testing techniques   74–5
Phased testing, value of   5, 73, 141, 142, 149, 175–6
Photographs, use of, in hands-off tests   41, 46, 58, 76
Pictorial tests   63
Pilot tests:
  five important points in   123, 125
  necessity for, in questionnaire-framing   24, 93, 123–5
Planning, scoring of tests in   106–9
Planning skills, tests for   58–62
Pleasantness, rating for   16
Politeness, rating for   16
Process:
  assessment of, in performance tests   97
  setting standards for assessing   97–100
Process of product?, in task analysis   16–17
Products or process?, in task analysis   16
Progress testing   73
Psycho-motor skills   11
Punch press, tests involving   36–7
Purpose of test, to be clearly stated to candidate   116

Quality:
  setting test standards for   83–8
  in analysis of task   16
Quantity, setting test standards for   92–3
Questionnaires, defects in   24

Questions, how to word, in questionnaire-framing   23–4
Quintamensional plan in questionnaires   23

Rating scales   90, 98
$r_{(bis)}$ 54
Reliability:
  and process of validation   157–62
  of criterion-referenced tests   163–5
  formulae   163–4
Remedial training, using tests as sources of information as to whether to undertake   141–3
Reply-paid envelopes, value of   22
Results:
  incongruity of, reasons for   139–40
  methods of displaying to trainees   141, 143
  determination, see Test results, interpreting and utilizing
Rub-away mask tests   65
Running costs   167

Safety precautions   15, 82
Safety regulations in task analysis   18
Scoring:
  fault-finding tests   100–2
  planning tests   106–9
  for various methods, see also:
    diagnostic tests, scoring in;
    dimension-orientated marking schemes;
    fault-finding tests, scoring of tests in;
    marking of essay-type questions;
    marking schems;
    marksheets;
    parallel marking systems;
    planning, scoring tests in;
    weighting system of scoring;
Scrap, assessing amount of, during tests   82
Security and tests   130

Index

Self-training 143–4
Sequence of questions, importance of, in questionnaire-framing 22
Service manuals and task analysis 17
Short-answer tests 45–8, 62
Shorthand, analysis task involving 16
Simulators 66–9, 76, 101
Skill:
  categories of 10–11
  choosing technique to test 72
  definitions of 8–9
Skilled performance, concept of 8–10
Skill sample test 38, 41
Sliding window test 65
Speed, measuring work-, for a given task 81, 93–6
Split-half methods 162
Staff, availability of, for testing 75–6
Stem (of a question), definition of 49
Supporting knowledge in task analysis 17
Standards, establishing, for assessment of test performance 79–82
Stanine scale 148–9
Switching-in of faults 67–8
System development costs 167
System maintenance costs 168

Tables (figures) and task analysis 17
Tab-tests 65, 101, 102
Tape recorders at interviews 21
Taper-plug test piece 41, 43, 84, 85–7
Task:
  analysis of 13–33:
    behavioural specification 26–33
    criticality 15
    difficulty (candidate's) 15
    frequency 14
    how to collect information 18–26:
      personal experience 20
      consulting colleagues 20
      survey 20

Task: *(continued)*
    interview 20
    who to interview 21–2
    questionnaire 22–3
    direct observation 24–6
    product or process? 16
    safety regulations 18
    standard of performance 16
    supporting knowledge 17
    working conditions 17
  importance, measuring by frequency 14–15
  specification when implementing tests 115–16
Temperature, considering, in task analysis 17
Test battery: profile or multiple cut-off method? 134–8
Test manual 130
Test performance, assessing 79–112:
  fault-finding etc., scoring for, 100–2
  injection-moulding 102
  envelopes test 102
  graded composition scales 92
  on-the-job measures 82
  planning etc., scoring for 106–9
  process
    checklists 97–8
    rating scales 98–100
  quality, measuring 83–8
  quantity, measuring 92–3
  speed of work, measuring 93–6
  standard, establishing a 79–82
  summary 109–12
Test results, interpreting and Utilizing 132–50
  criterion-referenced tests 134–5
  normative results 138–9
  pass/fail situation 132–4
  ready-made tests with norms 139
  test battery: profile or multiple cut-off method? 134–8
  trouble-shooting with results determination methods 139–40
  utilizing tests and results 140–50:
    classifying candidates 141

Index

Test results, interpreting and
  Utilizing *(continued)*
    tests as sources of information
      for remedial training 141–3
    self-testing 143–4
    trainability tests and assessments
      144–6
    assessing performance of
      instructors 147–8
    assessing overall training centre
      performance 148
    comparing training methods
      148–50
Testing, purpose of 4–6, 72–4
Testing system, eight important points
  to enquire about 167
Testing techniques 35–69:
  hands-off method 41–69
    fixed sequence 44–64
    variable sequence 44, 64–9
  hands-on method 36–41
    sampling 38–41
  choosing between 71–8
    administrative situation 75–7
    attitudes towards testing 74
    purpose of 72–4
    skill and knowledge 72
    type and level of personnel 74–5
  summary of, in table form 78
Tests:
  as sources of information for
    remedial training 141–3
  implementing and administering
    115–30:
    candidate's instructions 116–19
    examiner's instructions 119
    marking schemes 119–22
      see also Scoring
    marksheets 122–3
    pilot tests 123–5
    security 130
    task specification 115–16
    test manual 130
    timetabling and layout tests
      125–9
  involving calculations 44
  involving selection of one correct
    answer 49–53

Tests: *(continued)*
  table of comparative costs of
    various 77
  when candidate supplies answer 44–8
  with norms, ready-made 138–9
Time allowed:
  to be checked first by pilot test-
    ing 123
  in the analysis of a task 15
  timetabling of tests 125–9
Total job test 36
Trainability tests and assessments
  144–6
Training centre, assessing overall
  performance of 148
Training methods, comparing various
  148–50
Training objectives, need to be
  detailed about 33
Training, purpose of 4–6
Trouble-shooting:
  ability, measuring of 66, 69
  following test results 139–40
True/false questions 54
Truing test 92–3
Turner's skills, testing 41
Typing, analysing a task involving 16

Utilization of results of tests, *see*
  Utilizing tests and results *under*
  Test results, interpreting and
  Utilizing

Validation checklist 165–6
Validation, process of 152–79:
  of performance tests 153–7
  evaluation, process of 167–8
    costs 167–8
  reliability 157–62
    of criterion-referenced tests
      163–5
  validation checklist 165–6
    hands-off tests 166
    hands-on tests 165–6
  validity of tests, examples
    assessing 168–78

194

Index

Validity of Tests, five examples of 168–78
   types of performance 155
Variable sequence testing techniques 44, 64–9
Veeder counters 92

Weighting system of scoring 138
Wording of questions in questionnaire-framing 23–4

Working conditions in task analysis 17
Work sample test 38–9, 41
Work-speed, measuring 93–6
Written and performance tests, distinguished and discussed 2–3

Zone of uncertainty, concept of 141